FAT IS A FEMINIST ISSUE

Susie Orbach is a psychoanalyst, psychotherapist, writer and co-founder of The Women's Therapy Centre in London and The Women's Therapy Centre in New York. Her books include *Hunger Strike, What's Really Going on Here?, Towards Emotional Literacy, Susie Orbach On Eating and The Impossibility of Sex*. She lectures widely nationally and internationally in the UK, Europe and North America, has written for several magazines and newspapers, and has provided consultation advice for organisations from the NHS to the World Bank. She continues to help many individuals and couples from her practice in London. She was a visiting Professor at the London School of Economics for ten years. She is a member of www.endangeredbodies.org.

FAT IS A FEMINIST ISSUE

Book One

The Anti-Diet Guide

&

Book Two

Conquering Compulsive Eating

Susie Orbach

arrow books

6 8 10 9 7

Arrow Books
20 Vauxhall Bridge Road
London SW1V 2SA

Previously published in two separate volumes

Arrow Books is part of the Penguin Random House group of companies
whose addresses can be found at global.penguinrandomhouse.com

Penguin
Random House
UK

First published in Great Britain by Arrow Books in 1998

www.penguin.co.uk

A CIP catalogue record for this book is available from the British Library.

ISBN 9781784753092

Printed and bound in Great Britain by Clays Ltd, Elcograf S.p.A.

Penguin Random House is committed to a sustainable future
for our business, our readers and our planet. This book is made
from Forest Stewardship Council® certified paper.

MIX
Paper from
responsible sources
FSC® C018179

FIFI Today

It's 2016, almost forty years since FIFI explored the relationship between women's individual experience and the political and social meanings of body, of food, of fatness and of thinness. Since then, the little-known problem of women's troubled relationship with food and their bodies has exploded year on year, capturing the minds, bodies, appetites and stomachs of girls as young as six to women in care homes.

Food and bodies have become challenging for girls and women (and increasingly boys and men) across age, across class, across ethnicity and geography. This serious situation is almost taken for granted. Many of the people who come to therapy propelled by other issues – insecurity, loss of a partner, troubles with intimacy and so on – have eating behaviours which would qualify for an eating disorder 'diagnosis'. They don't, however, expect to find relief from their eating and body difficulties. They don't even raise these issues except in passing because being troubled in relation to food, appetite and desire is integrated into their sense of self. It is the price of modernity. They see their mothers, sisters, grandmothers and aunts similarly troubled and, as with the bound feet of yesteryear, they expect to go on being troubled and just managing. Body troubles are an expression of a new social phenomenon and politics, something hidden, something hurtful and yet in plain view.

Meanwhile there is now a parallel explosion of what has become the field of Eating Disorders – a new speciality of counselling, psychotherapy, psychiatry, endocrinology and internal medicine – with junior and senior specialists, journals and clinics, some of which are funded by venture capital who see the treatment of eating difficulties and body troubles as a profitable growth area. Back in 1978 there were very few writings that addressed the issue; none for the public and certainly none that either looked at women's struggles with their bodies in a cultural context, nor ones that proposed solutions.

The women I was writing about came from the United States, Canada and the UK. They were aged from fourteen to sixty-five. They included grandmothers, foster parents and single women. They came from working-class backgrounds and middle- and upper-middle-income occupations. They were mainly white. During the years the book has been in print, women (and indeed some men) from every continent and social background have told me of its significance for them and their eating difficulties as the ubiquity of visual culture has gobbled up and subverted the variety of body types, shapes, ages and sizes, subsuming everything into the westernised, digitally enhanced aesthetic.

Alas, this book has come to speak to women all over the world. Something that an author might be expected to take pleasure in, but in this instance it has the taste of tragedy. The rapacious industries that together create and exploit the twin ideas that we must all be beautiful and in a narrowly defined way, have created a uniform aesthetic that circles the globe bringing a damaging limiting visual grammar causing immense hurt and anguish. It penetrates our eyes and our screens, and diminishes our ideas about the possibilities of being in a female body.

This hurt isn't trivial. Images aren't trivial. They work on our ideas of who we can be and these include how we need to display and present ourselves and what we can eat in order to match these images. They undermine the sense that bodies are varied. To be a girl, to be a woman is to embody the brand of woman which lives within a binary which proclaims thin as OK and other – non-thin – bodies as wanting. Thin is now aspirational; it purports to be a passport of entry into modernity. It is the ambition and sign of belonging in a world in which division between those who have and those who don't has also – ludicrously and horrifyingly – come to be demarcated by size and shape. As American English swallows up indigenous languages all over the world, so too the huge variety of body types is being lost. They are being re-sculpted and remodelled to meet today's narrowing aesthetic.

In classrooms around the world girls as young as six worry about food. They mimic the 'worked on' bodies they see staring out at them from music videos, TV soaps, the catwalk, magazines and billboards. They don't know yet that digital manipulation is ubiquitous[1]. They don't know yet that the glamorous celebrities they follow use lighting and well-thought-out camera angles to make them appear to have longer legs, smaller waists, larger breasts and rounder bums. But no matter even if they do. They plan for their own future surgeries on games apps designed for 10-year-olds[2]. Body transformation is no longer experienced as a problem but as a potential they will be able to take up. They don't know that cosmetic surgery is another industry which undermines them with its promises of security by giving them uniform labia, noses, cheekbones, breasts and so on. For them, body transformation is exciting and will be as unquestioned as colouring one's hair. They don't know that body dissatisfaction is not inevitable. They don't know that body dissatisfaction is the outcome of multiple commercial pressures. They experience it as personal, as something they need to fix, as something they want to fix, as something that is a delight to fix. Fixing what's 'wrong' becomes a sign of engagement and personal power. The way their body looks, they learn, will be as important as their jobs, whether as a yummy mummy, a doctor, a teacher, an engineer or a personal assistant.

Bodies today have almost come to define the way our lives can be lived. Without a body that a girl feels all right about, nothing much in her life feels OK. Her body causes her trouble and worry. All the normal difficulties of growing up, dealing with the conflicts, choices and angsts of adolescence, sexuality, parents and schooling get subsumed under a preoccupation to get her body right. Concerns about whether her still-developing body will be like the current fashionable figure, whether she will be found acceptable, pretty, sexy and desirable, and whether her size, shape and the way she looks are good enough, consumes her thoughts and hopes, affecting even her educational achievements.[3]

Being online is the prevailing experience for many of us today and more especially for young people. Only 40,000 of the 4.3 million 15 to 18-year-olds in the UK are not connected pretty much all their waking hours. The 4.26 million meanwhile post approximately seven selfies of themselves each week in the search for approval. Each selfie that a girl posts in the search for 'likes' takes an average of twelve minutes to get right. That doesn't of course include the time taken to dress and make up for it. The physical self, or rather its representation, is being curated. Approval matters and yet it is elusive. Girls surveyed say that they would feel good with 124 likes, as compared to the 26 they actually average[4]. Beauty has been democratised with the notion that all of us can (and should) be goddesses, models, X-Factor winners. We just have to fix our bodies. If we don't, we risk being attacked for how we look. Online trolls target women's bodies when they don't like their ideas or post unflattering 'revenge' photos in relationship break-ups. Attacking a woman's body is seen as fair game.

In this context where physical attractiveness has become so crucial, so narrowly defined and so apparently available for purchase, the struggle to feel safe and good in one's body dominates. When we pause to recognise it, it hurts and it can enrage. What an extraordinary expenditure of human energy.

While we are aware of the many efforts we make to look good, exercise, and eat well, the underlying questions about why and how we have come to be so concerned about our bodies is just taken as a given, written into our consciousness. We don't, importantly, become passive victims; we actively make it our own cause. We embrace the challenge. Yet, in doing so we can make decisions which are not only damaging to our well-being; but inadvertently create and then reinforce an anguished relationship to food and the body.

Whatever point we choose in the life cycle, we can see the evidence of our cultural preoccupation with food and body image. The growth of elective caesarean deliveries at 36 weeks, designed to avoid the increase in weight associated with the last month of pregnancy and lose that tummy more quickly - although most women don't significantly gain weight in the last two to four weeks anyway - is illustrative. In Brazil, a tummy tuck can be offered at the same time, with the disturbing result that the most treasured moments of early parent–baby bonding may be hampered by a mother's discomfort and recovery from double surgery.

The impact of this kind of decision on the mother and baby extends beyond the actual pregnancy and birth.[5] Quite unintentionally, the woman's ability to breastfeed and nurture her new-born can be clouded by concerns about her own appearance and appetite. Most new mothers inevitably feel some nervousness about whether they can respond well to their baby's needs. Of course, every new mum wants to give her baby a good start in life, and if she has weight or eating problems she will be eager to make sure that she doesn't pass these on.[6] But, sadly, the push to return to a pre-pregnancy figure, and the premium on doing so speedily, brings eating anxieties right into the early feeding relationship. The statement by Victoria Beckham that she ran six days a week after giving birth and the pictures of Rachida Dati, the French politician glammed up and in high heels five days after giving birth become taken up as the new norms of the early post-pregnancy period. They unintentionally induce confusion and envy: how is a new mother to be? Is she to present herself for display or is she to take this precious time and discover the rhythms she will create with her baby?

The earliest weeks of life begin the process of bonding outside the womb. It is a time of sleeplessness, of joy, of relief, of confusion and of wonderment in which the baby is welcomed into the world. Its delicate urges and needs are translated for it by the parent who herself is making the psychological and physical adjustment to becoming a parent, either for the first time or to this particular baby. Everything about the early post-partum weeks is suffused with a mix of delight, concern, interest, love and exhaustion. To have trepidation about one's own eating or needing to return to the state of the pre-pregnant body enters the emotional field and gets into the heart of this most intimate of relationships, inducing in mothers a sense that they have to be on high alert with their appetites while watching what their baby eats. The early feeding relationship thus can become infused with anxiety.

The basic appetite mechanism then may not develop in a straightforward manner but arc towards the influence of emotional states on eating. Unsurprisingly, many children grow up with confusion knitted into their appetites. They learn from early on that eating is somewhat fraught. They learn about good foods and bad foods and may not know that eating is something you only need to do when prompted by hunger.

When ideas about body size predominate, some foods become designated good while those considered bad gain a special attraction. The fact that nutritional theory changes constantly and diet hocus pocus and marketing fads fill the web, extolling the joys of juicing or giving up protein, gluten, carbs or fats, only adds to the confusion. As children become more independent and have pocket money to spend, they become interested in making food choices that veer towards everything a parent wishes they weren't interested in, partly because of course it is pitched to them as special. It becomes an aspect of the befuddling of appetites which has been an aspect of the food industry's aim for several decades.

As food activists from different perspectives[7] have been telling us, the food industry is up to no good. We now know about the exploitation of the rainforest to feed an induced hunger for meat – a hunger stimulated by the industrialization of cattle rearing; of the development of GM foods to control farmers, of the adulteration of basic foods. We can all see the proliferation of cheap, tasty, addictive snacks, which while appearing 'healthy' and filling, are quite the opposite and a big part of the industry's activity.[8] The food industry's profits increase the more they sell and the more they reduce the cost of producing, transporting and storing the food. Over the past few decades we have been accustomed to a wider availability of relatively cheap food, but the problem is that lots of these have stabilisers and artificial flavours added to them to increase their shelf life. Moreover they are produced to maximise the 'bliss point' without quite delivering satisfaction, so that the impulse is to keep on going for the sugary or salty or cheesy taste and texture that becomes sensually addictive. Sometimes, or perhaps I should say, often, these snacks aren't even foods but a collection of chemicals which, according to Tim Spector and Giulia Enders, are reducing our microbial intake and rendering our guts like a conveyer belt to our bottoms rather than transforming and distributing nutrients to our bodies and brains.

Of course, the industry is canny. If we don't like these so-called foodstuffs we can choose the fresher and more organic options. If we don't like mass-produced food we can purchase the unprocessed or gourmet lines. Beautiful cooking programmes and food shops are one response to this. We then crave the beauty of real food and unadulterated ingredients. But for many, the food emporiums and cook books become a form of food porn – what the market temptingly offers (especially to women who feel they must constrain their appetites) rather than how food could be for us all.

The food industry caters to all of our appetites, whims and budgets and the latest in nutritional theory. Reduce fat? No problem. Water, sugars and cellulose fillers can give texture and ersatz taste. As I write there is yet another struggle to rein in the food industry's promiscuous use of sugar. Despite high-profile campaigns and a report by Public Health England in October 2015, the power of the industry is strong enough to resist pressure to reform. We aren't talking about the necessary sugar in cakes and buns but the sugar that is inserted into prepared savoury foods and so-called fruit drinks.

Food is caught in a battlefield between the consumer and those who wish to increase or restrain – or preferably both – our eating. In this atmosphere; eating has become a psychological, moral, medical, aesthetic and cultural statement. Eating certain foods becomes equated with moral value, almost a holiness. To eat them is to accord oneself a sense of goodness. To refrain is wrong. Tempted as I am to give the examples of what's considered good, I can't; it changes constantly. Tim Spector's fascinating recent work[9] points to metabolic difference in twins leading their bodies to absorb and use the same portions of food differently and causing significant weight differences because of epigenetic influences – influences outside of the womb such as antibiotics - and yet the moral argument, the health argument and the aesthetic argument are all deployed to maintain a fat-thin binary that profits industries while hurting individuals.

The health food lobby is complicit in this game too. Even the nutritionist can become colonised[10]. Michele Simon[11] has detailed how the continuing education of nutritionists is often subsidized by the big food companies who use webinars, the underwriting of conferences, conference sessions and industry-funded research directed to showing the efficacy of their particular products and food groups. It can then be hard for nutritionists to recognise that their learning base may be influenced and tainted by such funding. This bears on funding for research showing the efficacy of the weight loss industry too, an industry that is owned in large part by the big food conglomerates. In his research for The Men Who Made Us Fat and The Men Who Made Us Thin[12], Jacques Peretti talks with a weight loss industry senior executive who freely admits that recidivism is the basis of its profit. For the industry to thrive it must fail its customers repeatedly so that they return time after time. That part of the NHS budget is now funding such dubious weight loss plans is reprehensible.

As in traditional market economics, there is a free market for the food companies to sell their wares, to offer the freedom of choice and stimulate desire in us who have to regulate ourselves lest we be fat. For 'fat' is designated bad and this means that individuals find themselves avoiding certain food groups, describing their aspiration as *healthy* eating, getting involved in orthorexic behaviour or eating minimally during the week and binging on weekends, as a way of managing food. Bulimic behaviours become unremarkable and commonplace. In a perverse interference with appetite to ensure that one is not eating too much, restraint is offered as the righteous alternative to the devil's path of indulgence.

The fear word of today is obesity. Many more people in the west are growing wider and wider. We know that certain fats, corns and sugars, particularly of the long-shelf-life variety, coupled with a sedentary lifestyle, make our bodies work less efficiently[13]. We know that sugar substitutes may affect metabolism adversely so that people gain rather than achieve the promised weight loss.[14] A recent study[15] published in Obesity Research and Clinical Practice shows that weight loss is not simply predicated on calories in and calories out. In calling for further investigation of their conclusion that 'multiple factors beyond diet and physical activity are associated with increases in body weight', they are suggesting that the ways the health industry is framing the question and evidence is insufficient. The quality of the foodstuffs that are ingested is questioned. Tim Spector's work leads him to posit that 'The diminution in our microbes and our processed, sugary, fatty diets have joined forces to produce the perfect obesity storm'[16]. He worries that our microbes are being depopulated by sterile foods, which in turn create epigenetic changes causing our digestion to work; or rather not work; in its intended ways. His work helps us to understand the growth in girth. It has also helped me to understand how the message of FIFI to eat when you are hungry, to eat what you really desire, to pay attention to how the food feels as you eat it, to stop when you are full, and assess how it feels after you've eaten it, needs to be modified. It needs to be modified in one simple way: to encourage people to choose foods that start from natural ingredients rather than from a chemical base. All manner of foods – cheesecake, sausages, potatoes, biscuits, pasta etc. – depending on one's individual body, will sit absolutely fine if they are made from real cheese, real meat, real cream, butter, flour etc. It is the horror of food-industry practices that has made non-foods such as aspartame enter into an eating culture which now harms us. This is not to say that we won't be drawn to eat industrial concoctions and they must be avoided; but it is to say that as people struggle to find their hungers and satisfactions, it will be important to observe whether non-food foods satisfy in a sustainable way or whether they induce the desire for more and more; without offering an end point from the inside of the body rather than the end of the packet. Often with non-food foods, there is a rush to finish them so that their pull will be silenced by their disappearance. They tantalise and their promise can be so much more than their delivery.

In addition to the ingestion of non-foods and the adulteration of even the most cherished of foods, we must also factor in that the extreme pressure on people to be thin creates, in part, a mindset that they are fat when they are not fat. This mindset, this sense that one is too large or too fat, has penetrated our awareness so that girls and women, boys and men, become increasingly self-conscious of their body size. They restrict their food when they needn't, and if done consistently this can muck about with their set-point[17] which controls their metabolism. The implications of food deprivation leading to extreme thinness during pregnancy and the consequences for children who then have a propensity to towards obesity is an often overlooked factor in all the debates about body size[18]. This was found in the Dutch famine during the war but is now occurring for entirely different and troubling reasons to do with the tyrannical hold of thinness.

Our society sets few limits on corporate power. In an ingenious sell, freedom is vested in the individual's right to choose[19]. Health is an individual decision. Freedom is also vested in the corporate right to a free market in which to sell wares of a more than dubious nature. Thin is one such dubious sell and foods that are not foods is another such dubious sell. With the individual accountable for their own fate, personal responsibility is extolled. It's as though we didn't have sewage systems and we then blamed the individual for contracting infections and urinary tract problems. Governments need to take on the food industry on the one hand and, on the other, address the widespread and hidden problems of troubled eating which beset so many. *It is this hidden problem of troubled eating which is the true public health emergency and the epidemic that needs confronting. Obesity is as much as studied skinniness an expression of troubled eating.*

Fat is no longer an objective word meaning adipose tissue. It is a word heavily laden with negative value and discomforting emotions. Even to have a book title *Fat Is A Feminist Issue* is to risk turning off potential readers. Culturally we are encouraged to find fat an affront. Negativity screams so intensely from the word that we are unable to sort out the facts from the fantasies.

While we've become accustomed to training our eyes on the tobacco industry's nefarious doings, the escapades of the food industry often go unnoticed. Well known diet companies continue to sell their wares despite their appalling recidivism rate of 90%.[20] The sell here is a revolving door. If you fall off the wagon you are welcomed back to purchase more pre-prepared foods and support. Oprah's recent association with Weight Watchers is a testament to how profitable such companies are. They appear to speak to women's discontent and confusion about their eating. The sell is to accompany you through life. There seems to be no notion that you will find – as you do in this book – nourishing and delicious ways to eat when you are hungry, stop when you are full and, most importantly, be free from food and body obsessions, counting points, calories or grams. Sadly, slimming companies who now rebrand themselves as helping you to eat well, serve only a small percentage of their customers in anything but the short term. The camaraderie they offer, the structures of group leaders are there to bind you to a product – the group, the goods with an emotional, quasi-nutritional or substitute nutritional, price tag. Zoe Heller, head of nutrition for Weight Watchers, told the Parliamentary Inquiry on Body Image in 2012 that a 5% weight loss was all they expected. This extraordinary admission from a slimming company, that this is all the weight loss they anticipate, nevertheless targets its services at those who believe they have so much more weight to lose.

But let's not forget the other players who are also responsible for driving the Obesity Agenda and categorising it as the number one health problem in the western world. The new rise in obesity is not only simple growth in girth, although it is also that. Some of it is to do with the avail-

ability of non-food foods which harm us, some to do with
the sedentary life, some to do with the revising of the Body
Mass Index (the BMI) downwards over the past fifteen years
so that if you are Brad Pitt or George Bush, you are now
considered overweight. Despite the evidence from the
Center for Disease Control at the National Institute of
Health that the most protective weight is a BMI of 27.5,
this is considered overweight.[21] As Paul Campos and J. Eric
Oliver[22] recount in their attempts to understand the rise in
the obesity stats which concerned them both, they were
separately amazed to discover the industry push behind the
classification of obesity which include the recalibration of
what constitutes 'overweight' so that for example, overnight
36 million Americans woke up to find that they were obese.

But let's take an even wider snapshot. In her book
Dispensing with the Truth, Alice Mundy details the million-
dollar funding that commercial weight-loss groups contributed to the campaign 'Shape Up America'. This campaign
was part of a strategy to turn obesity into a disease to be
treated by the pharmaceutical, diet and medical industries.
'Think of it,' Mundy writes, 'as Obesity Inc.', which is how
I did think when I went to my local Boots on the day that
GlaxoSmithKline's Alli (pronounced as one would a friend)
went on sale. At the pharmacy counter, women, not in any
way large, queued up to buy the new miracle fat blocker.
The pharmacist accepted that these women needed to lose
weight even without much physical sign to point to and
despite evidence from the professional journals, which shows
that fitness, not fat, determines our mortality. Obesity Inc.
doesn't like the message that you can be fat, fit and healthy.

And then there is the fitness industry. What could be
better than being fit, we've all come to believe? And what
could be better than us taking personal responsibility for our

fitness? Once again the neo-liberal agenda is in full force. As the Nobel Prize-winning economists Akerlof and Shiller[23] detail, the activities of the so-called free market make individuals the prey of business schemes. They show how the health club industry in the US is another way to coin money as a $22 billion industry seduces over 50 million customers to pay monthly contracts; even though many of them would save a considerable amount if they paid by the visit.

The pursuit of money and profit is behind much of the beauty and fashion industry initiatives which in turn rest on the fat - thin binary in which thin is aspirational and essential (despite the fact that more clothes in the UK are sold above size 12 then below). Consider the role of branding in these industries and the safety and feel-good identification offered through purchasing 'names'. Consider the increasing floor space the cosmetic companies take up in a department store. Consider the links between the producers of fashion and the abject position of the seamstresses in Vietnam, Bangladesh, Pakistan. Consider the despoiling of the earth and water of an industry which uses intense chemical dyes in the mass preparation of cotton. Consider the wealth of fashion retailers and designers who regularly, like their compatriots in the beauty industry, rank in the Rich List[24]. Consider too how the ideology of 'choice' operates to encourage us to spend copiously on fast fashion and branded clothing. The curating of self-image is implied as essential, and essential too is a kind of body fascism, a tyranny of thin and the sense that we should all be one size. This is not only unrealistic, it is unhealthy and unattainable. But despite the fact that one size does not fit all, the desire to conform and to see reflected back in our mirrors an approximation of what we see on billboards, magazines and screens is compelling. The uniformity of the visual imagery that we are exposed to constructs our relationship to our personal bodies.

We may think it doesn't, we may think that style and aesthetics are just a bit of fun, but now we have evidence that tells us that we have been seriously underestimating the impact that visual culture has on us. In 1995 TV was first introduced to Fiji; showing many imported US shows.[25] In 1998, only three years later, 11.9% of the teenage girls were hanging over the toilet bowl with bulimia, a previously unknown behaviour. They wanted to be modern, to look like the girls they saw on US shows. This shocking fact reverberates in my mind when I try to understand the growth of eating and body-image problems today and the factors that have accelerated them globally. It is not only key for the young women of Fiji, it is key for young women in England, Ireland, Scotland, Wales, Europe, North and South America, Japan, Korea, India and increasingly those countries brought into globalism. When one considers the facts from Fiji alongside the phenomenon of 35,000 cases of women's noses being reshaped in Iran under the Hijab, and Chinese women's legs being broken and prostheses inserted in order to create a few extra centimetres of height, and Nigerian women thinking they are too fat, a picture emerges of body insecurity, even body hatred, becoming a major export of the western world.

What binds people together in the global village is an ability to identify with and recognise one another speedily through consuming and specifically through consuming the brands, clothes, food and music we wear, eat or listen to. In this global marketplace a woman's body shape has in itself become a brand, her brand, her membership and entitlement to occupy space. Her body has to fit for her to feel she belongs and is recognised as belonging. As women have fought to expand the ways in which they can act in and on the world, they have been given back a picture of femininity that is ever more homogeneous and diminutive. Yes, diversity appears to rule because models of all colours and ethnic groups now promote today's look, but the ethnic variations are all circumscribed within a small body variation whose main architecture is skinny and long.

If we read the zeitgeist and the research[26] and track the blogs, we can see how unsatisfactory women find this state of affairs. There are a whole slew of voices from Kate Winslet to star bloggers[27] contesting the use of this mono-visual culture and seemingly innocuous; but truly pernicious; internet sites. They yearn for a wider representation of beauty, one which shows that beauty comes in many different sizes. They reject the notion that thin is all. They reject that physical attractiveness should be a base line before you can start to live. Health at Every Size campaigns as the new peace movement and they have more than a point: www.haescommunity.org. The international activist group www.endangeredbodies.org, of which I am a member, successfully campaigned to remove the Facebook emoticon 'fat' as a feeling. And singers like Pink in her song 'Fuckin' Perfect' reject the horrors of having to look and project perfection; while Nina Nesbitt blogs and sings about these pressures. Meanwhile there have been some promising advertising initiatives which have been trying to expand and extend the pictures of girls and women we see around us and these are being met by women with enormous pleasure. It is refreshing and heartening but it is not enough.

It is not my argument that thin is bad and fat is good. That would be an absurd position. I am writing about the emotional meanings that we have bequeathed to fat and thin. More often than not, for the individual, fat isn't about the physical: it is in their own mind and in their articulation of what they believe fat to be. For them; fat is demonic and thin is wonderful. In accepting these notions we are missing more complex and contradictory meanings and ideas we ascribe to fatness and thinness. If these were understood, it could help the individual find ways to live in her body without constantly criticising it. It is in this sense that I use the words fat and thin: as symbolic rather than actual. *Fat Is A Feminist Issue* seeks to helps us encounter these richer meanings while providing a model for a different kind of eating – a sustainable way to feed one's body and be a size that is right for oneself. It offers a way to feel entitled to eat – an all too rare pleasure in a climate of guilt.

A central message of this book is that dieting and food deprivation schemes don't ultimately work[28]. If dieting's aim is to temper eating and lose weight, the evidence is in the opposite direction. Dieting leads to weight gain and troubled eating. Worse than that, it undermines the individual's capacity to feed herself well. It leads to food confusion, compulsive eating and body distress. The messages of the diet/health industries fail to keep up with even the most minimal of research, let alone the interesting work on epigenetics[29] which shows us how very individual our bodies are and how useless these dietetic manipulations are. The diet/health industries don't follow science, and it bears repeating, because their profits depend upon failure.

But we needn't despair. There is both an individual and a group way out. The psychological exercises and the political critique this book offers are designed to enable the individual to live in her body with more ease and with an ability to enjoy her hunger and her appetite and to defy with others the heinous attack on girls' and women's bodies.

The ideas and practices I detail came out of a women's group at the height of Second Wave Feminism. I went to the Alternate U(niversity) on Sixth Avenue and 14th Street in New York City and was intrigued by the notice of a meeting on compulsive eating and self-image. Its – at that time – rather abstract title produced a vague worry that this might be somewhat trivial or superficial. Nevertheless it drew me. What could it quite mean? Were we now to apply the ways of talking in women's groups about men, sex, work, war and children to bodies and eating?

I anticipated an analysis of the food, fashion and beauty industries or the meaning of 'thin' in wealthy countries and 'fat' in poorer ones, perhaps a discussion of nutritional and agricultural policies in the United States and the 'developing world'. I wondered how we might explore the topic of women's troubled eating in the context of a political vocabulary – a vocabulary that looked at patriarchy, the family, gender and the role of corporations. I was quizzical but interested.

Back then we believed ourselves happy in our blue jeans and work shirts. We wore the clothes of rebellion and did not care what was especially fashionable, provocative or appealing to others. Or did we?

One by one we shared how we felt about our bodies, being attractive, food, eating, thinness, fatness, adverts and fashion and how this related to the economic structure. We detailed our previous food histories and traded horror stories of diet doctors, psychiatrists, diet organisations, health farms, summer camps and fasting. We knew that all our previous attempts at getting our bodies the right weight and shape had not worked. Many of us had achieved the size we believed we wanted to be after considerable struggles, only to discover that we were perched there for a shorter time than the sizes we disliked and mostly dwelled in. We wondered *why* we had wanted our bodies so much thinner. We did not understand why we could not keep 'it' off, why every time we neared the goal 'it' would creep up, or why we always broke our diets.

Why were we plagued by our body size and shape?

We began asking new questions and coming up with new answers. We were a self-help group at the time when energy from the Women's Liberation Movement sparked us all into rethinking many previously held assumptions. The creativity of women coming together prepared a fertile soil in which new ideas, feminist ideas, nurtured and developed in countless consciousness-raising groups, in mass marches and demonstrations, in organised political campaigns, found new applications and usefulness. Looking at the body and compulsive eating became one such area.[30]

Compulsive eating is a painful and, on the surface, self-destructive, activity. But feminism and psychoanalysis have taught us that activities that appear to be self-destructive are invariably adaptations, attempts to cope with the world. In our group, we turned our strongly held ideas about dieting and thinness upside down.

Carol Munter, who had convened the group, told us of her friend who lost weight without dieting. Slowly and unsurely we stopped dieting. Nothing terrible happened. My world did not collapse. Carol raised a central question: maybe there was a reluctance to be thin. I dismissed that out of hand. Of course I wanted to be thin, I would be . . . The dots turned out to hold the answer. Who I would be thin was, I imagined, different from who *I* was. I decided I did not want to be thin, there was not much in it. You were more hassled by men, you became a sex object. You were constantly evaluating yourself from the outside. No, I definitely did not want to be thin . . . I developed a new political reason for not being thin – I was not going to be like the fashion magazines wanted me to be; I was a Jewish beatnik and I would be *zaftig*. I relaxed, ate what I wanted, and wore clothes that were expressive of me. I even felt a little smug. I ignored the diet sheets in the newspapers. I enjoyed the different food phases I was going through and I walked down the street feeling increasingly confident.

But the dots nagged. Why was I afraid of being thin?

The things I was frightened of came into view. I confronted them, always asking myself, how would it help to be 'fat' in this situation? What *in reality* would be more troublesome if I were 'thin'? As the images of my 'fat' and 'thin' personality conflated, I began to lose weight. I wasn't so large to begin with so *I began to understand that fat and thin are more powerful as states of mind than they are as literal translations of size.* Today for the vast majority of girls and women feeling fat,[31] it is similarly what fat and thin mean that is enabling or disabling.

As the group and our explorations progressed, I felt a deep satisfaction that I could be a size that felt good for me while no longer being preoccupied with food. I promised myself I would not be responsible for depriving myself of the food I liked. I had learned a crucial lesson – that I could be, indeed I was, the same person thin as I was fat. Satisfied, I left the group. Together we had developed a theory and practice that made sense. Carol and I went on to help other women sort through this problem. We ran groups. We became psychotherapists and worked with women individually and together for five years.

Fat is a Feminist Issue, written back then, was my effort to share this work. At an individual level this book, written as a self-help manual, has been used by hundreds of thousands of women to help them manage their food and bodies in this toxic culture. It is also the case that many therapists have been incorporating this method into their own work.

And of course it was written to put an end to this stealing of women's bodies and lives. No such luck. We will need a movement not scared to trivialise this subject, not scared to see the players outside of ourselves and the ways in which they live inside of ourselves if we are to save future generations from the horrors of body and eating troubles. Such a movement is gathering pace in many different places. It has to contend with its own notion that in the face of the world's many troubles, focus on the body can seem insignificant. But of course it isn't. In every struggle, women's bodies have a story to tell, carry cultural and political meanings and reflect social inequality in complex ways. To all women who suffer from the problems of compulsive eating, I hope that the accumulated experience of other women as expressed in this book will speak to you. I hope you will find ways to contest what is still visited upon us.

To all of you approaching this book, I hope it has meaning for you. I hope you can find a personal body peace.

SUSIE ORBACH
London, 2016

[1]By and large, the approach has been either to try to remove the resultant obesity or to treat the underlying cause of distress that has produced compulsive eating. Compulsive eating has never been strictly defined but what it has meant for me and the women I have worked with is:

- Eating when you are not physically hungry.
- Feeling out of control around food, submerged by either dieting or gorging.
- Spending a good deal of time thinking and worrying about food and fatness.
- Scouring the latest diet for vital information.
- Feeling awful about yourself as someone who is out of control.
- Feeling awful about your body.

Our approach has been to see compulsive eating as *both* a symptom and a problem in itself. It is a symptom in the sense that the compulsive eater does not know how to cope with whatever underlies this behaviour and turns to food. On the other hand, the compulsive eating syndrome is so highly developed and painfully absorbing that it has to be addressed directly as the problem too. Consequently, we address both aspects. We explore and demystify the symptom to find out what is being expressed in the desire to be fat, in the fear of thinness and in the wish to fill and starve ourselves.

At the same time we attempt to intervene directly so that the feelings and behaviour around food can change.

---

[1] Thompson, P.B., (2015) *From Field to Fork: Food Ethics for Everyone* Oxford University Press, Oxford

ying problems need to be exposed and separated, though not necessarily worked through. The perspective is always to see the social dimensions that have led women to choose compulsive eating as an adaptation to sexist pressure in contemporary society.

BOOK ONE

The Anti-Diet Guide

For
Eleanor Anguti,
Carol Bloom
and
Lela Zaphiropoulos

Contents

Prologue

Obesity and overeating have joined sex as central issues in the lives of many women today. In the United States, 50% of women are estimated to be overweight. Every women's magazine has a diet column. Diet doctors and clinics flourish. The names of diet foods are now part of our general vocabulary. Physical fitness and beauty are every woman's goals. While this preoccupation with fat and food has become so common that we tend to take it for granted, being fat, feeling fat and the compulsion to overeat are, in fact, serious and painful experiences for the women involved.

Being fat isolates and invalidates a woman. Almost inevitably, the explanations offered for fatness point a finger at the failure of women themselves to control their weight, control their appetites and control their impulses. Women suffering from the problem of compulsive eating endure a double anguish: feeling out of step with the rest of society, and believing that it is all their own fault.

The number of women who have problems with weight and compulsive eating is large and growing. Owing to the emotional distress involved and the fact that the many varied solutions offered to women in the past have not worked, a new psychotherapy to deal with compulsive eating has had to evolve within the context of the movement for women's liberation. This new psychotherapy represents a feminist rethinking of traditional psychoanalysis.

A psychoanalytic approach has much to offer towards a solution to compulsive eating problems. It provides ways for exploring the roots of such problems in early experiences. It shows us how we develop our adult personalities, most

5

importantly our sexual identity – how a female baby becomes a girl and then a woman, and how a male baby becomes a boy and then a man. Psychoanalytic insight helps us to understand what getting fat and overeating mean to individual women – by explaining their conscious or unconscious acts.

An approach based exclusively on classical psychoanalysis, without a feminist perspective is, however, inadequate. Since the Second World War, psychiatry has, by and large, told unhappy women that their discontent represents an inability to resolve the 'Oedipal constellation'. Female fatness has been diagnosed as an obsessive-compulsive symptom related to separation-individuation, narcissism and insufficient ego development.[1] Being overweight is seen as a deviance and anti-men. Overeating and obesity have been reduced to character defects, rather than perceived as the expression of painful and conflicting experiences. Furthermore, rather than attempting to uncover and confront women's bad feelings about their bodies or towards food, professionals concerned themselves with the problem of how to get the women thin. So, after the psychiatrists, analysts and clinical psychologists proved unsuccessful, experimental workers looked for biological and even genetic reasons for obesity. None of these approaches has had convincing, lasting results. None of them has addressed the central issues of compulsive eating which are rooted in the social inequality of women.

A feminist perspective to the problem of women's compulsive eating is essential if we are to move on from the ineffective blame-the-victim approach[2] and the unsatisfactory adjustment model of treatment. While psychoanalysis gives us useful tools to discover the deepest sources of emotional distress, feminism insists that those painful personal experiences derive from the social context into which female babies are born, and within which they develop to become adult women. The fact that compulsive eating is over-whelmingly a woman's problem suggests that it has something to do with the experience of being female in our society. Feminism argues that being fat represents an attempt to break free of society's sex stereotypes. Getting fat can thus be understood as a definite and purposeful act; it is a directed, conscious or unconscious, challenge to sex-role stereotyping and culturally defined experience of womanhood.

Fat is a social disease, and fat is a feminist issue. Fat is *not* about lack of self-control or lack of will power. Fat *is* about protection, sex, nurturance, strength, boundaries, mothering, substance, assertion and rage. It is a response to the inequality of the sexes. Fat expresses experiences of women today in ways that are seldom examined and even more seldom treated. While becoming fat does not alter the roots of sexual oppression, an examination of the underlying causes or unconscious motivation that lead women to compulsive eating suggests new treatment possibilities. Unlike most weight-reducing schemes, our new therapeutic approach does not reinforce the oppressive social roles that lead women into compulsive eating in the first place. What is it about the social position of women that leads them to respond to it by getting fat?

The current idelogical justification for inequality of the sexes has been built on the concept of the innate differences between women and men. Women alone can give birth to and breast-feed their infants and, as a result, a primary dependency relationship develops between mother and child. While this biological capacity is the only known genetic difference between men and women,[3] it is used as the basis on which to divide unequally women and men's labour, power, roles and expectations. The division of labour has become institutionalised. Woman's capacity to reproduce and provide nourishment has relegated her to the care and socialisation of children.

The relegation of women to the social roles of wife and mother has several significant consequences that contribute to the problem of fat. First, in order to become a wife and mother, a woman has to have a man. Getting a man is presented as an almost unattainable and yet essential goal. To get a man, a woman has to learn to regard herself as an item, a commodity, a sex object. Much of her experience and identity depends on how she and others see her. As John Berger says in *Ways of Seeing:*

> Men *act* and women *appear*. Men look at women. Women watch themselves being looked at. This determines not only most relations between men and women, but also the relation of women to themselves.[4]

This emphasis on presentation as the central aspect of a woman's existence makes her extremely self-conscious. It demands that she occupy herself with a self-image that others will find pleasing and attractive – an image that will immediately convey what kind of woman she is. She must observe and evaluate herself, scrutinising every detail of herself as though she were an outside judge. She attempts to make herself in the image of womanhood presented by billboards, newspapers, magazines and television. The media present women either in a sexual context or within the family, reflecting a woman's two prescribed roles, first as a sex object, and then as a mother. She is brought up to marry by 'catching' a man with her good looks and pleasing manner. To do this she must look appealing, earthy, sensual, sexual, virginal, innocent, reliable, daring, mysterious, coquettish and thin. In other words, she offers her self-image on the marriage marketplace.

As a married woman, her sexuality will be sanctioned and her economic needs will be looked after. She will have achieved the first step of womanhood.

Since women are taught to see themselves from the outside as candidates for men, they become prey to the huge fashion and diet industries that first set up the ideal images and then exhort women to meet them. The message is loud and clear – the woman's body is not her own. The woman's body is not satisfactory as it is. It must be thin, free of 'unwanted hair,' deodorised, perfumed and clothed. It must conform to an ideal physical type. Family and school socialisation teaches girls to groom themselves properly. Furthermore, the job is never-ending, for the image changes from year to year. In the early 1960s, the only way to feel acceptable was to be skinny and flat chested with long straight hair. The first of these was achieved by near starvation, the second, by binding one's breasts with an ace bandage and the third, by ironing one's hair. Then in the early 1970s, the look was curly hair and full breasts. Just as styles in clothes change seasonally, so women's bodies are expected to change to fit these fashions. Long and skinny one year, petite and demure the next, women are continually manipulated by images of proper womanhood, which are extremely powerful because they are presented as the only reality. To ignore them means to risk being an outcast. Women are urged to conform, to help out the economy by continuous consumption of goods and clothing that are quickly made unwearable by the next season's fashion styles in clothes and body shapes. In the background, a ten billion dollar industry waits to remould bodies to the latest fashion. In this way, women are caught in an attempt to conform to a standard that is *externally* defined and constantly changing. But these models of femininity are experienced by women as unreal, frightening and unattainable. They produce a picture that is far removed from the reality of women's day-to-day lives.

The one constant in these images is that a woman must be thin. For many women, compulsive eating and being fat have become one way to avoid being marketed or seen as the ideal woman: 'My fat says "screw you" to all who want me to be the perfect mom, sweetheart, maid and whore. Take me for who *I* am, not for who I'm supposed to be. If you are really interested in *me*, you can wade through the layers and find out who I am.' In this way, fat expresses a rebellion against the powerlessness of the woman, against the pressure to look and act in a certain way and against being evaluated on her ability to create an image of herself.

Becoming fat is, thus, a woman's response to the first step in the process of fulfilling a prescribed social role which requires her to shape herself to an externally imposed image in order to catch a man. But a second stage in this process takes place after she achieves that goal, after she has become a wife and mother.

For a mother, everyone else's needs come first. Mothers are the unpaid managers of small, essential, complex and demanding organisations. They may not control the financial arrangements of this minicorporation or the major decisions on location or capital expenditure, but they do generally control the day-to-day operations. For her keep, the mother works an estimated ten hours a day (eighteen, if she has a second job outside the home) making sure that the food is purchased and prepared, the children's clothes, toys and books are in place, and that the father's effects are at the ready. She makes the house habitable, clean and comfy; she does the social secretarial work of arranging for the family to spend time with relatives and friends; she provides a baby-sitting and chauffeur-escort service for her children.

As babies and children, we are all cared for. As adults, however, women are expected to feed and clean not only their babies but also their husbands, and only then, themselves.

In this role women experience particular pressure over food and eating. After the birth of each baby, breasts or bottle becomes a major issue. The mother is often made to feel insecure about her adequacy to perform her fundamental job. In the hospital the baby is weighed after each feed to see if the mother's breasts have enough milk. Pediatricians and baby-care books bombard the new mother with authoritative but conflicting advice about, for example, scheduled versus demand feeding, composition of the formula or the introduction of solid foods. As her children grow older, a woman continues to be reminded that her feeding skills are inadequate. To the tune of billions of dollars a year, the food industry counsels her on how, when and what she should feed her charges. The advertisements cajole her into providing nutritious breakfasts, munchy snacks, and wholesome dinners. Media preoccupation with good housekeeping and, particularly, with good food and good feeding, serves as a yardstick by which to measure the mother's everfailing performance. This preoccupation colonises food preparation so that the housewife is presented with a list of 'do's' and 'don'ts' so contradictory that it is a wonder that anything gets produced in the kitchen at all. It is not surprising that a woman quickly learns not to trust her own impulses, either in feeding her family or in listening to her own needs when she feeds herself.

During the period in her life which is devoted to child rearing, the woman is constantly making sure that others' lives run smoothly. She does this without thinking seriously that she is working at a full-time job. Her own experience of everyday life is as midwife to others' activities. While she is preparing her children to become future workers, and enabling her husband to be a more 'effective' producer, her role is to produce and reproduce workers. In this capacity she is constantly giving out without receiving the credit that would validate her social worth.

In a capitalist society everyone is defined by their job. A higher status is given to business*men*, academics and professionals than to production and service workers. Women's work in the home falls into the service and production category. Although often described as menial, deemed creative, dismissed as easy, or revered as god-given, women's work is seen as existing outside the production process and therefore devalued. Women as a group are allowed less expression than the men in their social class. However oppressed men are by a class society, they hold more power than women. Every man has to watch out for his boss. Every woman has to watch out lest her man not approve. The standards and views of the day are male. Women are seen as different from normal people (who are men), they are seen as 'other'.[5] They are not accepted as equal human beings with men. Their full identity is not supported by the society in which they grow up. This leads to confusion for women. Women are trapped in the role of an alien, yet delegated responsibility for making sure that others' lives are productive.

Since women are not accepted as equal human beings but are nevertheless expected to devote enormous energy to the lives of others, the distinctions between their own lives and the lives of those close to them may become blurred. Merging with others, feeding others, not knowing how to make space for themselves are frequent themes for women. Mothers are constantly giving out and feeding the world; everyone else's needs are primary. That they feel confusion about their own bodily needs is not surprising and there may be few ways of noting their personal concerns. A form of giving to and replenishing oneself is through food. 'I eat a lot because I'm always stoking myself up for the day's encounters. I look after my family, my mother and any number of people who pass in and out of my day. I feel empty with all this giving so I eat to fill up the spaces and give me sustenance to go on giving to the world.' The resulting fat has the function of making the space for which women crave. It is an attempt to answer the question, 'If I am constantly giving myself to everyone, where do I begin and end?' We want to look and be substantial. We want to be bigger than society will let us. We want to take up as much space as the other sex. 'If I get bigger like a man then maybe I'll get taken seriously as is a man.'

What happens to the woman who does not fit the social role? Although the image of ideal sexual object and all-competent mother is socially pervasive, it is not only limiting and unattainable, but it also fails to correspond to the reality of many, many women's lives today. Most women today do still marry and have children. But many also continue to work outside the home after marriage, either to meet economic needs or in an attempt to break the limits of their social role. Women continually juggle with the many different aspects of their personalities which are developed and expressed at great cost against this unfriendly background. In this context, just as many women first become fat in an attempt to avoid being made into sexual objects at the beginning of their adult lives, so many women remain fat as a way of neutralising their sexual identity in the eyes of others who are important to them as their life progresses. In this way, they can hope to be taken seriously in their working lives outside the home. It is unusual for women to be accepted for their competence in this sphere.

When they lose weight, that is, begin to look like a perfect female, they find themselves being treated frivolously by their male colleagues. When women are thin, they *are* treated frivolously: thin-sexy-incompetent worker. But if a woman loses weight, she herself may not yet be able to separate thinness from the packaged sexuality around her which simultaneously defines her as incompetent. It is difficult to conform to one image that society would have you fit (thin) without also being the other image (sexy female). 'When I'm fat, I feel I can hold my own. Whenever I get thin I feel I'm being treated like a little doll who doesn't know which end is up.'

We have seen how fat is a symbolic rejection of the limitations of women's role, an adaptation that many women use in the burdensome attempt to pursue their individual lives within the proscriptions of their social function. But in order to understand more about the way that overweight and, in particular, overeating, function in the lives of individual women, we must examine the process by which they are initially taught their social role. It is a complex and ironic process, for women are prepared for this life of inequality by other women who themselves suffer its limitations – their mothers. The feminist perspective reveals that compulsive eating is, in fact, an expression of the complex relationships between mothers and daughters.

If a woman's social role is to become a mother, nurturing – feeding the family in the widest possible sense – is the mother's central job. By and large, it is only within the family that a woman has any social power. Her competence as a mother and her ability to be an emotional support for her family defines her and provides her with a recognised context within which to exist. For a mother, a crucial part of the maternal role is to help her daughter, as her mother did before her, to make a smooth transition into the female social role. From her mother, the young girl learns who she herself is and can be. The mother provides her with a model of feminine behaviour, and directs the daughter's behaviour in particular ways.

But the world the mother must present to her daughter is one of unequal relationships, between parent and child, authority and powerlessness, man and woman. The child is exposed to the world of power relationships by a unit that itself produces and reproduces perhaps the most fundamental of these inequalities. Within the family, an inferior sense of self is instilled into little girls.[6] While it is obvious that the growing-up process for girls and boys is vastly different, what may be less apparent is that to prepare her daughter for a life of inequality, the mother tries to hold back her child's desires to be a powerful, autonomous, self-directed, energetic and productive human being. From an early age, the young girl is encouraged to accept this rupture in her development and is guided to cope with this loss by putting her energy into taking care of others. Her own needs for emotional support and growth will be satisfied if she can convert them into giving to others.

Meanwhile, little boys are taught to accept emotional support without learning how to give this kind of nurturing and loving in return. Therefore, when a young woman finally achieves the social reward of marriage, she finds that it rarely provides either the nuture she still needs, or an opportunity for independence and self-development. To be a woman is to live with the tension of giving and not getting; and the mother and daughter involved in the process leading to this conclusion are inevitably bound up in ambivalence, difficulty and conflict.

If we look at it from the mother's point of view, the

process of leading her daughter to adult womanhood is ambivalent for several reasons. The first is the question of independence. The mother, who has been prepared for a life of giving, finds her feeding, nurturing and child-rearing capacity – so integral to her success in her social role – satisfied. She needs to be needed and has indeed fulfilled herself as a 'good mother' by attentively feeding her child. Thus, mothers do and do not want their daughters to leave them. They do because the maternal role also requires them to prepare their daughters for eventual independence: to fail at this is to fail at motherhood. On the other hand, to succeed at this signals the end of motherhood. We have seen that of the limited roles that have been available to women in this century, motherhood is the only one in which women have legitimate power. Therefore, their personal success at being mothers results in their loss of power. Their personal success is a dead end; it does not lead on to the creation of a new, equally powerful role.

The mother's ambivalence is, however, even more painful in that mothers do and do not want their daughters to be like them. For a daughter to be like her mother is a way, at least partially, to validate the mother's life. But, the mother's life remains an invalidated life and the daughter's act of reproducing her mother's lifestyle can be no more than a perpetuation of powerlessness. In her love for her daughter, the mother must inevitably want a different life for her.

Nevertheless, mothers may feel ambivalent about the changing opportunities available to their daughters which were not available to them. They may be jealous of these opportunities, and fearful of their daughters' welfare in a world they know to be hostile to women, at the same time as they acquire some indirect satisfaction at their daughters'

16

ambition and success. While a mother must be a m[...]
daughter can be ambitious and engaged in the world.

Let us now look at these conflicts from the daughter's
point of view. Daughters do and do not want to leave their
mothers. For a daughter to leave is for her to become
independent, part of the world, to signal her emergence as
a female adult. However, this autonomy itself causes problems. As we have seen, independence in the world is not
yet an option for female adults. Daughters feel ambivalent
about their opportunities in the world; they are ill-prepared
to take them up, as they have learned both from the culture
at large and from their own mothers.

Daughters identify with the powerlessness of their
mothers as women in a patriarchal society. They have been
brought up to be like their mothers. But daughters both
do and do not want to be like their mothers. While they
identify with their mothers as women, as givers, as caretakers, they may nevertheless desire a different experience
of womanhood. In leaving, in moving outside the prescribed
female role, the daughter may feel she is betraying her
mother or is showing her up by doing 'better'. She may
also feel nervous about being on shaky, untested ground.
Furthermore, if a daughter identifies with her mother's
powerlessness, she may see her role as that of taking care
of her mother – to provide her mother with the love, care
and interest she never received. She becomes her mother's
mother? Leaving becomes even more of a betrayal.

How do these ambivalences and conflicts in the
mother-daughter relationship come to express themselves
in fat, food and feeding? How is each adult woman who
suffers from compulsive eating expressing what happened
to her with her mother. It is obvious that feeding plays
a crucial part in the relationship of mother and child,

whatever the child's sex. Within the whole spectrum of nurturing activities expected of mothers, physical feeding is the most fundamental – indeed, instinctive. A mother's breasts provide food for her children, virtually without any conscious act on her own part, whereas all other nurturing activities, including the vital provision of emotional support, must be learned.

Because of her ambivalence towards her daughter, a mother's willingness to provide her with sensitive nurturing, both physically and emotionally, can be under-mined. Both female and male babies experience their first love relationships with the mother, but early on the mother must withhold a certain degree of support and sustenance from her daughter, in order to teach her the ways of womanhood. This has specific consequences. In *Little Girls*,[7] Elena Gianini Belotti cites a study of mothers' atti-tudes and actions when feeding their babies. In a sample of babies of both sexes, 99% of boys were breast-fed, while only 66% of girls were. Girls were weaned significantly earlier than boys and spent 50% less time feeding (in the case of breast- and bottle-feeds this meant much smaller feeds than the boys'). Thus, daughters are often fed less well, less attentively and less sensitively than they need. Inappropriate and insensitive physical feeding is subse-quently paralleled unconsciously by inadequate emotional feeding.

While unconsciously the mother may not be nurturing her daughter well, she gives up feeding her daughter only reluctantly. In the absence of an alternative role, the distinc-tion between herself and her child now outside the womb may become blurred. The mother may see her child as a product, a possession or an extension of herself. Thus, the mother has an interest in retaining control over how much, what, when and how her child eats. She needs to encourage this initial dependency for her own social survival.

There may be great ambivalence about feeding and nurturing. A mother must make sure her daughter is not overfed in case she becomes greedy and overweight – a terrible fate for a girl. She must make sure the child looks healthy – this is normally associated with a certain roundness – and she needs the child to depend on her; for who else is she, if she is not seen as mother? Yet she may also dislike this dependency, which ties her down, drains her and prevents her from directing her energies elsewhere. Finally, she must prepare her daughter to become the future nurturer and feeder of someone else – her daughter's future child, lover, husband or parents. She must teach her daughter to be concerned with feeding and nourishing others at the cost of not fully developing herself.

Meanwhile, on the daughter's side, as she develops from child to woman, the daughter's feeding of herself can become a symbolic response to both the physical and emotional deprivation she suffered as a child, an expression of her fraught intimacy with her mother. As the child gets more adept, she begins to feed herself and select her own foods, producing a developing sense of independence of the mother. But this break causes conflict for the daughter. On the one hand, the daughter wants to move away and learn to take care of herself; on the other hand, this ability to nurture herself suggests a rejection of the mother. This rejection takes on a deep significance because of the social limitation of the woman's role in patriarchal society. If the mother is not needed as mother, who will she be? The daughter feels guilty about destroying her mother's only role. As she seeks emotional sustenance through other social relationships, the adult daughter may continue to suffer deprivation, as her own partner has, very often, not learned to give. She turns to eating in the search for love, comfort, warmth and support – for that indefinable something that seems never to be there.

Compulsive eating becomes a way of expressing either side of this conflict. In overfeeding herself, the daughter may be trying to reject her mother's role while at the same time reproaching the mother for inadequate nurturing; or she may be attempting to retain a sense of identity with her mother. Popular culture abounds with evidence of the symbolic value that food and fat hold between mothers and daughters. In *Lady Oracle*,[8] for example, Margaret Atwood shows how the daughter's fat becomes a weapon in her battle with her mother. When her mother gives Joan a clothing allowance as an incentive to reduce, Joan deliberately buys clothes that flaunt her size and finally, with the purchase of a lime-green carcoat, succeeds in reducing her mother to tears:

> My mother had never cried where I could see her and I was dismayed, but elated too at this evidence of my power, my only power. I had defeated her; I wouldn't ever let her make me over in her image, thin and beautiful.

Similarly, in the movie, *Summer Wishes, Winter Dreams*, when the mother criticises her daughter's size, the latter blasts back that her fat is her own, that it is something for which she alone is responsible, that it is something her mother cannot take away too.

Women engaged in exploring their compulsive eating in relation to their mothers have come to the following varied realisations:

My fat says to my mother: 'I'm substantial. I can protect myself. I can go out into the world.'

My fat says to my mother: 'Look at me. I'm a mess; I don't know how to take care of myself. You can still be my mother.'

My fat says to my mother: 'I'm going out in the world. I can't take you with me but I can take a part of you that's connected to me. My body is from yours. My fat is connected to you. This way I can still have you with me.'

My fat says to my mother: 'I'm leaving you but I still need you. My fat lets you know I'm not really able to take care of myself.'

For the compulsive eater, fat has much symbolic meaning which makes sense within a feminist context. Fat is a response to the many oppressive manifestations of a sexist culture. Fat is a way of saying 'no' to powerlessness and self-denial, to a limiting sexual expression which demands that females look and act a certain way, and to an image of womanhood that defines a specific social role. Fat offends Western ideals of female beauty and, as such, every 'over-weight' woman creates a crack in the popular culture's ability to make us mere products. Fat also expresses the tension in the mother-daughter relationship, the relationship which has been allocated the feminisation of the female. This relationship is bound to be difficult in a patriarchal society because it demands that the already oppressed mothers become the teachers, preparers and enforcers of the oppression that society will visit on their daughters.

While fat serves the symbolic function of rejecting the way by which society distorts women and their relationships

21

with others, particularly in the critical relationship between mothers and daughters, getting fat remains an unhappy and unsatisfactory attempt to resolve these conflicts. It is a painful price to pay, whether a woman is trying to conform to society's expectations or attempting to forge a new identity.

When something is 'amiss' in this way, we can expect a psychological imbalance and reaction. Few things could be more 'amiss' than the attempt of a patriarchal culture to inhibit a young girl's desires to be creative and expressive, to push her almost exclusively into restrictive gender-linked activities, thoughts and feelings. A woman's psychological development is structured in such a way as to prepare her for a life of inequality, but this straitjacket is not accepted lightly and invariably causes a 'reaction'. Psychological disturbance often distorts a person's physiological capacity: ability to eat, sleep, talk or enjoy sexual activity. I suggest that one of the reasons we find so many women suffering from eating disorders is because the social relationship between feeder and fed, between mother and daughter, fraught as it is with ambivalence and hostility, becomes a suitable mechanism for distortion and rebellion.

An examination of the symbolic meanings of fat provides insight into individual woman's experience in patriarchal culture. Fat is an adaptation to the oppression of women and, as such, it may be an unsatisfying personal solution and an ineffectual political attack. It is to this problem that our compulsive eating therapy speaks, and it is within a feminist context that this is developed in the following chapters.

CHAPTER ONE

What Is Fat About for the Compulsive Eater?

Many people who are compulsive eaters underestimate the connection between their eating and body size. The compulsive eater often experiences her eating as chaotic, out of control, self-destructive and an example of her lack of will power. At the same time, however, she may say that really she just likes to eat a lot and is too greedy for her own good and that if it were not for the pounds and inches all this eating put on, she would be quite content. Some women say that if only there was a magic pill that allowed them to eat and eat incessantly while remaining at their ideal size, they would be quite happy. Indeed, women have had bypass surgery to achieve this state. So it is clear that people do see a connection between overeating and obesity and they attempt, through various deprivation schemes, to keep their overeating to a minimum so that they are not too fat.

What is crucial about this connection from the point of view of breaking the cycle of compulsive eating/dieting, however, is something often overlooked or misunderstood, both by compulsive eaters themselves and by those who try to help them. This is the idea that compulsive eating is linked to a desire to get fat. Now this point is not very obvious and can be difficult to understand. However, it is vital that we address it when trying to understand the immovability of the compulsive eater's seemingly bizarre relationship with food.

If one recognises that compulsive eating habits express an interest in being large, many things fall into place and the possibility of breaking the addiction to food is there.

Compulsive eating is a very, very painful activity. Behind the self-deprecating jokes is a person who suffers enormously. Much of her life is centred on food, what she can and cannot eat, what she will or will not eat, what she has or has not eaten and when she will or will not eat next. Typically, she cannot leave one mouthful of food on her plate and finds herself eating both at mealtimes and all through the day, evening or night. Much of her eating is done in secret or with eating friends, while at public meals she is the professional dieter and much admired for her abstinence. If she wants to eat cake she will go to the bakery and pretend that the cheesecake she buys is for her daughter or a friend, she will have it wrapped and only dare to eat it out in the open when she thinks no one will spot her. Alternatively she will buy some candy and hide it in her pocket, stealthily putting it into her mouth while she walks or drives along the street. The obsession with food carries with it an enormous amount of self-disgust, loathing and shame. These feelings arise from the experience of being out of control around food and compulsive eaters try numerous ways to discipline themselves. Many think that if they do not have access to food they will be all right. Therefore, if a compulsive eater lives alone her kitchen closets and refrigerator will probably contain only the most meagre range of foods. The kitchen will seem almost medicinal with its skimmed milk, cottage cheese, diet sodas and sugar-free jellies that masquerade as real food.

Alison, a 29 year-old zoologist, explained the pitfalls in her system of banning enjoyable foods from her apartment. She woke up in the middle of the night and felt driven to eat. She had been bingeing all evening so there was virtually nothing except dry cereal in the apartment left to eat. For the last two weeks she had had in mind a batch of homemade chocolate-chip cookies she had baked for Greg, her upstairs neighbour. Greg had gone away on vacation and Alison knew that there were still some cookies left because, while watering his plants, she noticed the cookie tin sitting on the kitchen counter. She got out of bed and took the keys to get into his apartment, found the cookies and stood there eating them all. She felt she could not just have one or two because that would not be enough, and if she ate a substantial number, when he returned, Greg would realise some were missing. Alison's solution was to stand in his freezing cold apartment and eat the lot hoping that when he returned he would not remember that he had left any cookies at all.

If the compulsive eater lives with others, the kitchen is more likely to be full of appetising foods that she denies herself or feels she must deny herself. Helen, a 50 year-old mother of two who has been watching her weight for the last 33 years, is so petrified of the food in her house that she has arranged with her husband that he lock the kitchen door at night. She has a coffee percolator by her bed and celery and carrots on ice and she is banned from the kitchen on all occasions except when preparing family meals and eating her dietetic version of them. Her situation is just an extreme example of what many compulsive eaters go through in their attempts to stay away from food.

Helen brought her husband in on her problem but for Alison it was of paramount importance that nobody else knew that she was eating in that way. Many women with compulsive eating problems find it excruciatingly painful that others should think that they themselves are large because of the amount they eat. They cannot bear other people making the connection between food intake and body size. This explains, in part, the public side of the compulsive eater who eats sparingly. Other women feel differently. A highly publicised method for weight control is a procedure of wiring the jaws together. The women involved in this treatment have been extremely large – well over 250lb [113kg]. While their teeth are braced and wired they subsist on a liquid diet. The braces are loosened once a week so that the teeth can be brushed.

These various ways of coping with the situation, although particularly extreme, capture the desperation that many compulsive eaters experience, and illustrate how compulsive eating is both a very painful activity and one which is enormously hard to give up. When people repeatedly act in a way that causes them a lot of pain we look to the possible reasons that are involved. Labeling such behaviour simply as self-destructive, for example, does not increase one's understanding of the forces behind compulsive eating. Instead, it judges the activity negatively and this provides yet another reason for the compulsive eater to adopt a self-deprecating attitude which is relieved only by a binge or yet another timetable to lose the weight. It is our experience that before an habitual activity – in this instance, eating compulsively – can be given up, the reasons for it need to be explored. As I argued earlier, getting fat is a very definite and purposeful act connected to women's social position. Before giving up compulsive eating the meanings of the fat for the individual woman need to be explored. In giving up compulsive eating she is almost certainly going to stabilise at a lower weight. In order to feel at home with this new constant weight, and, more importantly, her smaller size, the compulsive eater needs to understand what her previous interest has been in being overweight and in being preoccupied with food intake. If she can understand how her fat has served her she can begin to give it up.

In this chapter, I shall describe six important steps we take in the groups:

1. To demonstrate that the compulsive eater has an interest in being fat.

2. To show that this interest is largely unconscious.

3. Specific exercises are done to bring this theme to a woman's consciousness.

4. Once this interest in being fat is recognised, the meanings for each individual woman can be explored.

5. Then we ask whether the fat does what it is supposed to do.

6. We help each woman reclaim aspects of herself that she has previously attributed solely to the fat.

Because fatness has such negative connotations in our culture it may be hard to imagine that anyone could have an interest in getting fat.

- To be fat means to get into the subway and worry about whether you can fit into the allotted space.

- To be fat means to compare yourself to every other woman, looking for the ones whose own fat can make you relax.

- To be fat means to be outgoing and jovial to make up for what you think are your deficiencies.

- To be fat means to refuse invitations to go to the beach or dancing.

- To be fat means to be excluded from contemporary mass culture, from fashion, sports and the outdoor life.

- To be fat is to be a constant embarrassment to yourself and your friends.

- To be fat is to worry every time a camera is in view.

- To be fat means to feel ashamed for existing.

- To be fat means having to wait until you are thin to live.

- To be fat means to have no needs.

- To be fat means to be constantly trying to lose weight.

- To be fat means to take care of others' needs.

- To be fat means never saying 'no'.

- To be fat means to have an excuse for failure.

- To be fat means to be a little different.

- To be fat means to wait for the man who will love you despite the fat – the man who will fight through the layers.

• To be fat, nowadays, means to be told by women friends that 'Men aren't where it's at', even before you have had a chance to know.

Above all, the fat woman wants to hide. Paradoxically, her lot in life is to be perpetually noticed.

These popular conceptions of fatness, while accurate, present an incomplete picture of the compulsive eater's experience. There is also something positive to be gained from being fat that we must explore. I am not suggesting that the desire to be fat is a conscious one. Indeed, I would argue that people are largely unaware of it, and it is not at all easy to discuss this in the abstract. In the groups we do the following exercise to provide us with insight into some of the ways in which fat serves us. I suggest you close your eyes for ten minutes and have someone read you the following fantasy exercise:

Imagine yourself in a social situation . . . this could be at work, at home, at a party, whatever . . . notice what you are wearing . . . whether you are sitting or standing . . . whom you are talking to, or having something to do with . . . Now imagine yourself getting fatter, in the same social situation . . . you are now quite large . . . What does it feel like? . . . Notice what you are wearing . . . whether you are sitting or standing . . . Notice all the details in this situation . . . how are you getting on with the people around you? . . . Are you an active participant or do you feel excluded? . . . Are you having to make more or less of an effort? . . . Now see if you can detect any messages that this very fat you has to say to the world . . . Is there any way in which you can see it serving

you? . . . Are there any benefits you see from being this
fat in this situation? . . .

When we do this exercise in the groups we get a variety
of responses and many are what one might expect. They
include feeling like a freak, an outsider, or a blob or
assuming that whomever one had contact with was doing
so out of pity or was also a freak. But more significantly,
people were able to see a new meaning in the fat. For
some, the fantasy sparked feelings of confidence and
substance as though the fat represented concrete strength.
For others, being fat felt very safe as though it were an
excuse for failure and that in worrying about body size
the women did not have to think about any other possible
problems in their lives. Some women felt that being fat
protected them insofar as it allowed them to contain their
feelings; other women talked of feeling comfortable in their
bigness and warmth and having plenty of love to give to
others. However, the most common benefits that women
saw in being large had to do with a sexual protection. In
seeing herself as fat, a woman is often able to desexualise
herself; the fat prevents her from considering herself as
sexual. Having done the exercise, so many women report
feeling relaxed at a party, not feeling they were on show
or had to compete but were comfortably talking to female
friends. Others felt the fat separated them from the kind
of women they had ambivalent feelings about – the ones
whom they perceived as self-involved, trivial and vain.
Others felt that it meant they could hold their own and
keep unwanted intruders away. Many women felt a relief
at not having to conceive of themselves as sexual. Fatness
took them out of the category of woman and put them
in the androgynous state of 'big girl'.

As people in the groups are slowly able to incorporate these positive aspects and benefits into their views of fatness, they begin to develop a different self-image. The image of fatness then is no longer one-sidedly negative, inextricably tied up with an ugly vision. Instead of regarding themselves as hopeless, helpless or willfully destructive, they can see that their compulsive eating has had some purpose, that it has had a function. As this function becomes more apparent it is possible to be more generous to yourself, to regard the compulsive eating and the attempt to get fat as a way in which you have handled particularly difficult situations. The compulsive eating can then be looked on as an attempt to adapt to a set of circumstances rather than as irrational, 'crazy' behaviour.

I would now like to explore just why these images of largeness are comforting. What is it that women are saying they feel more capable of when they are fat?

Many women experience the social expectations placed on them as unattainable, unrealistic, undesirable, burdensome and oppressive. Central among these expectations is the feeling that women should be, on the one hand, decorative, attractive and an embellishment to the surroundings and on the other hand, that they should do the hard concrete work of raising the children, running households, while at the same time maintaining jobs outside the home. For many women the physical model of the shy, retiring flower, demurely smiling beneath lowered eyelashes, is too frail and insubstantial to accomplish the daily tasks of living that are their responsibility. As such, to these women the fat represents substance and strength. Harriet, a 35 year-old community worker who lives with her husband and two children, put it this way: 'I had the feeling that my fat gives me substance and physical presence in the world. It allows me to do all the things I have to do. In the fantasy I saw myself in my office sitting at my desk and taking up an enormous amount of space. I felt the capacity to do anything I needed to do – challenge my boss and fight more effectively for the community group that I'm there to serve. I felt my strength in this exaggeration of my size. Then in my fantasy I went home, and with the realisation of the extra bulk it struck me that I walked into an antagonistic situation with my fat as my armour. As I walk into the house I am reminded of all the tasks that have to be done there that I either execute personally or direct others to do. I feel quite angry about all this, both about feeling so bossy but, of course, also because the terrain of the household is mine – and not by choice. So I see the fat in the situation as making me feel like a sergeant major – big and authoritative. When I go through this fantasy of seeing myself thin, what immediately strikes me is just how fragile and little I feel, almost as though I might disappear or be blown away.'

Barbara, a 27 year-old book-jacket designer, talked about the annoying expectations of many of her male colleagues. She felt that her bulk and substance was an expression of her need to be noticed as a productive human being rather than a decorative accompaniment to the environment. She felt that whenever she looked the slightest bit sexy – and this corresponded to the way she looked when she was thin – her colleagues only reacted to the sexual aspect of her. She experienced this as both a frightening demand and also a deflection from her work. As it is for so many women, taking her work seriously was quite a struggle for Barbara. She had grown up with the idea that she would work for a couple of years after school and then get married and have children. But ideas had changed and by the time she left college she wanted to work to have a career rather than for a stop-gap measure. This decision was not trivial; she felt she had a lot of support for her change of mind because all her friends were also pursuing work as a central part of their lives. But Barbara was in conflict about her capacity to be a good worker, not because her art work was erratic, second-rate or inadequate but because she was battling with an unconscious idea that taking herself seriously in her work life was inappropriate. In the group we were able to expose this conflict and Barbara saw how difficult it was for her to be thin/sexual on the job because she and the men there collaborated in trivialising her. She felt the only way she could hold on to that aspect of herself that was involved in a career was by having an extra layer covering her femaleness. As she said, 'The fat made me one of the boys'.

In the group we also worked to expose the conflict that Barbara felt about the different models of adult female behaviour; the one she grew up with which was modelled not only on her mother's life but also on a popular conception of femininity in the 1950s and early 1960s; and a model that she and her contemporaries were struggling to articulate, a view of womanhood that was less limiting and struck at the very roots of women's oppression within the family. This conflict is, in my experience, a difficult and painful one for many women and not one that will be resolved by a sudden flash of insight. In the groups it is important to realise that the goal is not necessarily to resolve this or any other conflict which may lie at the root of the compulsive eating. What is important, however, is that the conflict be brought to light, that the woman should understand that it exists and that eating compulsively is not going to make it go away – it may cover it. The fat may provide for something less threatening to worry about. But the critical issue is to make the woman acknowledge the conflict so that it need not be expressed indirectly and hidden from the person who is experiencing it. This acknowledgment then becomes a powerful weapon in the fight against compulsive eating. It is very reassuring to discover that there are substantial reasons for why one is eating in such a seemingly inexplicable way. It provides one with the tools; thus when Barbara, for instance, noticed that she was bingeing, she could ask herself what was really troubling her. If she did not come up with any spontaneous answer she could review her day or events leading up to the binge and see if there were any incidents that particularly encapsulated her conflict about who she could be as a woman in the world. In this way she could decode her own behaviour. This then gave her a chance to intervene on her own behalf and she could move on to ask herself whether being fat in that particular situation was really going to help her out.

So one meaning of the fat is the woman's need for recognition in a work setting. But another theme that frequently comes up is almost diametrically opposed to this. It is often the case that people's fat fantasies are widely different and that even within the same person the fat may express many different meanings. Barbara, for example, could see the use of the fat in her attempt to be taken seriously at work, but at the same time we discovered her fat also symbolised her fear of being successful both in work and courtship. Her fear of success, of course, stems largely from the social position of a young woman of today growing up with contradictory messages about what she can accomplish. Stepping outside what has been laid out for one is frightening. A useful, protective device is to make

34

the assumption that one will fail; in Barbara's view the excess weight provided her with an excuse should she not succeed in love and work. She found out that she could not bear the idea that her work life or love life would not be satisfying, once she had committed herself to trying to have both. She felt sure that if there were failure on either score, it would be attributable to a character weakness on her part. This idea, in turn, was so painful that she focused instead on her weight as an excuse in the case of potential failure. As long as she was overweight, and love and career did not quite work out as she hoped, she could imagine that if she were thin, everything would be just fine. Thus, this fantasy allowed her to exert some control over her circumstances as though in an inspired weight loss she would be able to sort out social attitudes to women at work and love relationships with men.

In Barbara's case the fat served two distinct purposes, albeit somewhat contradictory ones. Firstly, it provided her with a way to express competence on the job; secondly, if she did not succeed at work or in her love life she could blame her excess weight. As these two themes emerged in the course of her therapy, Barbara was able to see that getting fat was a personal adaptation she had made in trying to cope with a very difficult situation. In addition to being able to expose the conflict, she was able to see the dilemma of a young career woman today and how she felt she had to deny or solve the difficulties facing her entirely on her own. Other women in the group identified with what Barbara was going through and, as they began to share their difficulties, they broke their individual isolation and feelings of impotence which had in part led to the weight gain.

Failure and success are powerful concepts within our world. Very early on we absorb the idea that a limit has been set on what is available and we learn to compete for what is around. If we are successful we are rewarded, and if we are unsuccessful our lot is to suffer. When we are very young it is hard to see quite how the odds are stacked or in whose favour, and the competition seems fair – with failure or success being the individual's fault or triumph. As we get older, we may question the basic assumptions behind the scramble or even how the pie is divided up, whether it is the number of possible 'A's in a class or the division of labour itself. But ideas absorbed and structured into the personality die hard, and feel almost impenetrably lodged. While we may reject the notion of competition because of the devastating effects it has wrought in relationships between people as well as in world politics, we may nevertheless find ourselves unwittingly competitive. Competitive feelings get triggered in a situation of scarcity where there is not enough to go round, or where only a certain number of people can be rewarded. The apprehension of possible exclusion or denial can foster either a desire to compete individually for some of the scarce resource or to sort out cooperatively a way to deal with the shortage. Another alternative is to opt out of the competition. But by and large, as we grow up we are encouraged to compete against others. In school this is expressed through grades or which team you make or your position in class. But girls and boys, women and men, are trained to cope with scarcity and competition in different ways. The cliché of 'let the boy win at tennis' expresses an aspect of the competition between women and men. We learn that if there is a game between the sexes in which one side has to lose, we had better make sure we are the losers. In general, men are taught to compete against other men for jobs and status. They gain prestige in the world of work by being better than other men, and they measure their success by comparing it with that of others. Although women also exist in the world of work, men are rarely encouraged to compete against women because they do not tend to take women's presence in traditional male preserves very seriously. Similarly, women are strongly discouraged from competing with men or each other at work. Women are forced to compete with each other for the man who will help the winner secure her social position. A woman's success in the world continues largely to be regarded as a reflection of her husband's status. In this battle for social survival, women are essentially competing on the basis of their sexual appeal while other aspects of their personality are viewed as attributes to be paraded in the attempt to secure a man.

Women's liberation is challenging this value system for both women and men. However, those of us in our twenties and upward have grown up with these values and ideas and, although they are being shaken up, they nevertheless continue to play a significant part in our personalities. Often we do not realise how much a part of us they are. When we do notice these competitive feelings, we find them distasteful and inappropriate in a changing world and try to suppress, hide or ignore them.

The acknowledgment of a whole range of competitive feelings is difficult for many women and often we attempt to cover these feelings by getting fat. The fat has several functions in this regard.

1. It provides space and protection for the feelings. Without the fat a woman might worry unconsciously that her feelings will be exposed. There would be no difficulty in getting thin if the competitive feelings could find no

place to hide and just disappeared. But problems like that never do just disappear; they either get actively repressed and reappear in another form; or they become exaggerated and completely exposed; or they get acknowledged with the potential for being worked through.

2.   The feeling of being fat–outsize – larger than life, removes the possibility of competing since everyone knows that 'fat women can't win and, in fact, aren't even in the same game'.

3.   In the very act of compulsive eating – the most frequent route to getting fat – one may be attempting to blot out competitive feelings that may have been stirred up. Again, we see the dual function of compulsive eating – to dull the feeling that is difficult to cope with and to provide a way for the energy behind the worry (in this case feeling competitive) to be harnessed to a more familiar concern about body size.

Compulsive eating also helps out in other circumstances when women are frightened to show certain emotions. These are feelings such as anger, that women are afraid to show because they are considered inappropriate for women, many of whom have been hurt when they expressed them.

A preparation for a life of inequality inevitably leads to many of these turbulent and hence socially unacceptable feelings in women. In addition to difficulties with competition in which women are expected to lose on all fronts except the sexual one where she must succeed in getting her man in order to move towards adulthood, other feelings engendered by social situations can be swallowed up by the fat.

Anger is a particularly difficult emotion for women to

accept in themselves. Jennifer is a 48 year-old teacher in London. She is married and has two sons, aged 18 and 20. Professionally competent and well recognised for her work in inner-city education, she has had a history of compulsive eating since she got married. Jennifer was an orphan, brought up by many different foster parents. She never felt safe or loved in any of the homes in which she stayed and at eighteen she received a scholarship to college and left her last foster parents permanently. At that point she was truly on her own with no pretence that anyone around her was taking care of her. She felt quite strong and able to cope, and remembers feeling particularly relieved that she did not have to pretend to be grateful for every ounce of attention paid to her. She roomed with other young women and felt quite envious of their family life. When she was 25 she got married to Doug, a draughtsman, and for the first time found herself in a stable family environment. Jennifer decided to work for a couple of years so that they would feel more secure financially. It was at that time Jennifer noticed that she was becoming preoccupied with her food intake, and her weight began to fluctuate wildly. Jennifer knew that psychological issues often got expressed in weight gain or loss but just could not pinpoint what was going on because she felt that for the first time her life was making some kind of sense and she felt a security that she had not thought possible before. Both of her pregnancies proceeded relatively comfortably. Jennifer took four years off from her work as a teacher and then went for further training before resuming a full-time job. The family stayed in the same neighbourhood for 20 years and Jennifer developed some solid friendships and, as she put it, 'a real feeling of community'. Yet she continued to eat in a way she found quite disagreeable, alternately picking and shoveling. The only way she could understand this behaviour was by seeing it as an expression of how inadequate she felt her own parenting had been. She saw herself continuing the previous pattern of erratic caring of herself. This insight provided her with some relief but the eating problem still continued. In the course of her therapy, we did a fantasy of Jennifer fat and thin with her foster parents in the same room. In a response to a question about what the fat was saying to her many foster parents, Jennifer was suddenly overcome by enormous feelings of rage. She experienced the fat as all the poisonous, venomous feelings she had stored up through the many years of being shuffled about. She felt that if the fat itself had a mouth it would shriek hateful and angry thoughts to all those people who had supposedly cared for her. Her fat was a way to keep quiet about all those feelings but she also experienced it as an indictment of the inadequate parenting she had had. As we discussed it more, she said that without it nobody would know that she had suffered and people would take it for granted that she could just float through life quite easily, that she was like everyone else. Once she had felt these feelings of rage much of her compulsive eating made sense. She began to notice that whenever she felt angry, with her kids, at school or with Doug, she rushed to eat to swallow the feelings. To feel the anger was to put herself in jeopardy – she felt a tape going through her head every time she got angry, it said: 'Nice girls don't. Be grateful or you'll be thrown out.' These sentences were those that were taught to her very early on indeed. To express anger or disappointment in a foster home was unacceptable and carried with it not only this exclusion from the female sex but also the fear of abandonment and rejection. If she got angry at her foster parents she would be sent back. The discovery of the roots of the compulsive eating eased the situation for Jennifer. She began to allow herself to experience anger directly and risk the consequences instead of eating it away. She also became aware of her anxiety about levels of insecurity she felt within her own family as though if she expressed displeasure at something she would be turfed out. On most levels she felt quite safe with Doug and it was, in fact, this safety that had allowed that historic anger and rage to emerge – albeit indirectly – in the first place. Jennifer was caught in a changing situation. As a youngster she had to put up and shut up. She could show no anger or rebellion. When she was able to leave these unsatisfactory homes and start her own family she felt more secure and in charge of the situation but she understandably carried past insecurities with her. The part of her that felt securely established with Doug, her career and the kids provided enough space for her to reject the dreadful past she had had but she was not quite able to do that openly and expressed that rejection by eating compulsively.

In Jennifer's case, her fat was a delayed response to a series of extremely precarious and deprived home circumstances. It was not until she had set up her own home that she found herself eating erratically and yoyo-ing on the scales. This pattern – becoming obsessively involved with food after the troublesome events have passed – is quite common. There seems to be a psychological mechanism that works in the following way for some people: a girl grows up in a difficult environment, but needs to survive it as much intact as possible in order to get out. Any expression of breakdown or weakness would only prolong the imprisonment and make escape more difficult. All her resources are harnessed so that she can endure the horrible circumstances and prepare for an exit. She finally leaves this setting and puts herself in a safer place. As she begins to relax in her new-found safety and lets her defences down all the wretched feelings from the past have a chance to come up. It is not as though in leaving the situation she has left the feelings behind. The safety and security of the new situation provides for a detoxification process. But these feelings are very powerful and very often extremely painful and the human organism may respond by trying to continue to ward them off. In the case of someone who starts compulsive eating at this point, what is happening is that the feelings are coming up but are experienced as too dangerous to confront. The woman turns to compulsive eating to anesthetise the feelings and cover them with a layer of fat. The feelings do not get expressed and cleansed; instead they get transformed into a symptom which then has to be demystified before it can be made to go away.

I should now like to discuss why the expression of anger is so difficult for women. In Jennifer's case, there was an explicit threat of expulsion should she express anger at her treatment but in general, women are actively discouraged from expressing anger, rage, resentment and hostility. We are raised to be demure and accept what we are given with no complaints. We all learn how little girls are made of sugar and spice and all things nice. So we try hard not to show our anger or even feel it ourselves. When we rebel and show dissatisfaction we learn we are nasty and greedy. Whether we realise it or not we are being taught to accept silently a second-class citizenship. Secondary status is further compounded by having our anger denied us. Anger provides a way for people to challenge injustices at whatever level – be it a child's anger in response to a punitive parent or the collective anger of others fighting to have their day-care centres restored.

But there are few models of righteously angry women for us to follow. Indeed, I think most of us are pretty frightened around an angry woman – so unfamiliar is the sight. Anger, as a legitimate emotion for many women, has no cultural validation. Little girls are encouraged to cry if they do not get what they are wanting instead of angrily protesting; 'There, there, dear.' In Edward Albee's play *Who's Afraid of Virginia Woolf*, Martha, the angry wife who protests against the life of a helpmate, is portrayed as a bitch and a harridan. Much of popular culture attests to the negative value we place on women's rage. It is not surprising, therefore, to find that for many women, the unconscious motivation behind the weight gain is a flight from anger. In this case, the symbolic meaning of the fat is a 'Fuck you!'

Behind the suppression of anger lies one of the most important themes for women today. Gaining weight to express anger, to be able to say, 'Fuck you', is only a part of a larger problem. Expressing anger is an assertive act. Assertion for women is difficult. Consider these typical situations:

Ann is extremely tired after a long day at work. She plans to spend the evening alone just resting, watching television and reading. Her neighbour Jack calls up and asks if she would not mind helping out by baby-sitting for his children for an hour while he and his wife go to the store. Ann feels she must be cooperative but knows from past experience that the hour is rarely such and the whole evening will be gone. Reluctantly, she goes next door. At 11:30 p.m. Jack and Penny return. They have been to the store and the movies. Ann is at this point angry but blames herself for having agreed to baby-sit without conditions in the first place. She goes home muttering to herself and eats.

Bill and Roz planned to go to the movies together. Bill calls Roz up from work to check that it will be all right for him to bring some friends home to dinner. Roz, who had already started cooking, takes his decision as a *fait accompli* and reluctantly agrees, feeling she has no right to refuse. She goes into the kitchen and starts banging around fixing dinner and feeling very moody. She assumes that Bill has forgotten about their movie date and she feels rejected. She feels put upon as she is cooking but also feels guilty for being so ungenerous and unspontaneous. She noshes her way through the cooking and when Bill and his friends sit down for supper she shovels the food into her mouth, at this point angry about her inability to assert herself in the first place.

In both situations Ann and Roz feel unentitled to demand what they actually want. Ann is afraid to set limits on her own altruism and Roz does not stand up for herself and the movie date. Both women blame themselves for not having asserted themselves and also for feeling selfish enough even to conceive of their own wants in the first place. They both eat away the bad feelings and focus the negative feelings on the food rather than addressing the difficult issue of assertion. *They feel safer using their mouths to feed themselves than using them to talk and be assertive. They imagine that their fat is making the statement for them while the suffering prevents the words from coming out.* None of this is conscious, the seeds for this behaviour have been planted in the mother–daughter relationship in which the mother encourages the girl child to adopt a pleasing manner. The mother prepares her daughter for a life in which major decisions are made for her rather than by her. *The girl will be taught to accept that her needs come second and that keeping quiet is safer than assertion.* Consequently, women are confused and afraid to act on their own behalf. To do so often makes one appear aggressive and *that* has such negative connotations for women that it feels less dangerous to adopt an acquiescent stance. So for women, there is great confusion between unassertive, assertive and aggressive behaviour. The recent rush of courses and self-help assertion-training books is witness to the magnitude of this problem. And there have been unfortunate consequences for women who have risked stepping out of line in the past. *Women have been condemned as castrating or domineering when they have attempted to assert their rights.*

There are, in addition, other consequences about being unassertive that add to the problem. If one is not trained to be assertive it is quite hard to define how much you will or will not give to others. By and large, women are taught to nurture the world. As one psychoanalyst, Mercy Heatley, put it, women are the 'sewage treatment plants' for the family and, as such, are always giving emotionally to others. In discussing what their fat and food symbolised to them many women have described it as being a kind of 'fuel for the furnace', a private storehouse they can draw on when they need to be replenished in order to go on feeding others. For some women, however, the fat in this case represents a rejection of just this kind of service to others. In the woman's mind the excess weight is a message to others to keep away and not make any demands, almost a 'Can't you see I've got enough on my hands without worrying about anyone else.' For others, it is a statement which embodies both these feelings – the fat expresses a shapeless capacity to both absorb and repel outside demands. So the fat expresses both an attempt to be separate from others while, at the same time, a woman's sheer size encompasses everything around her. It is as though the woman can take on everyone else's needs without them actually penetrating her – the weight acts as a shock absorber for others and as a cushion against her becoming too affected.

As I have said in discussing responses to the fat fantasy, the most frequently stated advantage women saw in being fat had to do with sexual protection. It is almost as though through the protective aspects of the fat, women are saying they must deny their own sexuality in order to be seen as a person. *To expose their sexuality means that others will deny them their personhood.* In adolescence, girls are supposed to magically transfer their friendship interest in boys to a sexual one – they learn a ritual called dating. This sudden transition can be quite formidable and difficult to cope with. As Mary, a 27 year-old doctor, put it, 'When I was about six or seven years old, girls and boys used to play together. Then we were separated out and, until the age of eleven, contact with boys was fairly limited, particularly as I went to an all-girls school during that period. Then at twelve I went to a coed junior high school and looked forward to playing with the boys again. Their games seemed more exciting and I really missed the adventures they got up to. However, something weird seemed to be happening; instead of fooling around together we were supposed to fix ourselves up real pretty and accumulate dates. This was a way for us to continue to hang out with the guys. But along with this went a whole series of rules and regulations about kissing and touching – it seemed to me as if in order to play with the fellows I had to put out. This was quite disconcerting, not because I didn't like kissing, which I did, but because it seemed that all of a sudden girls and boys were really different and had to relate to each other within a rigid set-up. It was really quite confusing for all of us and everything seemed downhill from there on. Sports were divided and we had the great job of cheering the boys on. I kept feeling that if this is going to be what being grown up is all about I'll keep my puppy fat on and try and avoid this whole dating trip.'

So Mary spent the next 15 years, as she put it, 'slightly overweight'. She noticed during the course of her therapy that her eating binges occurred almost uniformly when she was in any kind of potentially sexual situation. She would gorge away before going to a party, for instance, and convince herself that she was too big to be considered sexual. This allowed her a kind of ease to relate to people at the party – women and men – on her terms rather than on the exchange value of her body. The example of Mary shows quite clearly how the fat is conceived as providing a means of removal from the sexualising and hence, also competitive aspects of relationships for women.

This sexual division has wide-ranging consequences. Many women have shared the feeling that being fat was a way to stand out in a crowd, to be noticeable, to be different without having to invest as much as they assume thin, attractive women do.

Several women have mentioned that their sex was a disappointment to their parents. Rita remembers eating energetically in order to get big, to prove her existence. Quite strikingly, she stopped bingeing for the first time when she got pregnant. When she had life inside her she felt this was ample evidence of her right to exist. If Rita could reproduce, she had a real role, as a mother, even if she had felt unwanted as a child.

These varied explanations of the meanings behind the fat, from eating as protection to eating as an expression of anger, will not necessarily provide the key for everyone who feels they have this problem. Because the syndrome of compulsive eating, compulsive dieting, weight loss and weight gain is so highly developed and, in a sense, so absorbing a preoccupation in itself, it may be hard to get outside it enough to realise just what it is doing for you. In a sense, compulsive eating provides a beautiful, insulated world: obsessing about how terrible you are for overeating leads to feelings of self-disgust; these feelings have no outlet and are quickly covered up or numbed by the intake of food or banished by the fantasy of reincarnation after the plan for the new diet has been made. All negative feelings get harnessed to complaints and self-loathing about body size and eating habits and the fat provides a less threatening issue to worry about than other possible problems. It may also be true that while the fat has one meaning for you today, it has had quite another when it originally developed. In other words, the historic reasons and driving force behind the impulse to get fat in the first place may be quite different from its current significance, so it often proves useful to look back and see how getting fat has helped people at certain times in their lives. In order to tap this information in the groups we do weight histories to reveal when the 'problem' first started. I should like to illustrate this point by drawing on some case histories of women I have worked with. Some of the historic reasons that I will outline will be of clearly feminist content and others will be less explicitly so, though in each example it will be obvious what feminine personality-development has meant to each of the women whose lives I am describing.

Rea was an only child. Her parents had high expectations for her which included academic excellence, sociability and beauty. She felt pressed by these demands to be the perfect, happy child and felt that she did not have much space in which to develop her own independence. She became quite overweight in adolescence and it was to this period that we returned to examine when she came into therapy in her early thirties. Her fat began to make sense set against the background of intense parental concern that she be successful. Rea did not see herself in the same light as did her parents. She felt inadequate. She felt that she was a selfish, ungrateful and bad person. She felt that she could not cope with her parents' demands and that she would be increasingly incompetent. Her fat expressed both the resentment at having to be so perfect and the need to hide and contain the bad person she felt she was inside. She feared being thin because she felt she would then be everything her parents wanted; she would be in their image and without a self.

Jane, a 55 year-old legal secretary, put on weight after her mother's death. Up to the age of 25, Jane had been quite thin and fairly relaxed about her body image. She was an only child, her father died when she was a teenager and she was very close to her mother. She married when she was 22 but shortly afterwards her husband Tom was sent overseas to fight in World War II. When her baby girl Carol was 18 months old Tom returned from the war. About a year later Jane's mother died of cancer. For the preceding year and a half she had been losing a lot of weight and looked very thin and ill. When Jane officially stopped mourning she began to put on weight. By the time she was 27 she was 25–30lb [11–14kg] heavier than she had ever been before, except during her pregnancy. She was quite staggered by the increase in her size and at first she put it down to lack of exercise after Carol's birth. Friends suggested that maybe she had enjoyed pregnancy so much that her excess weight was a desire to look continually pregnant. But this explanation made little sense to Jane because her pregnancy had not been the easiest time for her. A psychiatrist friend at the time expounded that she wanted to look pregnant so she could get the attention and praise from Tom he assumed she had missed at the time of her genuine pregnancy. The weight stayed on and eventually, as standards in fashion and health demanded slimness, Jane started the round of diets and diet doctors. Outwardly Jane had a fairly contented home life – she and Tom really liked each other and Carol, their only child, kept up continued contact with them after she had grown up and left home. However, Tom reported that almost every night Jane cried out in her sleep for *her* mother. In the course of therapy this piece of information from Tom was discussed in detail. Jane came to understand that the weight gain had much to do with the loss of her mother, as she said, 'My mother died tragically of cancer. She became very thin before her death. I've had a need to feel big ever since then and worried, I suppose, that if I get thin I might disappear or die like her.' Facing her mother's death and her own fears about dying if she became thin allowed Jane to determine a size for herself that was both physically and psychologically comfortable. As it turned out, Jane felt that she no longer wished to be as svelte as she imagined she might and her weight stabilised at about 15lb [7kg] lower than it had been.

Death has been a factor in the fat for other women with whom I have worked. Sheila, a 28 year-old graduate student, had lost her older brother Ivan when he was 12 and she was 10. She gained weight from that time on and in the group we discovered that the origin of becoming fat had had two distinct symbolic meanings. Sheila felt the oversized body allowed her to carry her brother with her. She remembered that she had really enjoyed being with him and played with him a lot. Ivan had been the pride and joy of the family, first born and male it was antici-pated that he would fulfil his parents' ambitions. About two years after his death they had another child, Maureen. Sheila felt a great deal of responsibility for being both a little mother to Maureen and a son to her parents. To her, what a son meant was quite distinct from what being a daughter had meant. It demanded that she be very good at sports, achieve scholastically and plan for a successful career of which her parents could be proud. In being a daughter she was expected to do decently at school but a career was to come second to a successful love life. In her adolescence, Sheila's father took her to ball games. She enjoyed being one of the boys and having a much more developed rela-tionship with her father than she had had before she became a teenager. In the therapy, what emerged was a guilt for feeling good that she could have so much of her father. She imagined that if her brother had lived, this would not have been the case. Symbolically, she felt the second meaning of her fat was to round out her curves – to make her less feminine so she could look more the part of a son. When she had lost weight over the years she took with her the same desire to look boyish and she was always annoyed that she still had hips and breasts and could not achieve the androgynous body she wanted.

Sheila had been trying to cope with the problem of how to be the teenage son and the little mother. This latter aspect is one showed by many girls at even earlier ages than Sheila. Often a 7 year-old daughter will be expected to be mother's little helper or substitute in looking after the babies that follow her.

Melinda, the eldest girl in a family of seven, recalls a blissful early childhood when she and her older brother would play together. When she was 7 years old her mother had another baby. It seemed to Melinda that her childhood was over; not only did she have to share her mother with yet another child but she was expected to, and indeed did, carry out many grown-up tasks. As more and more babies came, Melinda became a second mommy to them so that at 18 when she left home she felt well trained to start her own family. She became large instead, however, explaining that if she looked like a big earth mother no one would assume she was at all available. She had had her lot for the moment!

This mothering learned so early on leads many women to teach their daughters to deprive and deny themselves. Florence and her daughter Laura both had compulsive eating problems. Florence's ideology was that eating goodies was an indulgence – and a disgusting one at that. She felt it was indecent to give into oneself with almost any form of pleasure, but particularly bodily pleasures. Food and sex were inviting and exciting but one must stay away from them. Florence ate sparingly all year round. On vacation when she overate she felt guilty and on her return would immediately put herself on the Mayo Clinic Diet to lose the excess. She was iron-willed and very self-controlled but terribly afraid of food. Her husband hid his candies in the glove compartment of his car and she considered his love of dessert a sign of his character weakness. Laura rebelled against this code of self-denial. She despised her mother's meanness with herself and characterised her as compulsively thin. She felt her mother never gave herself pleasure with food or sex. Laura chose the opposite route and tried to get pleasure from both activities. However, since the food and sex were both experienced behind closed doors with one ear open for her mother's intrusions, Laura could not be as much in control as she wanted and her eating expressed these tensions. In the group, she learned to eat just for herself and her own pleasure without having to get so big as though to prove her mother was right. She did not have to be ostracised by her size in order to give to herself.

Because of the prevailing position of women in the family, mothers also deny themselves in situations where there just is not enough to go round. They make sure that in a situation of shortage their husbands and children have as much as possible. If a mother fails to provide enough food on the table she feels herself a failure. When prices soar, a mother with a fixed income has less and less to spend on the family shopping and even though she experiences this along with all other housekeepers, it is she alone who must face the family and the complaints and disappointment if the food is not up to scratch. In the depression of the 1930s this was particularly acute; money was very scarce and there was never enough food on the table. Mothers talking about this period say they held back so there would be enough for the rest of the family – they could always make do, *they* were not at school using their brains or out on the streets looking for work everyday, so they felt it was only right that they should suffer.

Carolyn, one of the daughters of that time who subsequently became fat, said, 'When I was young it was depression time. My mother would go hungry and try to be sure to provide enough food for us kids, which there wasn't. When I got married I had enough food for the first time in my life and I feel like I'm eating to protect myself against those terrible feelings of hunger I had as a child.'

Rose, Carolyn's daughter, born at the end of the Second World War, remembers battles she had with her mother who worried lest she not eat enough – she recalled all the spoonfuls she ate for the poor starving children in Europe, never understanding how eating extra would help them.

Rose remained quite slender until the age of 17 when she left home to travel round Europe. When she returned, her parents greeted her with approval about her gain in weight. She, however, was quite unhappy being that big – she felt it made her too like them. She got involved with the diet-binge syndrome for the next 12 years. The following themes were explored in her therapy. When she had lived at home, a way to rebel against her parents had been to be thin. Not only were both her parents overweight but they also constantly encouraged her to eat. When she left home, she gained weight as an expression of her conflict about giving up her parents. The fat was a way to take with her a part of her home life – her parents. One of the most critical parts of her therapy was the termination process. Rose had at this point lost about

25lb [11kg] and stabilised at a weight she felt fitted her frame. The anticipated separation from the therapist and from the fat brought forth issues related to Rose's child-hood struggles to separate herself from her mother. For Rose, these battles about food symbolised her attempts to strike out on her own, to define herself and develop some independence from her mother. As the conflict was brought to light – that is, both Rose's interest in developing a sepa-rate identity and her fear of it because of the social and psychological dangers she perceived if she were separate from her mother – she could feel a safety for the first time in determining her own food intake. Her body for her then expressed this surer feeling of independence; it was defined and self-contained and not 'all fat, stuck like a mayonnaisey glue to my mother'.

Body size means different things to different women. In Rose's case being large was being stuck, capitulating, it meant accepting all those extra spoonfuls of food she had not wanted; in Barbara's case it was an attempt to desex-ualise herself in the face of her work colleagues; for Harriet it represented strength and substance; for Jane, her anger, and so on. Not only will fat have different meanings for different women but at different times the meanings will take on more, or less, significance.

At the beginning of a compulsive eating group a woman may only be able to see the fat as a graphic symbol of everything she dislikes in herself. She may describe it as the ghastly manifestation of the ugliness and horridness she feels inside. The fat both covers and exposes her perceived terribleness. As the group goes on in time and other women share their stories, this same woman may well be able to separate that fat from a definition of ugliness and explore some of the ways her fat has served her in the past. She will be able to see that the fat was an attempt to take care of herself under a difficult set of circumstances. As she moves towards a conscious acceptance of this aspect of the fat she can utilise the self-protective impulse in a different way. As she is able to understand that she became fat as a response – to mother, to society, to various situations – she can begin to remove the judgment that it was good or it was bad. *It just was.* It is extremely painful and difficult, if not impossible, to change if one has a negative self-image. An understanding of the dynamics behind getting fat can help remove the judgment. When the judgment is given up and you can accept that the fat just was, you can go on to the question of, 'Is it serving me well now?'

It is necessary for those who work in the area of the unconscious to explain about the existence of an unconscious life which has its own force and symbols. These symbols then need to be translated into the language of everyday experience so that we can explore them. Then, as conscious people, we need to intervene to question the rational and seemingly irrational fears and fantasies that rise from the land of dreams and motives. I find myself in a situation where I have asked the reader to consider that compulsive eating is linked to an unconscious desire to get fat. I have further argued that in order to give up the fat this motivation must be exposed. I will now propose, however, that the protective function the fat is meant to serve is one step away from the truth – that the fat itself does not actually do the job it is meant to do. By attributing to the fat a powerful protective role, a woman sets herself up for a situation in which a life without the fat would be a defenceless one. This is a frightening proposition indeed. We aim to offer the compulsive eater another option, that of seeing that the qualities she feels are in the weight are, instead, characteristics that she herself possesses but has assigned to the fat. In drawing on various aspects of the histories of women with whom I have worked, I have suggested that the discovery of the meaning of the fat has subsequently led to a reappraisal of whether it is the fat *itself* which actually keeps people away, desexualises one, helps contain the angry, (hurt, disappointed) feelings or provides substance. If, indeed, it is not the fat itself that has done all these things but rather the individual, two questions arise:

1. How and why has the individual woman withheld this power from herself and attributed it solely to the fat?

2. How can she reappropriate this power so that she feels it to be more a part of her essential self – who she is? This is so that when she gives up the weight she is not giving up the main methods in which she has dealt with the world.

The first question speaks to an issue of crucial importance that arises from the socialisation of women. Women are systematically discouraged from taking responsibility for various activities, actions, even thoughts. Men both act for them and describe their experience. While women's experience is exceedingly rich, it is rarely described or heard. Only in literature have women consistently had a voice and a wide audience. In the areas in which women, almost without exception, have taken enormous responsibility – in child-rearing, nurturing and housekeeping – their actions are not seen as defined and delineated because they are described as natural and inevitable. If it is natural you must do it. If it is natural it does not count. Hence it is devalued.

Now the paradox lies in the fact that so many of the women described in this chapter have, in fact, defied this stereotype of femininity. They have purposefully gone out into the world and taken on responsibilities that fall outside the scope of their role expectations. But they are caught in a sense of self which denies their power and this self-devaluation seems inexplicable unless it is considered as a consequence of living in a culture that has withheld social power from women and demonstrates this by denying and punishing those who violate prescribed social roles. It is not hard to see how a woman might adopt a self-image that is in tune with the idea that women are powerless. In doing so she accustoms herself to the idea that it is not *her* who has direct power but her 'unowned' fat. If it is *her* who can keep people away and not simply her fat then she becomes more in charge of herself. If she is more in charge of herself and acts more for herself in a determined way, will what she wants be attainable? Or will she be punished and rejected by others for daring to define herself rather than fitting in with others' expectations of herself? A further paradox is encapsulated in the compulsive eater whose imagined sense of herself thin is as the powerfully attractive sexual woman. As she subscribes to the image of the thin, sexual woman – a view offered to her consistently by the mass media – she reaches for the elusive power that this image promises but does not deliver. It is precisely this non-recognition of the person in the thin sexual image that causes her unconsciously to reject this thinness. For many women, 'thin-sexy-powerful' is an experience that lasts no more than the fleeting moment when she makes her entrance, her initial impact. After that, her image is appropriated by others and translates into 'thin-sexy-powerless' and at the same time she may find

no way to handle being thin, sexy and in charge.
critical question of how women can define and
their own sexuality that is being grappled with so often in
the fat/thin dilemma. And it is the lack of support for a
redefinition that compounds the woman's relinquishing her
own power to her fat. This, then, is an explanation both for
the occurrence of a symptom and its tenacity. Giving up
a symptom and owning the power assigned to it means
you are taking yourself seriously. Taking themselves seriously has been a risky business for women. It is helpful to
remember here that in both the attempt to conform to
appropriate female behaviour and the attempt to reject it,
women pay heavily. The issue that confronts us is whether
we will risk being punished for rebelling or accept being
punished for following feminine roles. As many women
have pointed out, the very words 'mother' and 'wife' conjure
up self-denial while the alternative images of women –
career woman, single parent, lesbian – provoke hostility and
ostracisation.

Having described the conventions by which women
have been forced to exist I think it clarifies why we might
choose something else – the fat – to act for us.
Reappropriation of your power (temporarily given to the
fat) involves a reevaluation of yourself. This very reevaluation produces a change in consciousness and with the
awareness of what has been given away, we can slowly
incorporate into our new self-image what belongs to us.
In owning the power of the fat we can give it up.

CHAPTER TWO

What Is Thin About for the Compulsive Eater?

We know that every woman wants to be thin. Our images of womanhood are almost synonymous with thinness. If we are thin we shall feel healthier, lighter and less restricted. Our sex lives will be easier and more satisfying. We shall have more energy and vigour. We shall be able to buy nice clothes and decorate our bodies, winning approval from our lovers, families and friends. We shall be the woman in the advertisements who lives the good life; we shall be able to project a variety of images – athletic, sexy or elegant. We shall set a good example to our children. No doctors will ever again yell at us to take off the excess weight. We shall be admired. We shall be beautiful. We shall never have to be ashamed about our bodies, at the beach, in a store trying to buy clothes or in a tightly packed automobile. We shall be light enough to sit on someone's knee and lithe enough to dance. If we stand out in a crowd it will be because we are lovely, not 'repulsive'. We shall sit down in any position comfortably, not worrying where the flab shows. We shall sweat less and smell nicer. We shall feel good going to parties. We shall be able to eat in public without courting disfavour. We shall not have to make excuses for liking food.

These images and desires bombard our consciousness

daily. In seeing ourselves thin, we can all find something positive with which to identify. When we are fat we crave thinness as we crave the food, searching within it for the solution to our varied problems.

But the fact is that while many of us want to be thin many millions of women are overweight or concerned with body size. One of the theses of this book is not obvious. Women fear being thin; fat has its purposes and advantages. Our experience shows that many women are positively afraid of being thin. Woman's conscious experience is of wanting to be thin, but her body size can belie this intention suggesting that in the same way that fat plays an active role in our lives, so thinness is the other side of the coin. Being fat serves the compulsive eater in a protective way; being thin is a fearful state – the woman is exposed to the very things she attempted to get away from when she got fat in the first place.

In trying to absorb this idea, I suggest you close your eyes for two minutes and think about a social situation that you were involved in today. This might have been an incident at work, at the shops or in the home.

Now carefully go over what happened in that particular situation . . . Notice what you were wearing . . . whether you were standing or sitting and how you were getting on with the people around you . . . Were you an active participant or did you feel excluded? . . . Be aware of as many details as possible . . .

Now imagine yourself thin in exactly the same situation . . . Notice particularly what you are wearing and how you feel in your body. Are you sitting or standing? . . . How are you getting on with the people around you? . . . Notice particularly if there is a difference in the way you are getting on with others now . . . Do you feel more or less included? . . . Are people wanting different things from you? . . .

When you have become familiar with the details of the situation, see if you are aware of any negative feelings that being thin engenders in you. Is there anything frightening about being thin in this place?

When women in the groups I work with try this fantasy exercise they are often very surprised at the kinds of things they find out about themselves. After an initial joyful experience of seeing themselves thin they contact feelings and ideas associated with thinness that sound like the following:

1.   They feel cold and ungiving.

2.   They feel angular, almost too defined, and self-involved.

3.   They feel admired to the point of having expectations laid on them. They feel they will not be able to keep people at bay – particularly those with a sexual interest.

4.   They do not know how to cope with their own sexual desires; they feel free to be sexual now but unsure of the implications.

5.   They feel they command too much power.

6.   They do not know how to define the boundaries around themselves and feel invaded by others' attention because they will not know how to fend it off. They are worried about where they exist in this new admiration.

7.   They feel uncomfortable amongst other women who throw competitive glances.

8.   They are worried by the need to have everything worked out – to have their lives fit together. They feel

there are no longer any excuses for the difficulties they face in their lives. They feel they must give up all the pain that their fat has expressed. They are particularly concerned that when they are thin they will have no room to feel blue, and that no one will see their neediness. It is very important to realise that concern about body size, as reflected by these themes, is a constant preoccupation for women because these images are the only socially accept-able models of feminine behaviour.

I should like to take each of these feelings in turn and show why they are such common fears when women do that fantasy exercise.

1.   The fear that being thin means to be emotionally cold is a familiar one. We know how very deeply our iden-tities are formed around the model of the woman as a giving, caring person. Experiencing oneself as cold and ungiving is in direct conflict with this very basic notion we learn as little girls. How many of us can comfortably accept that there are aspects of ourselves that reject this giving, nurturing woman? We fear being cold so much because we rarely allow ourselves to show this side of our personalities.

Annie, a 58 year-old teacher and expectant grandmother, said, 'All my life I've striven to create a warm and loving place around me. If I imagine myself thin now, I feel icy and frozen, like an emaciated version of myself. I feel I wouldn't fit into my life. It would be as if I'd stopped being lively, warm and giving which is how I see myself now.' Just as we think one candy means we eat the whole roll, so we worry that showing any coldness means we shall be cold people. We are expected to be caring and giving and, furthermore, we expect this from ourselves. So many of our daily relationships centre on our capacity to nurture others. To be cold, even temporarily, is virtually to deny our own sexual identity.

2. Being angular and too defined causes problems because we are so used to having our personalities defined for us. By this I mean that we tune our antennae to adjust to others' expectations of us because our social position has discouraged us from forging our own identities.

We are defined to fit the traditional female stereotypes. When we struggle for self-definition, we are met with curiosity, lack of support and even hostility. Diane, a Canadian psychiatrist in therapy for compulsive eating, expressed a common fear. She worried that if she were thin, people would think that she was really only interested in herself and not in others. If she looked thin and beautiful (in her mind, the two go together), that would mean she was vain and self-involved since thinness was something she had to work hard to attain. Diane felt her fatness covered her feelings of self-importance; if she were thin, these feelings would be apparent. Since Diane's work was to help others, the idea that she might be so involved with herself horrified her. Her discomfort was of a kind familiar to many women. We grow up to be concerned with others and often feel guilty when we notice that we have our own needs, desires and concerns which really come first. For Diane, the dilemma was particularly acute and she noticed that she stuffed several cookies down her mouth just before sessions with her patients. By doing this, she felt she was accomplishing two things: she ensured that she remained big – which to her meant being stable and reliable; and she was preventing herself from betraying her feelings of self-involvement when she was

64

working with someone. Stuffing down the cookies she stuffed her feelings.

3.   Being admired is also not without its difficulties. If we are admired when we are thin we often feel that it is only our bodies that are being appreciated. A woman's body has been her primary asset; how she sees it measuring up against the bodies of other women is an important factor determining how she feels. How she looks will partly determine her choice of lovers and husband. It is important that she makes a good impression with her looks to a much greater extent than her male counterpart. This, of course, is a preposterous position – to be valued on the basis of current fashions of sexual attractiveness. What about the active, thinking part of us? Thus being thin carries with it worries about whether we shall be regarded as a complete person, rather than simply as a sexual one.

4.   The desire to be sexual is double-edged. On the one hand, many women associate thinness with sexual desirability, and they feel more in control of their choice of partners. As thin people they feel it is legitimate to select those in whom they are interested; as overweight people they feel they must wait for the man or woman who will fight through the layers to find the person. On the other hand, many women fear the new-found sexuality that being thin promises. Many feel that they will act on it in ways that are different from their current sexual behaviour. One of the worries that comes up time and time again in groups is, 'If I become thin and very attractive maybe I'll be turned on to other men apart from my husband and I don't want to jeopardise our relationship.' We have so little say over the determination of our sexuality and consequently it is often hard for us to feel, let alone act on, what we want sexually.

One woman I worked with spelled it out this way: 'If there is less of me, people will see more of me, I shall be exposed. What will be exposed is my sexuality. Fat, I hide it in cheerfulness and pretend I'm not sexual myself. Thin, I reveal a sexuality that is unformed and feels unfettered because I'm thin so rarely that I don't get used to feeling comfortable with my own sexuality.'

Images of female sexuality radiate from billboards, the television and the cinema. Advertisements for cars and tractors often show women draped over the goods. Female sexuality becomes a commodity in the eyes of both men and women.

The significance of this last point produces a further complication. Men's sexual objects are women. However, women's sexual objects are also women for sexuality is normally presented in female images. Therefore women become confused if they do not fit the image that has been set up for them. If a woman does not look like the sexually vital woman in the advertisement or on the fashion page, how dare she be sexual?

But why should thinness prove to be a problem of sexuality? For many, the answer lies in the fact that weight has been experienced as a way to avoid sexuality. While avoiding sexuality is a very painful way to cope, it may, nevertheless, be a safer option for women who fear that thinness is equated with sexual desirability. As with all the fantasies attached to thin, in the groups we work on new ways of saying 'no' and 'yes' to sexuality so that we can be whatever weight and at the same time still struggle to define our sexual needs. Thus, if fat has been a way of saying 'no' to sex we must learn to use our mouths to speak to assert the 'no' rather than hoping that the world will magically understand that the food we just put in our mouths was an attempt to say 'no.' Mouths have two important functions – to allow us to speak and to ingest food. Sometimes compulsive eaters worry that they do not know how to use their mouths in the first of these ways.

5. There are, as well, deeper levels of resistance to being thin. One of the fears many women discover they associate with being thin is that of feeling too powerful. In our culture, girls from a very early age are taught that their role in life is to be one of helpmate to a potent man. Their own sense of identity will develop from their husbands' positions; they will be the wife and loving mother, and the power behind the man. Girls are consistently discouraged from having power in their own right outside the mothering role. The meaning of being thin for many women is that they will be doing *too* well and will have exceeded their social place.

Power presents women with three interrelated problems: the first stems from cultural images of powerful women; the second from the way little girls are brought up; and the third, from the imagined or real consequences of being powerful. The few well-known examples we have of powerful women have either been equated with destruction, like Helen of Troy or Cleopatra, or they have been coupled with images of emasculated men, like Maggie of *Maggie and Jiggs*.

The all-powerful mother is only powerful *as mother*. Once father reenters the home, he reappropriates his authority from *his wife*. Thus, a little girl learns about power in a very confused way; her mother's power, the female power, is negated by that of her father but her father's power, male power, is generally equated with ruthlessness and competition.

In growing up, the young girl learns how to cope with second-class citizenship. Her mother teaches her to yield to others (as she herself does to her husband) and to expect others to define the shape of her world. Concepts of femininity exclude thinking of oneself as powerful and effective because to a woman, 'powerful' means 'selfish' – acting for oneself means depriving others.

Women risk social isolation if they become too powerful. If a woman is powerful and can take care of herself, she may worry that she will not need anyone else and that she will become too self-contained and alone. This fear is fostered by the reactions of others. Men frequently react against a woman's attempt to be powerful in her own right – 'What she needs is a man'.

Women are frequently no more encouraging to those women who try to act on their own behalf. They may feel threatened, jealous or betrayed. Thus if we exceed our social place by first conceiving of ourselves as powerful and then acting as powerful people, we may feel ourselves to be in jeopardy.

Work on this problem is an integral part of the groups. We explore why women have been taught to accept this secondary role and examine the power structure of individual families or school networks.

6. A very complicated fear which women almost invariably experience centres on the question of female boundaries. Psychoanalytic literature is full of references to the problem women have with boundary definition. What is meant by boundaries is the amount of space one takes up in the world – where one begins and where one ends. The reason why boundary issues are so difficult for women has social roots in the development of a feminine psychology. We know that the female role requires the woman to be a nurturing, caring person who gives emotional sustenance

to the people around her. She is required to merge her interests with those of others and seek her fulfillment in adjusting her needs and desires to others – mainly lovers and children with whom she is centrally involved. She is actively dissuaded from developing her autonomy economically and emotionally. Being fat expresses an attempt both to merge with others and, paradoxically, to provide an impenetrable wall around herself. Similarly, many women associate thinness with boundary issues. If the fat has been a way to express her separateness and her space, without it the woman will feel quite vulnerable and defenceless. Maggie, a 38 year-old clerk, put it this way: 'If I don't have all this weight *on me*, people will get in real close and I won't have any control or protection.' Drawings perhaps describe how these themes are experienced.

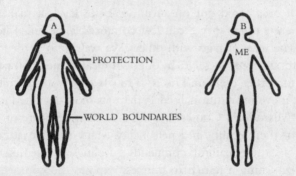

In figure A the woman is fat and experiences her true self as existing somewhere inside the fat. The fat provides physical protection against her believed vulnerability. She imagines that if she loses the weight she will be losing a protective coating against the world.

The loss of fixed boundaries of the self produces another of the terrifying states women have associated with loss of weight. This terror a woman may feel is the fear of people invading her. The fat may have allowed her to keep a certain distance from people. She imagines that it all has to do with the fat, that people themselves do not approach her and that she has little right to approach them. Thus, a woman will worry that while thin, people will encroach on her space in an active way and penetrate her. Once again, we see that the body states of fat and thin have been the way that compulsive eaters deal with the difficulties in their social relationships.

7.   An issue of enormous difficulty for women is that of competition. They have been forced to compete with each other in order to get the man who will supposedly take care of them and, in particular, to legitimise their sexuality. This competition between women is extremely fierce and painful even if only acted out on an unconscious level. It makes us assess each other so we can feel comfortable or uncomfortable when we engage with others. We walk into parties and unwittingly rank ourselves by our own attractiveness compared with the other women. This is so much a part of our culture that it is even institutionalised. Perhaps its most degraded form is the Miss World Contest in which women compete on the basis of their beauty and personality. Many women attempt to avoid these painful competitive feelings by getting fat. Contemplating a return to thinness exposes the competitive impulses. Many women are not sure how they will cope with either their own competitive desires or the animosity that they imagine they will rouse in other women.

8.   Finally, another of the most frequently expressed fears associated with being thin is crystallised by the statement made by Penny, a 24 year-old teacher. She felt that there were great chunks of her life that had not fallen into place

even though she enjoyed her work, friendships and love relationships. She had anticipated that if she could lose ten pounds everything in her life would run smoothly. The reason for this, she felt, was the excess weight. As we probed further together, we discovered that her image of thinness expressed competence and confidence. It allowed no space for anything to go wrong in her life – if she were thin what could possibly be a problem? If she were thin she would not know how to express her pain and sadness if she felt it. She realised that the extra weight provided her with a reason for why everything did not fit into place. Without that reason she worried about her capacity to be in charge of her life in the way that the absorbed media messages promised. As she put it: 'If I'm as thin as I really think I want to be I'll just have to get it together!'

Before moving on to detail the actual experience that compulsive eaters have had on the occasions when they have lost weight, it is important to point out that both the images and experiences of thinness contain contradictory messages. The same women attribute divergent worries to fatness and thinness. One might say, 'If I'm thin I'll feel weak and almost disappear'. Her fat self imagines that the weight gives her strength and substance. We may also discover, however, that for this same woman, thin also connotes a wiry kind of strength and fat its very opposite, a flabby indefinable quality – a blob.

Contradictory images are familiar to all of us in many of our daily activities. It is less commonly understood that the compulsive eater has contradictory feelings about body sizes. Nutritionists, psychologists, doctors and the diet and beauty columns of women's magazines rarely raise the issues that we have found so central in breaking the fat-thin, diet-binge cycle.

It is often the case that compulsive eaters' previous experiences of losing weight and becoming thin have been very difficult. There are many reasons for this which will be explored below but first, some preliminary remarks to provide a context for understanding the varied reasons.

The negative images associated with thinness are largely unconscious. This means that they are not readily accessible to people in their waking lives. The fantasy exercises in this book help to provide clues to finding out more about ideas we hold that we are not generally aware of. Unconscious ideas are as much a force in people's daily existence as the conscious desires, thoughts and actions we put into practice. The unconscious is an active part of all of us and when we attempt to change our behaviour or our feelings and it does not work, we look into the varied reasons that stand in our way. Social factors are critical determinants here and must never be underestimated, but our unconscious intent – formed by the repression of socially unacceptable desires – is a persuasive intervener and one that needs to be reckoned with. In addressing the issues of body size and self-image in the groups, we aim to help each other do the emotional work necessary so that this time being thin will be understood in all its rami-fications and the anticipated dangers will be minimised. This means that we will be working to:

1.   Explore the ideas that women hold on a conscious and unconscious level about thinness and fatness.

2.   Detach these ideas from body states so that the various qualities an individual ties up with her size will be attributed

to her directly and not to her thin self or her fat self. This will allow her to express different aspects of herself without regard to size.

3. Provide women with alternative ways, apart from eating, by which they can protect, assert and define themselves.

The fears of thinness that compulsive eaters hold based on previous experiences of losing weight centre on a number of themes. But the one feeling shared by nearly all compulsive eaters, whatever their own individual psychology, focuses on the effects of losing weight through a diet. Generally, the only way the compulsive eater has found to lose weight has been through a severe restriction of her food intake. Because her body size is such a crucial subject for her, in turning to a diet she invests it with the power to do wondrous things for her. In fact, many women report that once having decided to diet the amount of psychic energy required to actually mobilise, to drastically regulate themselves – is so enormous that they feel marvelous, pure, uncriticisable, almost high. Nothing disturbs them till they break it and the recriminations set in. Having deified dieting, the breaking of it signals a return to the tortuous state of compulsive eating.

For a woman the experience of depriving herself while on a diet operates on two levels. The one which produces the high allows her to continue the diet feeling self-righteous and contemptuous of her previous eating behaviour. But on another level, eating by rules and regulations is a constant reminder to the compulsive eater that she cannot be trusted. Thus, when she loses the weight, her experience of being normal sized and like everyone else is achieved only at the expense of her remaining in the prison of compulsive dieting, vigilantly fighting off the monster of compulsive eating, and keeping it at bay.

This battle to banish the bingeing puts the woman in an extremely precarious state. She is as worried as ever about what can and cannot go into her mouth and rarely does she feel confident that this particular diet will end her eating problem. Her days and nights are no less filled with worries of food intake and body size. If life for the compulsive eater is felt to be a process of continuous eating, then dieting exists outside life and is felt to be unreal. The addiction continues with all its concomitant obsessions: 'Will I be able to resist those French fries and desserts?' 'Will I be able to eat what Joyce is serving for dinner or will it be too fattening?' This tension adds to the feeling of distrust about her capacity to maintain the diet once the weight has been lost. The spectre of hugeness is always round the corner. The compulsive eater does not develop a confidence that she will remain thin. She has become a thin woman, someone who looks different and acts in different ways from her fat self, but a new woman whom she does not know very well. She is someone she is not sure she can trust or really get to know because she is unsure of how long she is going to be thin. If she is habitually thin for two months every year having dieted for one month, and fat for the remaining nine, then she is bound to be more familiar with her fat self. She really does not believe that her thin self is going to be around that long so she develops a suspicious relationship with it. Thus, her thin life has a precarious quality which is not conducive to self-confidence.

There is, in addition to all this, a new body to contend with, a smaller version of herself. (We tend to feel so small in our effect on the world, particularly as women, that reducing our physical presence feels almost bizarre.) Connected to this unfamiliarity with her body, is a drastic change in the woman's self-image. Many women report that they wore clothes that were quite unusual for themselves, not simply in the size that the label read, but also in the style that they had selected. Losing weight had held out the promise of fulfilling those aspects of dress they had denied themselves fat. This, for example, may have meant dressing attractively, a taboo idea for most overweight women. 'If I am fat, I must be horrible and don't deserve to have nice clothes.'

Having dressed in a different way when thin, these women acted differently with others but discovered that they were ill-equipped to deal with the reactions they stirred up. Kate, an anthropology graduate student, discovered that once, when thin, she had been to a party in tight blue jeans and a cheesecloth shirt (in place of her usual cover-up dress over pants) and her women friends, while initially complimentary and supportive, seemed to hover around when their husbands and lovers approached her. Kate was nervous that the other women felt jealous and would dislike her, but she did not know how to keep their husbands away. In the group, we discussed the various meanings of this new clothing. In the end, she was determined that the next time she lost weight, she would risk feeling good and sensual in her clothes without threatening her friends. She decided to share her new and fragile acceptance of her body with her friends and she reassured them that she was not interested in their lovers. This also helped her clear up her own confusion about dressing sensually and sexually.

Body image and protection are very important. In the

groups we try to address these two problems in the following ways: group members are encouraged to accept the physical aspects of being fat. Self-acceptance is the key task in the group; without it weight loss and breaking the addiction can only be temporary. We aim for a situation in which women can actually experience the ownership of their fat and the diverse meanings they have attributed to it. When they lose weight they can take its significance with them as necessary. They will not feel that they are losing a protective covering; they grow into their bodies and then they will feel that they have their whole bodies which they then can afford to compress. These diagrams help to show the process we aim for in the groups.

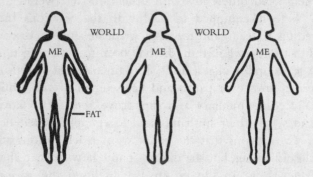

To help in the very difficult task of self-acceptance and the preparation for a new slim body and new self-image we employ the following strategies. Bear in mind that you first have to own something before you can lose it. You must first accept your body in its largeness before you can give it up. A full-length undistorted mirror is the first place to start. Group members set aside time each day – maybe just a couple of minutes at the outset – to observe their bodies. Most compulsive eaters are very aware of how their faces look but not in relation to the rest of their bodies. What we try to do in this exercise is to observe our bodies. We are using the mirror to see ourselves without judging the image it holds. This is both a frightening and difficult project for many women because one is so used to making a grimace and judgment on the few occasions we do see our whole bodies. We are so familiar with avoiding possibly unacceptable visions, keeping our heads down as we walk past shop windows lest we cast a glance at ourselves unaware and trigger negative feelings. So, in doing the exercise, a woman is asked initially to look at the reflected image of herself as she would a work of art, for example, a sculpture, getting to know its dimensions and texture. She is looking to find out where it begins and ends; where it curves or bumps in and out; what colour changes there are. The woman tries this in several different positions starting first by standing, then sitting – without having to hide half of her body – and finally, standing sideways. Some people have a greater ease doing this exercise dressed; others find it more manageable nude. So we start with what feels most comfortable and stay with that until the woman can have the experience of looking in the mirror and not flashing to feelings of disgust.

The second step in the mirror exercise is aimed to help you experience yourself existing throughout your body. Many women experience their fat as something that surrounds them with their true selves inside or, alternatively, that their fat trails them, taking up more room than it really does. So when a woman is standing in front of the mirror the emphasis in this part of the exercise is to feel herself *throughout* her body. She follows her breath on its course from her lungs through her body. The large thighs she may wish to reject are as much a part of her body as the wrist that seems so much more acceptable. Try to see the various parts of your body as connected. Start with your toes and remind yourself of how your toes are connected to your feet and your feet are connected to your ankles and your ankles are connected to your lower leg, and so on. It will provide you with a holistic view of your body. You will begin to experience yourself as existing through the fat.

This new approach has another function. If you can experience yourself as existing throughout the fat, then when you lose weight, you will not feel you have lost a protective covering; you will feel you have become compressed. This is because if you feel yourself all through the fat then what is all of you is part of you. In giving up the size you are making an exchange – you swap the fat for your own body, and that is power.

The drawings are worth repeating here because these will help towards an understanding of what we are trying to achieve in reducing the discrepancy between the fat self and the small interior physical self. We are aiming for a situation where the sequence, me:fat:world, is replaced by me:world.

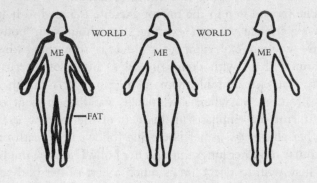

As I mentioned above, women report that when they have lost weight they have allowed themselves to wear very different clothes from those they wore when they considered their bodies as unacceptably large. A compulsive eater may have at least three wardrobes. These generally consist of one or two smocky-type items that will cover her at her absolute maximum weight; nondescript clothes for a medium weight; and clothes for when she was or will be thin which tend to be more stylish and varied and allow for a greater range of expression. The clothes in the larger sizes will almost undoubtedly be circumscribed by what is available in the shops and by what a compulsive eater thinks is permissible to wear. When you look at the clothing racks in sizes 18, 20 and up there is much less variety and styling than in the 10s and 12s. The taboos in people's minds against bright colours, horizontal stripes and good design for fat people correspond to what is available in the stores. By and large, cheap, stylish clothing is not available over size 14. It is therefore not surprising that when a woman loses weight she can experiment with projecting different images through her dressing, because for the first time alternative clothing is readily available. However, it is also true that as long as she feels her body size is unacceptable, she will be using her clothing to hide her body and avoid drawing attention to it. The initial goal of the groups is to give each woman a greater acceptance of her body. Without such acceptance we maintain that weight loss will be temporary because it will continue to trigger off frightening feelings. To avoid this state we do preparatory work in the area of body size, body image and dressing. We encourage the women to throw out or pack away or trade with other group members, all the clothes in their closets that do not currently fit them. This means that every morning, instead of confronting three sets of clothes (indeed, three different people in their closets) and torturing themselves about the 'thin' clothes that continually await and attack them, they will be looking at the clothes that do fit. Much of the compulsive eaters negative self-image gets expressed in the way she dresses and carries herself. This then produces a spiralling of self-hate. One woman I worked with said, 'I feel ashamed of my body and I just cover it as efficiently as possible in a big smock. Then I realise I don't like my clothes either, so I end up doubly hating myself.' Almost inevitably these self-rejecting feelings lead the compulsive eater to cram food into her mouth to assuage the feelings and then, of course, come renewed recriminations and resolutions to start yet another diet.

Having bared one's wardrobe, we are ready to move to step two. This involves experimenting with various images of yourself and dressing to express those now, not waiting until you are thin to wear the kinds of clothes in which you imagine yourself thin. It is not a criminal act to tuck in your blouse, shirt or sweater when overweight. It rarely makes you look larger to be more defined. This latter idea is one of the misconceptions we carry around supposing that loose clothing makes us look less big than fitted clothing. It may attract more attention. If so, that gives you the opportunity to work on reactions to one of the imagined consequences of being thin. Better to test it out and see how it feels while you still have the safety of the fat. It is important to test out your ideas of the images you want to express to find out what really feels good and what feels scary. In the groups, women can get some feedback for the images they are projecting; they can discuss whether there is a discrepancy between what they wish to project and are indeed projecting. Group members can also help each other go shopping for clothes or material to make garments[1] and

help each other through a day of real or imagined cri
sales staff and fellow shoppers.

Mirror work and dressing for now are thus two of the
basic techniques used in the group to help women both
accept their current body size and prepare for a smaller
one. In addition, we encourage group members to adopt
a self-image close to the one they imagine they will have
when thin. This has its physical aspects as well as emotional
ones, and an aim of the group is to work on the different
levels simultaneously.

Another of the preparatory exercises employed is to
imagine not only what you intend to project when thin
through your clothing but also through body position and
stance as well. Many women report that when they were
thin before, they sat, stood and danced quite differently,
generally adopting more open postures. These different
stances produced a variety of effects, some of which they
were comfortable with and others with which they were
not. The difficult ones mainly had to do with others'
responses and the women found that they did not know
how to deal with people's reactions. Putting on weight
again had been their only option. An illustration from my
work with Janet describes well her actual experience of
becoming thin in the past.

Janet is a 26 year-old social worker in a drug-addiction
agency. She grew up in Brooklyn, the eldest of three children in a middle-class Jewish family. She was of average
weight until she was thirteen. Her mother was slightly
overweight and from time to time was preoccupied with
dieting. At the dinner table her mother would often be
eating a modified version of the family meal – no potatoes or desserts. When Janet's body started to develop into
that of a woman she put on about 15lb [7kg]. She felt quite

h the changes going on in her body and
om the adolescent girls' magazines on
's new shape and the distressing feel-
ed puberty. She gravitated towards arti-
How to Look Like a Happy Teenager; What
bout the changes going on in your body.' Under
sy headlines these articles contained a ghastly message.
Janet learned there was something decidedly wrong about
her shape and was told that the answer lay in weight control.
Thus started 13 years of dieting and bingeing. Janet's initial
experience of terror and anxiety about her body changes
found no outlet except in these magazines. She had no
other place to explore the revulsion, excitement and fear
that she was feeling about periods, bras and pubic hair.
Indeed, her introduction to her menstrual periods itself was
quite confusing. Although prepared for the event so that
she was not initially frightened when the blood began,
she had no real way to understand the response from her
mother. On telling her, she was slapped on the cheek[2] and
offered congratulations. Subsequently, she overheard her
mother telephoning family friends to announce with pride
that Janet was a woman. Thus, an introduction to womanhood was accompanied by an act of violence. It was hard
for Janet to put together the slap and the congratulations:
The idea that she had done something wrong, or indeed
was all wrong, provided the basis for her to latch on to
those articles and advertisements which promised solutions
to one's failures through attaining the correct body size.
The very first diet she went on made her feel wonderful.
She experienced it as an act of independence from her
family. She would decide what to eat rather than eat whatever was put on the table. The diet had a double edged
function. She could try and transform her body and she

could establish her separateness from the family. She
performed adequately academically and went away to
college and graduate school. When I first met Janet she
had been working for two years, she had a large circle of
friends which included some close women friends, and had
been living with Alan, an architect, for over two years. With
one exception, she felt quite pleased with the way her life
was going, feeling herself to be quite active, social and
competent on the job. The one exception was her obsession with weight, dieting and body size. She was 5ft 2"
[157cm] and felt overweight at 130lb [59kg]. She had
successfully dieted many times to 112lb [51kg] but had
never maintained the weight loss for more than a few
months. Her current weight was not far off the maximum
she had ever been. In the course of the therapy we traced
the different times when her weight had increased and
decreased. As I have sketched out above we discussed in
detail the original feelings that had propelled her towards
the diet-binge syndrome. Two important discoveries were
made. The first was that many times Janet had geared up
to diet and, having lost the weight, felt herself attractive
enough to get sexually involved with men. These relationships varied in length but almost inevitably her eating went
through three phases when she was sexually involved. The
first phase, which lasted a week or so, was characterised by
a startling lack of interest in food. These were the only
times she was thirteen that Janet can remember actually not being preoccupied with her food intake. She ate
quite little and was not particularly aware of how it tasted.
The length of the second phase varied. With Alan she kept
quite close to her diet for about three months, with no
significant weight variation but with a considerable preoccupation and worry about food with days defined as 'good'

or 'bad' – depending on her intake. After three months they went on vacation together and Janet relaxed the proscription on her consumption of food although her obsession was just as great. Privately, she judged, worried or praised herself according to what passed between her lips. She resolved to diet when she got back from their vacation. Meanwhile, she ate a wide range of foods, particularly the kind of which she deprived herself during the previous months. When she and Alan returned to New York she had put on enough weight to convince herself that she must diet yet again. For the next fifteen months she yoyoed but became increasingly bored and unconvinced by the whole approach.

So one pattern was: weight loss to sexual involvement to weight gain. The other instances when she lost weight corresponded to big changes in her life – entry into high school, leaving home to go to college, leaving college and taking summer jobs, the beginning of the year she worked between college and graduate school and the return to New York City to work in the drug-addiction agency. Each one of these occasions represented Janet's growing independence and autonomy. She met them with confidence and a slim body and was quite perplexed as to why the impulse to eat compulsively returned shortly after she had settled in new surroundings.

In the course of the therapy, Janet described her experiences in sexual relationships and with new places, jobs and school challenges. What began to emerge was that the issues of separation and sexuality were more difficult for her than she had been aware of. In her sexual relationships she was able to see that she believed her acceptance was based on her looking a particular way and being thin. She received plenty of sexual attention which, although she enjoyed, threatened her – she did not know how to turn people away. She also did not know if she was as sexual inside as she projected outside because, in her periods of weight gain, she did not feel at all sexual and had not met with much sexual interest from others. In addition, she worried that she might become uncontrollably promiscuous if she were thin all the time. Her mother's attitude towards her was painful and confusing. Whereas her mother had previously encouraged dieting, she now passed comments on how Janet was looking pale and as if she might disappear. Janet had not become the thin, beautiful daughter her mother had wanted, and she was hurt by her mother's ambivalence towards her newfound self-acceptance. She was also confused by the reactions of men; she could not seem to please both her mother and men at the same time.

As we replayed her feelings frame by frame, Janet sensed the vulnerability she experienced in herself as a thin woman. She felt that she had become what everyone had encouraged her to be and was met by disapproval from her mother on the one hand, and abundant sexual interest from men on the other. She realised that she felt quite unable to handle these two kinds of attention. The disapproval from her mother made no sense to her and Janet felt angry as though she were being betrayed. She felt quite inadequate to handle all the sexual attention and felt that she had no way to say 'yes' or 'no' in a way which corresponded to her own desires. She felt she had no tools by which to select whomever she was interested in but, perhaps more confusing, she felt that now she had a beautiful body she was required to project the sexuality she had hidden in her overweight periods.

In dealing with the theme of separation, Janet realised

that as she had taken on the new challenges at school, college, and in her job, she had, indeed, been quite worried about what was expected of her. She had coped with her anxieties by attempting to take a hold of herself – putting herself on a stringent diet. When she started college she projected an image, and attempted to believe in that image of herself – one that expressed independence, competence, interest and general enthusiasm. Underneath this construct, and into the diet, were placed her fears of inadequacy, lone-liness, boredom and lack of security. She rarely allowed herself to have those feelings for more than an instant and set herself the task of living up to her idealised self-image as a thin person.

As she realised how ungenerous she had been to herself in her thin times, so it emerged how much of an invest-ment she had made in being thin whenever she put on weight. To be thin was a state that allowed no pain, no mistakes and represented independence and sexuality.

In the therapy we worked towards Janet's acknowledg-ment of just how scary her past experiences of being thin were. Having seen this, Janet looked to aspects of herself that she left behind in the fat. She began to incorporate those into an idea of herself thin. She learned how to be assertive so that she could say 'yes' or 'no' in sexual and other situations rather than being the victim of her body size. She looked at the feelings that seemed unacceptable while she was thin and began to articulate them directly rather than hiding them within the fat so that when she lost the weight again she was sure she could express them directly then and did not worry that she had no place to hide them. She allowed herself the possibility that she could be thin and have conflicts; that whatever conflicts she had with her mother, with her own sexuality, with her anger or whatever, they could all exist as part of her when thin. This did not mean resolving all the difficulties but acknowledging and accepting them. It meant giving up the idea that being thin meant that her life had to work out right all the time.

The actual progress of Janet's therapy was, of course, not a straightforward march with one theme unfolding after the other in the orderly fashion I described above. Insights and realisations come suddenly, fade away and come back again. Only through fantasy work, slow loss of weight, intermittent bingeing, and the hard work necessary to try out the insights in fearful situations, does such a complete picture emerge. Janet's therapy lasted fourteen months after which she had completely broken the compulsion and had lost weight. She stabilised at about 112–114lb [50–51kg]. Followup sessions verified that the understanding Janet had reached about her own experience of eating had permitted her to remain permanently at the weight she desired. She had found more direct and assertive ways for dealing with the problems of sexuality and womanhood than body size.

For Janet then, work on the meanings of fat and thin provided her with the opportunity to change her self-image. She closed the gap between her fantasies of who she would be thin and who she was in reality. This exploration and then abandonment of the thin fantasies allowed her to give up unrealistic expectations of personality change.

As we have seen, women unconsciously fear being thin. If one is thin then one is expected to fit the norm. If one is thin others will equate conforming in body size with conforming with stereotyped female behaviour. If one is thin, how can one be self-defining? It is precisely these confusions that have kept many women away from permanent thinness, and it is these underlying issues that need to be confronted so that a woman can experience the choice of being thin *and* herself.

It takes quite a bit of unraveling to separate the threads that push women to lose weight one week and gain it the next. In clarifying the tensions, I have tried to identify the varied reasons why thinness may be feared. A major question that needs to be confronted individually is, 'How will I be who I wish to be if I look as I am supposed to look?' Consideration of this question is essential and goes a long way towards providing solutions to being a thin woman in this culture.

CHAPTER THREE

The Experience of Hunger for the Compulsive Eater

The women I see have already tried many different ways to lose weight including hypnosis, Weight Watchers Inc., diet doctors, cellulose fillers, appetite suppressants and diuretics, Overeaters Anonymous and magic. All these methods are external schemes. Food intake is limited and particular foods — such as ice cream, cake and bread — are banned. This is all based on the principle that if you reduce your caloric intake (or carbohydrate intake) you will lose weight. Diets range from Stillman's Water Diet to Atkin's and the Mayo Clinic Diet, from the Banana Diet to the Drinking Person's Diet. A million diets and a million dieters. Millions of dollars too: 60 billion dollars is spent annually by the American public to get thin and stay thin.[1]

All these diets and weight-reduction schemes have two things in common. First, there is a devastatingly high rate of recidivism. Dieters lose weight by the ton but their success in keeping their weight down is less formidable.[2] Statistics are scarce but the maintenance rates are rumoured to be scandalously low. The second feature these schemes share is a stress on reinforcing the compulsive activity and an emphasis on cultural stereotypes of thinness and fatness.

None of these plans addresses the central issues behind

compulsive eating. Two of these issues are the experience of hunger and the need to break food addiction. 'Fat people' are not as aware of the actual mechanism of hunger as 'normal weight' non-compulsive eaters.[3] This means that compulsive eaters do not use their gurgling stomachs to tell them when to eat. Eating becomes so loaded with other meanings that a straightforward reaction to a hungry stomach is unusual. Indeed one of the features of compulsive eating is eating in such a way that physical hunger is never felt. The social stigma attached to being overweight accentuates this problem. Fat people in our culture feel the stigma in this way; 'Fat is bad, I should always be trying to lose weight and I definitely should not enjoy food.' In general, compulsive eaters divide food into categories of 'good foods' and 'bad foods'. All the diets work on the principle that food is dangerous. Only through rigorous deprivation can the compulsive eater redeem herself, lose weight and begin to enjoy life. So the mechanism of hunger on which 'normal' eaters rely is distorted. Years of guilty eating and mammoth deprivation schemes mean that the compulsive eater is very out of touch with the experience of hunger and the ability to satisfy it.

Distortions of the eating process cause confusion for the compulsive eater while the myriad of weight-reduction schemes infantilise her and reduce her control over her own eating to a minimum. As anyone who has ever dieted knows, the structure of a diet is rigid. Diets become moral straitjackets which confine the compulsive eater. *In turning to dieting, all the compulsiveness evident in overeating is now channeled into a new obsession – to staying on the diet.* Follow these rules, eat what the authorities tell you. Above all, do what women are so good at – deprive yourself. Even the so-called liberal diets ('Eat fat and grow slim', 'Enjoy as much food and vegetables as you like') rely on a structure that disenfranchises the woman from her own body. 'Eat bananas seven times a day; weigh 4oz [113g] of fish and 3oz [85g] of grated cheese; drink one glass of pulp-free orange juice a day and unlimited cups of black coffee or tea; use one bowl only and eat with chopsticks; always eat in the same place or at the same time; always eat a big breakfast; eat starch, cut out fat; cut out fat but eat high protein; lose weight and *get/hold your man*.' But never, never let yourself go or find out what you like to eat, when or how.

In the main, the compulsive eater knows two realities: compulsive eating (out of control) or compulsive dieting (imprisonment). To be a compulsive eater means to be a food junkie. Compulsive eaters crave their food as badly as a junkie craves heroin or an alcoholic thirsts for liquor. They spend much of their energy battling against their addiction. They are always going 'cold turkey' – dieting or fasting – or trying their methadone substitute – cottage cheese. While a drug addict or alcoholic is not continually struggling against the heroin or liquor, the compulsive eater is caught in an antagonistic relationship with the food she so wants. While the junkie may spend hours hustling the money and connection for the next fix, the compulsive eater will devote the same kind of psychic energy working out what to eat or not. In the end, as the heroin 'fixes' the drug addict and the liquor 'stuporises' the alcoholic, so the binge 'narcotises' the compulsive eater.

A curious aspect in the compulsive eater's addiction is that from a look at her kitchen or her public eating one might get the impression that certain foods are illegal. The presence of particular foods is so rare, and ingestion so clandestine, that one might be forgiven for assuming that criminal penalties are given for the possession and consumption of certain foods. It is as though foods are classified, with ice-cream sundaes and French fries as felonies; bananas and cream as misdemeanors and food in general as a violation. In fact, one well-known slimming organisation characterises food in just this way. Some foods are legal and can be eaten incessantly and in unlimited quantities, others are illegal and are to be eaten only in a restricted way. Thus the compulsive eater is encouraged to create her own jail sentence and in doing so she faces the world very much as does the junkie or alcoholic. This tension converts food into an enemy or an evil to be warded off constantly while at the same time it provides, however shortlived, a treat and comfort.

Unlike other addicts, however, the compulsive eater can find temporary relief in not eating. Not eating means she is being 'good' and conjures up immediate images of the rewards to come from thinness. Contrary to popular images of greed, the compulsive eater is quite frightened of food and what it can do to her. Short spells of withdrawal remove her from the responsibility of what she is putting in her mouth. The food is a drug, it is magical, it is poison, it is to keep one alive, it is suffocating, it is tantalising, but only very rarely is it seen as an essential enjoyable aspect of life. It is from this fear of food that the compulsive eater's large appetite springs. The compulsive eater can eat a lot of food. Often she does not taste the three boxes of cookies, ten celery stalks, four packets of potato chips and frozen pizza that she can consume at one sitting. The food is so guiltily eaten that enjoyment is limited. The feeling of insatiability is very strong and the compulsive eater will cram seemingly unappetising foods, like dry cereal, into her mouth during a binge. The food must be eaten quickly so that it is no longer dangerous. Once consumed, the crisis has passed and the compulsive eater is left with the familiar bad feelings following a binge.

Compulsive eating means eating without regard to the physiological cues which signal hunger. People who have never had difficulty distinguishing hunger pangs take it for granted that their bodies are wanting food then. They may be quite astonished by the extent to which this mechanism is so underutilised by the compulsive eater. For a compulsive eater it is an equally astonishing idea that people who do not have difficulty with food rely on their stomachs to tell them what, how much and when to eat. For the compulsive eater, food has taken on such additional significance that it has long since lost its obvious biological connection.

The word 'hunger' usually connotes the desire to eat. The body is depleted and needs nourishment. In its extreme form hunger becomes starvation. In its current Western setting the satisfaction of hunger is a social experience. While there is controversy about what exactly constitutes hunger, and what controls appetite and satisfaction, it is strikingly clear that the compulsive eater very rarely eats in response to the stomach cues which signal hunger.[4] Indeed, when we introduce this possibility as an important way out of the whole syndrome, people are eager to be reintroduced to aspects of their bodies they have ignored for so long. While one is rejecting one's body, an enormous alienation exists between it and oneself. This estrangement makes it hard to be receptive to signals from the body. If you have never felt your body was all right or acceptable but was cumbersome, unattractive or not pleasing in some way, it is quite a leap to trust what it has to say, as if an enemy territory were commanding. To listen to a body that has constantly been an unseemly colony is to own that body. To own your own body means to take its needs seriously and disregard many of the external values and measures to which you have attempted to mould it. This distortion of the hunger mechanism does not have a clear origin and it may begin very early on in life. What is clear is that many young women begin to tamper with this mechanism in an effort to transform their bodies at the time of puberty. An analogy may make this distortion process more graphic for those who have considerable difficulty envisaging hunger and an appropriate response. Take, for example, a tickle in the throat. This feeling is satisfied by a cough. A sneeze is preceded by a slight irritation in the nostrils. These reactions are virtually involuntary and few people suffer from the continual need to deny a cough or a sneeze, on the odd occasion it may be polite to stifle the sneeze or cough but not on a continuing basis.

Another example in which one acts less automatically is when one's bladder is full and there is a need to release the pressure. Again, most people will grow up with a confidence about knowing how to follow the signals that they need to urinate and the amount will vary considerably. Sometimes there will be a great deal of pressure on the bladder, sometimes less, but the information that one needs relief will become available quite obviously. These three physical activities are all under self-regulation and depend for satisfaction on recognition of the cues. This is true for the hunger mechanism too. The infant has the capacity to develop a harmonious relationship with its various bodily needs. It can learn to identify hunger cues and feel contented when satisfactorily fed. The confidence that there will be satisfaction is shaped by positive interaction with the environment. When a child cries from hunger and is fed, and cries for affection and gets held, then her cues will have been responded to appropriately and as the child develops she will be able to trust that she can both recognise and fulfil her needs.

Many women who have compulsive eating problems do not feel confident that they can recognise their signs of hunger and then eat to fulfil them. Not only has the hunger process been abused through years of dieting and bingeing but prepuberty eating is often remembered as tortured, interrupted and conflicted. In tracing back, we surmise that such a woman's very early signs of bodily needs were misinterpreted by her mother so that there is confusion over a variety of physical sensations. For example, if every time a child cries it is answered with food, then the food takes on the role of comforter. However, if a baby's diaper needs changing or a baby wants some kind of physical contact, providing food will give neither satisfaction or comfort, nor will it allow the infant to develop trust in its own body. Feeding in response to other bodily needs alienates a child from its body and interferes with the individual's ability to recognise both hunger and satisfaction. This early distortion may well be a contributing factor to many women's discomfort with their own bodies; a discomfort which is then readily available to manipulation by how society says one *should* look and what one *should* eat. Outside cues become powerful sources on which to rely in the absence of confidence that one can take care of one's own needs. Diet sheets and bakeries are equal contenders when a woman is seeking information about how to care for herself. Often compulsive eaters will describe their current eating in a way that confirms our impression that early satisfaction was interfered with. Daphne, a 32 year-old librarian, described much of her eating as a search for something that is missing. 'When I go to the refrigerator I'm quite aware that it is not food I am actually after but it's as though I'm looking for a missing piece.' The missing piece turns out to be a general unease and unsureness about whether she can provide adequately for her own needs.

This discourse on hunger and the distortion of the mechanism is not meant to put the blame on mothers for misinterpreting their children's body signals. It 'is true that in their role as primary caretakers, they often do misinterpret their infants' needs, but an explanation that stops there misses crucial issues that affect all women. The question is more *why* mothers give their children food when that is not what they may be wanting. Why is it that food is always at the ready to be offered when the child expresses discomfort? What are the social forces that produce this kind of mothering? We look for the answer in the social position of women. It is in her role as mother that a woman is unequivocally accepted. It is in her role as mother that she is counselled to be attentive and nurturing to her child. Nearly all of us will have grown up at a time when child care was seen to be the province of mothers. They were seen as the only ones who could adequately care for their children and establish the emotional bonding considered crucial for 'healthy' development. However, while considered the essential figure in the infant's daily life, the mother is not considered expert on child rearing. Instead, she will be encouraged to draw on the expertise of a wide range of specialists – pediatricians, child psychologists, analysts, nutritionists – who will tell her how, when and what she should or should not feed her child. Most 'experts' contradict each other as the fashion in child rearing changes and the different disciplines rush to fit their theories into prevailing ideologies.

Thus the mother is acclaimed on the one hand as *the* only suitable primary caretaker but on the other, is considered to be inadequately prepared to cope with this job and must rely on conflicting 'expert' opinions. It is in this situation that the woman comes to motherhood and the care of her child, and it is not surprising that she then distrusts her own reactions to her child's signals. Alternately deified and devalued, it is hard for her to feel secure about her own responses. One can well imagine how this insecurity is readily reinforced by other consequences of an enforced maternal role. As a mother, this is the chance in life to have an impact on shaping an aspect of one's world (through the child). This may set off in the mother feelings of delight, inadequacy, fear, insecurity, resentment or enthusiasm which are then expressed through her contact with the child. A mother's fears of inadequacy may cause her to overfeed her child by feeding it automatically every time it cries, just as her resentment at being its sole nurse may make her neglect it. But another factor may be involved: when a child cries and expresses its distress and, as the mother imagines, helplessness, she may see herself as the parent who must respond but also, find her own painful feelings of early deprivation reevoked. If *we* are 'inadequate mothers', we are also daughters of 'inadequate mothers' who were themselves daughters. If the early distortion in the feeding relationship is attributable to the social forces present in the mother-daughter relationship, then this will be as true for our mothers as daughters, and our mother's mothers as daughters. As long as a patriarchal culture demands that women bring up their daughters to accept an inferior social position, the mother's job will be fraught with tension and confusion which are often made manifest in the way mothers and daughters interact over the subject of food.

The experience of hunger, then, will not be the compulsive eater's motive for eating. She will not experience her eating as self-regulatory but as a kind of outside force tempting, pleasing and betraying her. Once overweight she will most probably adopt an attitude that says she is not entitled to eat, as though fatness can only be excused, or as if fat people only have a right to exist if they do not eat. Fat people move into a category quite apart from the rest of the population. While advertisers court us to eat more and more, slimming columns, doctors, fashion magazines and friends counsel those overweight to curtail their food intake. But to tell a compulsive eater to control something she feels is out of her control has the effect of making her feel powerless and guilty; powerless for being so apparently ineffectual and guilty for whatever food she does eat. This guilt further distances her from discovering what it is she would *like* to eat because she has become preoccupied with what she *should* or *should not* eat. Food is something to be feared, and to eat feels like committing a sin, for one feels so undeserving and unentitled. Eating takes place quickly and frequently furtively.

A compulsive eater would describe this experience in one of several ways:

1. FOOD AS SOCIAL: 'I'm never hungry at suppertime but I like everyone to eat together because it *feels* like we are a happy family if we eat together. Mealtimes are significant not for the food but for the appearance of family closeness.'

2. MOUTH HUNGER: 'I really need to put some food in my mouth although I don't feel hungry in my stomach.'

3. EATING PROPHYLACTICALLY: 'I'm not hungry at the moment but I might be hungry in a couple of hours and

I won't be able to get anything then, so I'd better have some food now.'

4.   DESERVED FOOD: 'I had a ghastly day. I think I'll cheer myself up with a nice nosh.'

5.   GUARANTEED PLEASURE: 'Eating goodies is the only way to give myself a real treat. It's the one pleasure that I know how to give myself.'

6.   NERVOUS EATING: 'I just have to have something. What can I cram into my mouth?'

7.   CELEBRATORY EATING: 'I had such a great day, one packet of Doritos corn chips can't possibly hurt me.'

8.   EATING OUT OF BOREDOM: 'I'm not in the mood to do anything at the moment . . . I'll fix myself a club sandwich.'

With compulsive dieting there is *also* no response to physiological hunger. The dieter is eating out of a prescribed set of rules saying what foods are allowed or forbidden; she is eating at specified mealtimes with little regard for what her body wants and when it wants it.

We work on the premise that compulsive eaters do not really allow themselves to eat, and consequently are either stuffing their mouths or depriving themselves. Every time a compulsive eater goes on a diet she is telling herself that there is something wrong with her so she must deprive herself. She defines her current self as reprehensible, so she decides to punish herself through denial. In this way, the compulsive eater rarely allows herself the direct pleasure that food can bring. A vicious circle ensues. While she may eat everything in sight when she is not dieting for fear of imminent deprivation, she is nevertheless not enjoying the food. 'I ate twenty cookies in ten minutes today. Tomorrow I'm going to put myself on a diet during which I won't be able to have any cookies, so I had to get all my cookie eating in today before I have to be good.' At the same time the 20 cookies are also a rebellion against the non-entitlement and deprivation.

This diet-binge syndrome can be broken by the compulsive eater when she begins to see herself as a 'normal' person, with fat being nothing more than a descriptive word, without connotating good or bad. If the compulsive eater can begin to experience herself as 'normal' then she can begin to eat like a 'normal' person. This means learning to recognise the difference between real hunger and psychological hunger, and eating accordingly. It means eating enough to satisfy one's hunger and eating whatever food satisfies that particular hunger (be it donuts or steak). After all, people without a compulsive eating problem do not deprive themselves of food by choice. In observing the eating behaviour of people who do not suffer over food, it is interesting to note just what a wide range of foods they do eat and how much at variance with conceptions of 'healthy diet' their daily intake may be. It is also important to realise that they occasionally overeat for pleasure. As this eating is not a substitute for other needs it does not have other connotations. It is the driving compulsion to stuff or starve that we are trying to dissolve rather than dictating 'correct' amounts of food intake.

To find out what, when and how much you might like to eat is not as simple as it seems. In addition, the pressure of the diet and fashion industry, which spends incalculable amounts of money making sure that women do not themselves decide what they would like to eat and wear, reinforces the idea that the compulsive eater is irresponsible, out of control, negligent and hateful.

On the psychological level the experience of hunger pangs can be quite scary. Some of the fear comes from an anxiety about one's ability to satisfy bodily hunger: 'If I'm not stuffing my face or starving myself, what should I do? How will I know how much to eat? Maybe I'll never want to stop.'

Another frightening factor is related to a challenge of the 'female-as-child' concept. For if you can respond to the hunger cues that your body does indeed transmit, this places you in a situation where you might actually satisfy yourself and begin to be in harmony with your body. This idea of being able to take care of yourself allows you to see the female as an adult with the rights and privileges that other adults (male adults) have. This means taking your own needs seriously and attempting to satisfy them for yourself. A woman is brought up to be attuned to and satisfy others' needs. The struggle to know what you want or need to eat changes the way you respond to others' needs. As you begin to trust the capacity to feed yourself you find a basis for being more explicit in relation to other needs. 'If I can take care of myself with food and say "yes" and "no" to what I am wanting or not wanting, then I can spell out for myself, *and* to others, desires in other areas and feel more in charge of other aspects of my life.' Being able to act on one's own needs is a novel experience and one overwhelmingly denied to women in this culture.

When the compulsive eater imagines herself as a thin female adult, when everything else in her life is supposed to hang together better, she has to conform to an image of womanhood rather than be confident with who she is. While this idea is fantasy, it is nevertheless a powerful and scary one: 'If I am thin, and look like a "real" woman, then I must be productive, energetic, together and loving.' The struggle to be female and self-defined is hard, with few supports for an expression of true female personhood.

In our work we spend a great deal of time uncovering and demystifying the various fantasies associated with fat and thin. At the same time we work together on the technical side, learning new ways to approach food and hunger. The steps that I outline here start with the idea that we are not going to judge whatever it is that we eat. Rather, we are going to observe the ways in which we eat. Learning not to judge one's food intake is not very easy. Years of attempting to follow the rules do not quickly fade away. To observe an aspect of the self which has been rejected time and time again requires a good deal of self-acceptance. Turning off one's judges – mothers, women's magazines, husbands, lovers, friends, diet doctors and nutritionists – requires trust in one's self. Being in a group with other women going through the same process can be of great assistance and support.

The first step is to learn about your eating patterns. This means pinpointing those times when you feel particularly vulnerable to attack by the food and to notice any occasions when you feel more at ease with it. By noting your food intake for a short period you will both gather data and develop a sense of yourself as an observer. As an observer you can begin to see that there is a part of you that eats and another part that does other things, including being an observer. Then you have broken away from the idea of yourself as being someone who is obsessed with food. You are ready to move on to becoming a 'normal' person who eats like 'normal' people.

Now the second step is taken. We move from observation to action. First, we begin to identify the difference between mouth hunger and stomach hunger. Risk going without food for a couple of waking hours until you experience some hunger sensations in your body. Most probably you will feel it in your stomach, though some people feel it in the chest or throat. When you feel the difference between the two types of hunger, see how it feels for a minute or so. Is it reassuring or scary? Do you associate pleasant or unpleasant memories with it? Often the first realised feelings of stomach hunger may produce painful associations which you will want to examine with your group or on your own. Mimi, a woman we worked with, discovered that when she allowed herself to experience hunger pangs, she got in touch with a whole other range of body emotions that she had successfully been trying to hide from herself. She felt sexual. These sexual feelings made her quite uncomfortable because she had come to think of sexuality as sinful, or not appropriate for herself. In talking about what this meant she was able to separate hunger pangs from guilt-producing sexuality. Another woman, Betty, remembered being hungry as a child when there was not enough food on the table. And Martha, whose family urged her to eat, discovered for herself that hungry feelings expressed capitulation to the family feeding situation. The process of working through these particular situations was enriched by a feminist understanding of the particular problems they each expressed. For instance, in examining Mimi's response to her sexual feelings we explored why and how she learned that sex was sinful for her, for women. In exploring Betty's hunger as a child we brought into focus the painful lot of mothers who hold back when there is not enough food and encourage the children to eat. Betty discovered that she actually denied herself more than necessary in an identification with her mother at the family table. To be a woman meant to be self-denying. Martha's giving in at the table reflected for her an ambivalence in separating from her family, a difficulty particularly acute for women where separation has traditionally occurred only at marriage. Looking at these associations in these ways can provide useful clues to the roots of your own particular history with food. Ultimately, when you have learned to give your body exactly what it wants you will be able to look forward to those hunger pangs because it is a message that your body is wanting something delicious.

The next step is to eat out of stomach hunger only as much as possible. Do not worry too much about this at first, because anyone with a history of compulsive eating is bound occasionally to eat from mouth hunger. But try to begin to see your body as a finely tuned instrument that likes to be lovingly cared for. When it is very hungry it might want quite a bit of nourishment; when it is only mildly hungry, quite a little less. In line with this, having learned about stomach hunger, try to locate precisely what food or liquid your body is hungry for. That is, once having experienced hunger pangs, work out what particular food or foods will satisfy that particular hunger. Sometimes this will be very easy and you will know right away what it is you are wanting, but often, particularly because of the years of 'shoulds' and regimens, you might not know and in this case you might find a two-minute fantasy exercise helpful. Close your eyes and ask yourself 'What kind of physical sensation do I have and how can I best satisfy it? Do I want something crunchy, salty, chewy, moist, sweet? Okay, I want some potato chips. Let me imagine myself eating some. No, that's not it. How about some plain chocolate . . . ?'

In this way before you eat the food you will have already imagined how it is most likely going to feel going down.

Taste the soup travelling down your throat, bite on the nuts, smell the fresh bread in your fantasy. Find the foods that fit the mood and then eat. Eat as much as your body is wanting. Really taste each mouthful. Enjoy yourself.

Quite frequently, no food will clearly present itself and this can mean one of two things. You are hungry but cannot find exactly what would make sense. Have a little of a food you enjoy and wait till you get a clear message. You may have let the hunger go on too long so that your stomach is jumping up and down and does not know how to be soothed. Alternatively you may not be hungry for food and it will be important for you to 'feed' yourself more appropriately with a hug, a cry, a bath, a telephone conversation or a run. If it *is* something else you are wanting, food will not satisfy the original desire. At the very most, it can provide a temporary relief from feelings that creep up. What is more disturbing is that eating at these times serves to mask other urges and distances you further from the capacity to take care of yourself. Sort out what emotional need you are asking the food to carry for you and ask yourself whether indeed it works. As you discover how unsatisfactory this way of operating is, consider alternative ways to cope with your needs. If you are accustomed to eating compulsively during especially upsetting times, it will be reassuring to know you can feed yourself according to hunger and leave space to feel the distress. As Carol Bloom puts it in her training manual,[5] 'Most compulsive eaters increase their non-nurturing eating during stress which usually makes them feel a lot worse. To not eat during those times (when you don't want to) is once again reinforcing a message to yourself, "I can take care of myself, I can give myself the support I need." "It's a way not to desert yourself when things get tough."'

For many people particular foods have special significance and correlate with particular moods and memories. Some like the calming effects of soup when they are feeling tense, carrots when they are angry or juice when they are feeling energetic. While I am not suggesting that you bite away your anger into a carrot and do not express it elsewhere, nevertheless food can be expressive. The main point is to pamper yourself with food – to allow every eating experience to be a pleasurable one – to see your stomach hunger as a signal for you to enjoy. Do not worry about regulation mealtimes or balanced meals. We do not believe in good foods or bad foods. *We believe that our bodies can tell us what to eat, how to have a nutritionally balanced food intake and how to lose weight.* The body is a self-regulatory system if allowed to operate. We are not concerned with caloric or carbohydrate value. Take a multivitamin pill every day until you feel that your body is as self-regulating as we propose it can be.

Now these suggestions – eat when you are hungry, eating as much as you want – may sound like a new set of rules that you are supposed to follow. In a sense they are. But we see them rather as helpful guidelines designed to let you trust your own bodily processes and as such, will not be experienced as 'shoulds' but as guides until you experience total trust. In a sense, the steps outlined above are no more than a frame-by-frame description of what goes on for 'normal' eaters.

Attention to the details of eating is a first step towards having a 'normal' relationship with food. As you can say 'yes' to a particular food so the possibility is there for you to say 'no' to particular foods at particular times. Saying 'no' is a great tool in self-definition but it is predicated on the ability to be able to say 'yes' in a wholesome, guilt-free way.

A few more tips in demystifying food may be helpful.

Try leaving a mouthful of every kind of food and drink you are ingesting on your plate, cup or glass. This will have two functions. On the one hand, it will begin to put the food at your control and reduce the feeling of insatiability; on the other, it will allow you to reject food. As you get more comfortable you will be able to define precisely how much food you are wanting. This exercise helped Elizabeth, a 38 year-old mother of three, who was brought up in England during the Second World War. It broke through a pattern she had established years back in trying to leave food on her plate. She had an image of her mother standing over her telling her she must not leave a crumb because soldiers had risked their lives getting the food to her. Food was rationed and goodies infrequent and Elizabeth felt she did not know when she would eat again.

Try loading up your house with 'bad foods' that you feel attracted to and scared of. One woman we worked with was persuaded to keep enough ingredients for seventy-five ice-cream sundaes with all the trimmings. When it was first suggested that she fill the refrigerator with ice cream, sauce, nuts and cream she exclaimed, 'But I'll eat it all!' The idea seemed so sinful to her. It was pointed out that if she had enough supplies for a minor army and could prove to herself that she did not want to consume it all at once, she would feel much more powerful and more in control of her food. She learned to love the ice cream and treat it as a friend to be called on when she wanted it rather than as an enemy to be conquered. She also took special care always to have plenty of her favourite brand or flavour. If you are really wanting to have coffee ice cream, the chocolate fudge in your refrigerator is a mediocre substitute. *It is worth going out to buy exactly what you want rather than just eating anything that is around.*

The only restrictions on this scheme are economic. It is unfortunate to have a yearning for fine smoked salmon when your pocket-book can only afford something cheaper. But really think about it. How much money did you used to spend on diet foods, diet books and binges?

In the groups we play a game to help focus on particular foods, and to destroy the idea that it is dangerous to have delicious foods in the house. We imagine that we have a special room filled with all of our favourite foods, and we see what it would be like to be surrounded with all of these wonderful taste possibilities. In the fantasy we see how it feels. Is it reassuring or scary to have all this goodness at one's fingertips? For most people it turns out that the initial flash makes them nervous. 'I'll never get out the door! I'll always be eating!' But then, sitting with the fantasy for a minute or two, we find that people feel safe and protected with all the food around. They even find they have other things to do apart from preparing and eating food. If the food is there, if they know that they are never again going to deprive themselves by their own hands, then they can begin to get on with the business of living, and to start to eat in order to live rather than living in order to eat.

All the work you do on locating your hunger and learning how to satisfy it can be accompanied by an examination of the psychological issues that interfere with your ability to satisfy your food needs. For example, if you experience difficulty in allowing yourself to feel hunger, pay attention to both the physical sensations in the body as well as the psychological factors that prevent you from hearing what your body might be wanting. The psychological issues might range from doubts about your ability to nurture yourself and what it would mean to nurture yourself, to whose power you might be jeopardising if you were to give to yourself. One woman discovered that, as she began to take her own needs seriously and specifically, she called into question her role in her family which was to take care of everybody else's needs while ignoring her own. Putting herself first in the food department was initially problematic for her. She felt she would be deserting her children. She found out subsequently that as she allowed herself to eat what she wanted, the whole family became more autonomous in that area. Mealtimes became much less tense affairs. Each member of the family chipped in to make something they wanted, and although there was some chaos while everyone was experimenting and messing up the kitchen, in the end each family member determined more of her or his own food intake and, as it turned out, took more responsibility in other areas of household labour.

Some people will find that as they begin to feel less addicted to food in general, certain foods will continue to have 'magical' qualities. One woman I was seeing inexplicably ate candy periodically during the day while she was at work. We discovered that the intake of sweets had to do with the attempt to sweeten herself, to make herself 'nice' when indeed she was feeling quite angry but felt that, 'Women shouldn't get mad; it's not nice. I'd better make myself like sweet and spice.' It turned out that she felt angry every time her boss treated her in a way that was particularly demeaning. Although she was paid to do research she was also expected to 'serve'. She was expected to prepare the coffee and entertain the various male clients that came to her office. These expectations were examples of the sexual inequality that so often operates in offices, and she, like many other women, experienced conflict and rage when 'feminised' in such a way. In the group we role-played ways for her to be more assertive with her boss and to discuss with him other options for the preparation of coffee. When a more equitable work situation was arrived at she found less need to cram her mouth furtively with candies. That is not to say that all her anger disappeared. There are bound to be frictions as long as there are bosses, but the anger was acknowledged and validated by the group for what it was and became separated from her eating activity.

In all that I have said it is important to remember that our goal is not primarily weight loss. *The goal is for the compulsive eater to break her addictive relationship towards food.* While weight loss is generally an important sign that the addiction is broken, our primary concern is that you begin to feel more comfortable about food. This cannot be stressed too strongly. *The problem that we seek to solve is addiction to food.* Continued obsession with weight loss or gain hinders the process of learning to love food and eating what your body is wanting. While this process is not a magical shortcut, its philosophy provides a basis for a more natural and relaxed relationship towards food, and our bodies.

CHAPTER FOUR

Self-Help

If you see yourself as a compulsive eater the chances are that you know other women in the same position. Indeed, it is likely that you have dieted, fasted or gorged with friends even though the compulsive eating may be experienced as a solitary and even masturbatory activity. Women with a compulsive eating problem tend to seek out others who will be sympathetic and understanding and it is largely true that the only people who can be really so are those who suffer from the same problem. If you do not feel close to anyone who shares this problem you can put up a notice in your college, community centre or women's centre, in order to contact others who might be interested in a self-help group. If you feel reluctant to work in a group, the exercises discussed can easily be done on your own. I do, however, suggest that you consider working in a group for the reasons I detail below.

There are several reasons for working on this issue in a group. Some are practical and others are related to the nature of the problem itself. On the practical level there are not enough people doing this work to satisfy the demand and interest for individual therapy dealing with compulsive eating. As more people who have had the problem and gone through it train and initiate work with others, there will be more options for those people who prefer one-to-one settings. But for now I should like to outline the advantages of group work and suggest a model for a self-help group.

For those who have not had friendships solidified on the basis of sharing eating obsessions, coming together with others who have the same problem can be an enormous relief. To be able to meet and talk with other women about this issue can help relieve those terrible feelings of being an isolated freak and a failure. Even for women who have talked endlessly about food obsessions with friends, the previous chats may have been circumscribed by the strictures of talking about diets or diet foods. Grouping with other women to explore explicitly one's relationship to fat and thin can provide a comforting and safe experience. *For some women it is like coming out of the closet. This may be particularly the case for those women who have managed to keep their weight within the cultural norm so that nobody else is aware of their problem.* For others, it is the relief of a supportive environment in which there is space for the grief and pain associated with a life centred on food to come out. They do not have to make excuses for being large or obsessed with food, they have a chance to be honest about the painful calculations they make every time food passes through their mouths, and the terror they face every morning wondering whether it is going to be a 'good day' or a 'bad day'. They do not have to pretend they eat like a bird. They get a chance, possibly for the first time ever, to discuss their eating openly and to explore the complicated feelings they may have about their bodies. For everyone in the group, it is possibly the first place they have been in which they feel they do not have to apologise for existing in the first place. Above all, the group offers help in getting through a problem that may seem insoluble on your own.

Beyond breaking the isolation there are, in addition, several other ways in which the group method can be beneficial. Within the group everyone has the same problem and so, although the compulsive eating is the reason which draws everyone together, in that assembling, the group can provide a means for a shift in the self-definition for individual members. What I mean by this is that by being in a group that accepts the part of one that is a compulsive eater – one can move beyond this limited concept of the self as a compulsive eater. As one can begin to see other compulsive eaters or fat women as having other attributes apart from the fat and can begin to see that fat has nothing to do with other values such as beauty, creativity, energy or caring, one can begin to see these attributes in oneself.

For example, when group member Joy can see another member, Mary, as a kind, quick and tough woman then Joy can look beyond her own self-definition as a fat person and see that she has additional qualities too. She can then begin to extend her view of fat so that it does not automatically trigger a response of repulsion or rejection. Fat can then be seen as one of a number of adjectives that can be coupled up with other adjectives – beautiful, gracious, horrid, awful, polite, nice or generous. The fat is seen as just a part of oneself, not the singular most defining characteristic. People are more than any of their parts or even the sum of their parts. If you have a big stomach on which you focus, you are nevertheless more than just a big stomach. However, if you have been defined by others or have defined yourself solely as someone of a particular size – and this definition has had negative connotations, as is the case with the adjective 'fat' – then it is hard for that part of yourself not to seem overwhelming. Expanding your definition of self to include other qualities in addition to the fat is crucial. This is so because at the point of giving up the fat you are then not throwing out all of yourself (a common fear) because you are more than the fat. Joan felt that her fat was the only thing she had in life that was all hers. She held on to her extra weight tenaciously, fearing that if she lost it, if she were to give up her fat, there would be no essential Joan left. The group was extremely important to her because she was forced to look at herself through others' eyes – others who accepted her size and sought additional characteristics in defining her. She recognised the uniqueness of others in the group, the particular configuration of their personalities which made them the people they were. She could see how they retained these characteristics at varying weights during the course of the group, and she was thus able to see her own essential uniqueness and individuality, not predicated on her fat.

In addition, the group serves other important functions. The fat conveys messages to the outside world. For example, many women say when discussing self-assertion that they do not know how to say 'yes' or 'no' directly. They have the fantasy that their fat is doing it for them. In the context of the group, where everyone's fat means something different, it is starkly demonstrated that having the fat speak for you does not necessarily get the message across. Of course, in the case of unassertive behaviour outside the group, the fat rarely succeeds in the job it is meant to do either, but the fantasy can cling. Within the group, not only *can* one begin to express oneself more directly but one *has* to. Without specific articulation the magical meaning of the individual's fat will never come through. Group members can support each other in their attempts to make the exchange – you have a forum for trying to use your mouth to speak and say what you are wanting, feeling or thinking instead of continuing to hope that the fat is doing it for you. Taking risks of this nature is often easier in groups. Group members who experience themselves as particularly unassertive can use the group to try out ways of asserting themselves. Group members can provide accurate feedback and encouragement. In a one-to-one situation the feedback is, of necessity, more limited.

When talking about images of thinness, some women have expressed the fantasy that 'When I am thin I will be competent, attractive, together, in good relationships . . . perfect.' Group members can help each other challenge such unreal expectations – they can demonstrate from their own past histories of times when they were thin that life was not wonderful and easy all the time. This can then aid others in giving up such notions of perfection which rely on a race against oneself in which one is bound to lose. But perhaps more instrumentally, it is likely that group members will be of varying sizes and that there will be one or two women who represent the ideal weight of others in the group. These women, the compulsive thins, so to speak, have kept the problem within physical bounds and are as thin as the culture demands its women to be. Despite this, they have not found that in thinness everything in their life runs smoothly, and this can be an enormously helpful lesson to those who imagine that being thin means that everything will be fine. Losing weight then can be seen as just that, rather than heralding a whole transformation of one's life.

As well as helping women redefine themselves, the group is also valuable in providing a direct way of dealing with compulsive eating itself. Within a compulsive eating group the focus of attention is always on what is the fat or thin expressing in one's life at the moment, or in one's past or in the here and now of the group. It is as though the protective functions of the fat, by being discussed and explored in the group, lose their power within that group and members have to search for new ways to protect themselves without relying on the weight. This then provides a learning experience in which group members can see that they have other protective mechanisms apart from the fat. This makes giving up the fat much less scary.

Inevitably, during the life of a group, people are at different sizes at different times. It can thus be noted that one can lose weight and nothing necessarily terrible happens. For example – Jill and Margot, who were different sizes, both feared their own 'promiscuity' if they were to lose weight. In both their cases their thin periods were times of intense sexual activity. In the course of the group both realised how scary these thin/sexual experiences had been and knew that before losing weight again they would have to promise themselves that hectic sexual activity did not automatically accompany being thin. Margot lost a good deal of weight first. She continued to reassure herself that she could be thin and not express her sexuality as long as she was scared. Meanwhile, Jill began to incorporate sexuality into her life, so that she gave up the idea of leaving sex only for thin times and then scaring herself with her sexual interest when slim. As Jill noticed Margot's new-found sexual selectivity she was very encouraged. She could see that sex was no longer bound up with weight in a deprivation/binge model of 'too fat to fuck' or 'thin and promiscuous'. For Jill and Margot then, each other's actions spelled important lessons. Jill saw that someone with whom she strongly identified could achieve something that had previously seemed so impossible – Margot had lost weight without becoming promiscuous. Similarly, Margot learned from Jill that it was possible to be sexual at any weight. This was particularly comforting because Margot wished to get pregnant and had connected many of her fears of pregnancy and motherhood with the idea that she would not be able to have sex if pregnant because she would be so large that she would be sexually undesirable. Jill's ability to be sexually involved at a higher weight than either had thought possible helped Margot recast her ideas about sexuality and size. She could see that Jill's size did not indeed preclude her from being sexual and attractive and she was heartened by this.

There are other important aids that emerge from working in a group setting which will become obvious as I detail a self-help model. At this point, though, I should like to spell out a few suggestions to help a group start.

It is my experience that the number of people in a group should not be too small. An optimum group would have between 5 and 10 members. Since it seems to take a while for a group to stabilise its membership – a few people always tend to drop out or move away – initially it is a good idea to form with slightly more than the number you desire. Age, size or cultural background seem to make little difference to the outcome of the group. Of course the similarity or difference in these factors will get expressed in the flavour and feeling of any particular group.

It is important to have a set length to the group session, one that does not vary from week to week. About 2½ hours makes sense for an eight-person group, or 1½ hours for a five-person group. A prescribed time is important for a couple of reasons. First, as in any therapy group, it designates those particular hours during which the group will purposefully focus on the psychological issue at hand. The session time should not be vague because the issue of definition – beginning and end – is a particularly critical one for compulsive eaters in all respects. Second, if the time is clearly defined then each member is likely to attempt to get her needs met from the group in a systematic way. This will cut into the feelings of insatiability and dissatisfaction that many compulsive eaters experience. These sessions then take on the additional significance, since an allotted time out of the daily routine of things is devoted to them. They become the time in the week that is guaranteed for reflection and exploration.

It is likely that everyone will come to the group with the expectation and desire that participation will produce dramatic and instant weight loss. While it is hard to banish such thoughts, it must be emphasised that weight loss is not the immediate goal. The aim of the group is to break the addictive relationship towards food, and the guidelines that follow point to that end. In achieving this goal the group will find it helpful to approach the problem on two levels simultaneously. One level is the exploration of the symbolic meanings of fatness and thinness for the individuals in the group. On the second level we work on new ways to approach food and hunger. But before moving into the specifics of the first few meetings, an important aside on what I understand about psychological processes.

Any symptom such as compulsive eating has occurred for a good reason. We do not produce symptoms unless we have no other routes to express distress. It is not wise to attempt to remove symptoms without providing insight into their origin and purposes. In addition, unless alternative strategies are developed for dealing with the conflicts that the symptoms were protecting an individual could feel quite helpless. This could lead to a hazardous situation in which, in an extreme case, the individual develops a new symptom. If we just remove a symptom, like compulsive eating, we are then not only devaluing it, in effect, saying it was just a bit of craziness that needed surgical removal, we are also risking – precisely because of its importance – a 'symptom switch'. It is not particularly helpful to give up compulsive eating one week to be hit by a new symptom (such as insomnia or anxiety) some time later. What I am suggesting here is that anxiety may occur if a woman begins to do all sorts of things she imagined she would do when thin without having sorted out what it is that worries her in those situations. Without the weight to rely on she may feel undefended and scared. If she is no longer eating to assuage these feelings and cannot contain them, she may well convert them into anxiety. I am using anxiety here to express a severe state of unease and helplessness, in which an individual is seemingly incapable of intervening on her own behalf.

Anxiety is a reaction to a feeling that is unacceptable, frightening or overwhelming. The individual finds the anxiety, however troublesome, safer than the tolerance of the trigger emotion or event. For example, Sara was extremely frightened by her angry feelings, imagining that they could kill her. She worried that if she allowed herself to come into contact with her anger for more than a split second, her rage would overpower her family and friends and wipe them out. This fantasy is quite common among women and is largely due to the taboo against the open expression of female fury. Sara then got frightened by her own anger and instead of being able to sit with the fantasy she became anxious. The diagram below may help to explain this process.

When Sara could accept that exploring her fantasy did not mean that she would carry it out – just because she felt like attacking all and sundry it did not mean she would – she no longer became anxious. She sat with her anger, it came and went and she felt in charge of it.

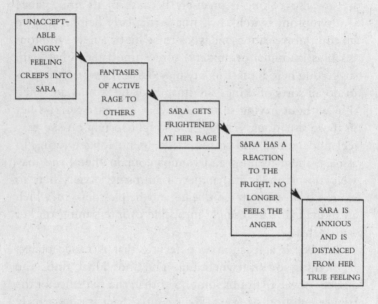

This digression about anxiety helps to explain how a rapid rejection of the compulsive eating can produce the same alienated symptom elsewhere unless sufficiently explored and incorporated. So I am concerned here to stress a few points:

1. Giving up the fat is a gradual process with emotional work being done at the same time.

2. The scary aspects of giving up the fat need to be faced.

3. Alternative ways of coping must be instituted.

4. Conflicts related to the eating and weight must be exposed.

These cautions are not, however, meant to suggest that it is necessary to restructure the whole personality before a symptom – such as compulsive eating – can be dissolved. It is our experience that, following the above lines, compulsive eating can be given up and that in learning to take care of oneself in the area of food an enormous self-confidence ensues.

When starting self-help groups we adopt the following structure for the initial meeting. The time is divided into two parts with the first half devoted to a preliminary exploration into the symbolic meanings of fat and thin for individual women. The second part is devoted to a discussion about food. Since you will presumably be doing this without a group leader it may be helpful for one group member to tape in advance the fantasy exercise that follows so that all members can participate during group time. If you do decide to tape it, leave good pauses where the dots are. The whole exercise should take around 15 minutes to read. Group members are asked to hold all the images in their heads during this time after which they will share their experiences with each other.

> *Get as comfortable as you can . . . Close your eyes . . .*
> *and imagine yourself at a party . . . You are getting fatter*
> *. . . you are now quite large . . . What does it feel like?*
> *. . . Take a note of your surroundings . . . How do you*
> *feel about them? . . . What kind of party is it? . . . What*
> *kinds of activities are going on? . . . Notice whether you*

121

are sitting or standing, or moving about . . . What are you wearing and how do you feel about your clothes? . . . What are they expressing? . . . Observe all the details in this situation . . . How are you interacting with the other people at the party? . . . Are you on your own or talking, dancing, eating with others? . . . Do you feel like an active participant or do you feel excluded? . . . Are you making the moves to have contact with others or are the other people at the party seeking you out? . . . Now see what this 'fat' you is saying to the people at the party . . . Does it have any specific messages? . . . Does it help you out in any way to be fat in this situation? . . . See if you can go beyond the feelings of revulsion you might have to locate any benefits you see from being this size at the party . . . Now imagine all the fat peeling and melting away and in the fantasy you are as thin as you might ever like to be . . . you are at the same party . . . What are you wearing now? . . . What do these clothes convey about you? . . . How do you feel in your body? . . . How are you getting on with the other people at the party? . . . Do you feel more or less included now? . . . Are people approaching you or are you making the first moves? . . . What is the quality of your contact with others? . . . See if you can locate anything scary about being thin at the party . . . see if you can get beyond how great it feels and notice any difficulties you might be having with being this thin . . . Now go back to being fat at the party . . . now thin again . . . Go back and forth between the two images and particularly notice the differences . . . When you are ready, open your eyes . . .

Now go around the room and share your fantasy. You will find that describing it in the present tense helps make the experience more vivid. For example, 'In my fantasy

I'm at a beach party. It's a very hot day and I'm wearing a terry-towelling robe over my swimsuit, trying not to draw attention to myself. I feel very awkward . . .' Do not worry if people's fantasies are both widely divergent and contradictory; the similarity of themes will emerge in due course. Be sure to use 'I', in order to give each person space to describe her experience in her own words. Generalising from individual experience can cause unnecessary friction if done prematurely. The exercise introduces in a concrete way the concepts outlined in the book. Inevitably, you will discover huge differences in your self-image fat and thin. You may find, for instance, that in the fat fantasy you are sitting chatting with another person while in your thin fantasy you are a sparkling wit and very much the centre of attention; or you may be on your own while fat and dancing with everybody when thin. In particular, the thin images may correspond to the popular conception of thinness discussed before, or your own experiences of being thin. In discussing your fantasies, bear in mind the kind of person you feel that you must/will become when thin. After you have sat with the image for a while see how it corresponds to your personality. Is the thin you a foreigner or, as some women comment, so decidedly different from your habitual self-image that you feel that you have two distinct personalities – fat and thin.

In our group, we raise the following questions both in the initial meeting and in subsequent meetings because they go to the very heart of the issue of how to find other means of protecting yourself which work as well as weight:

1. What of myself that emerged in my fat fantasy must I promise to take with me thin?

2. What did I find scary in my fat fantasy so I can promise myself I do not have to do it when I get thin?

In the fantasy, one group member, Maureen, was sitting with another person when fat, and had become a sparkling wit when thin. As she explored the qualities associated with these two different states she remarked on the safety and ease she felt chatting with her friend as compared to the driven and insecure quality associated with the sparkling wit. By recognising the negatives associated with thinness and the benefits of fatness, Maureen saw that, in order for her to lose weight permanently, she must allow herself the possibility that a thin her would not necessarily want to sparkle incessantly. She saw that her view of thinness, while superficially pleasurable and rewarding, was at great variance with her concept of her fat self, and that losing weight did not mean a complete personality change. Neither was the latter possible or desirable. Sparkling all the time for someone who enjoys relaxed conversation is unrealistic. *It is precisely this changed concept of self that puts the weight back on because it is enormously stressful trying to be someone entirely different when thin.* So Maureen had to promise herself that if she were to lose the weight she would not also have to lose the part of her that enjoyed relaxed chatting. She had to consider the possibility that her desire to chat, for example, was not an attribute of her fat but an aspect of her personality. Similarly, she had to consider that the part of her that wanted to be a sparkling wit did not have to wait to emerge until she was thin. Being overweight does not preclude one from being 'the star'. It does not mean one always has to be backstage waiting for thinness to bring you forth.

I have used Maureen's example for two reasons; not only

because of the frequency with which it comes up, but also to delineate the line of questioning to pursue. Obviously not everybody will find such a clear-cut discrepancy between a fat self-image and a thin self-image at an initial meeting. The fantasy exercise provides a way for the compulsive eater to enrich her view of what fat and thin mean to her. Then we can go on to ask what kinds of unreal expectations are attached to thinness, and what we imagine we shall be giving up in getting there. These questions are ones that need to be continually raised in the group and help to develop a self-image that does not vary with body size.

After everyone has shared their fantasies and, perhaps, seen common threads, we move on to consider the technical work of the group on ways to approach food and hunger. We do another fifteen-minute fantasy trip which aims to highlight current feelings towards food at the same time as suggesting new possibilities. Tape this or delegate one person to read it while the group gets as comfortable as possible:

Close your eyes . . . Now I should like you to imagine you are in your kitchen . . . Look around the room and make a note of all the food that is in it . . . in the refrigerator . . . closets . . . cookie tin . . . freezer . . . It probably is not too hard for you to form a complete picture because undoubtedly you know where everything is or is not, including any goodies or dietetic foods . . . Look around the room and see how it is affecting you . . . Is it painful to see how pathetic the foods are that you generally keep there or allow yourself to eat? . . . See what your kitchen says about you . . . Now go to your favourite supermarket or shopping mall or a place where there is a wide variety of stores under one roof – greengrocer, butcher, delicatessen, dairy, bakery, take-out food store – and I should like you to imagine that you have an unlimited amount of money to spend . . . Take a couple of supermarket carts and fill them up

*with all your favourite foods . . . Go up and down the aisles or
from counter to counter and carefully select the most appetising foods
. . . Be sure not to skimp . . . if you like cheesecake, take several,
take enough so you feel that there is no way you could possibly
eat it all in one sitting . . . be sure to get the specific ones you
really like . . . There is no hurry, you have plenty of time to get
whatever you want . . . Cast your eyes over the wonderful array of
foods and fill up your cart . . . Make sure you have everything you
need and then get into a cab with your boxes of food and go to
your home . . . There is nobody in the house and nobody will be
around for the rest of the day, the house — especially the kitchen —
is all yours for you to enjoy . . . Bring the food into the kitchen
and fill up the room with it . . . How do you feel surrounded by
all of this food just for you? . . . Does it feel sinful, or is it a very
joyful feeling? . . . Do you feel reassured or scared by the abundance of food just for you? . . . Just stay with the food and go
through the various moods that come up . . . remember nobody will
disturb you, the food is there just for you, enjoy it in whatever way
you want to . . . See if you can relax in the knowledge that you
will never again be deprived . . . And now I should like you to go
down the road to mail a letter . . . How do you feel about leaving
the house and all the food? . . . Does it give you a warm feeling
to know that when you go back it will still be there for you undisturbed? Or is it a relief to get away from it? . . . You have now
mailed the letter and are on your way back to the house
. . . Remember as you open the door that the food is all there just
for you and no one will interrupt you . . . How does it feel to be
back with the food? . . . If you found it reassuring before does it
continue to be so? If you found it scary can you find anything
comforting in being in the kitchen with all this food? . . . Slowly come
back to this room here with the knowledge that your kitchen is full
of beautiful foods to eat that nobody is going to take away from you
. . . and, when you are ready, open your eyes . . .*

Responses to this fantasy trip vary enormously but, as you will find, it rarely generates anything but dramatic reactions. These range from huge feelings of relief at having so much food available and the permission to enjoy it, to horror, fright and worries about one's ability actually to be in a room with all that food, from urges to throw it away or throw it around the room, to even lying in it. For many women, the trip to the mailbox provides much-needed relief from the claustrophobic feeling of being surrounded by 'tempting' foods; for others, it is a serene break from a kitchen that has been transformed into a beautiful nurturing environment. The fantasy pinpoints our deeply held worries about food and provides a good starting point for a discussion about just how much compulsive eaters deprive themselves of the enjoyment of food and just how much food has been converted into an enemy. In conveying a permissive idea towards food we are attempting to make inroads into the conception that because one is a compulsive eater or overweight, one must deprive oneself of food. The central idea to be conveyed is, in fact, precisely the opposite and it rests on a challenge to the premise that a compulsive eater never really allows herself to eat. She is always acting out of a model that says, 'I'm too fat, I must deny myself certain foods.' This sets up a paradigm in which she is either dieting or eating a lot of food in preparation for tomorrow's diet, when she must be 'good'. The diet is invariably broken by a binge hardly enjoyed because of its driven and stolen quality. Then follows a period of 'chaotic eating' and eventually a new diet plan as the chart below illustrates. None of this kind of eating contains within it a positive attitude towards food but rests on a frenetic struggle to control one's food intake.

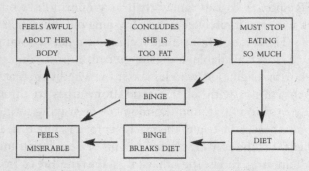

· This continual struggle to control one's food intake is a propelling factor in compulsive eating. The aim of our method is to redefine, for the compulsive eater, both the function of food and her entitlement to it. *People need food in order to live. Food is a life-giving source and not something to be avoided.* As long as there is plenty, food can be enjoyed. This idea, while hardly revolutionary, sounds staggering for someone who has been using food for other purposes. In due course I will discuss ways to implement this method but what is important in the first meeting is that group members share their daily experiences and fears about food.

This then, is the outline for the first meeting. Subsequent sessions will benefit from continuing work on the two levels – people's experiences with food that week and themes in relation to fat and thin although the time for doing this need not be structured so rigidly. The self-help groups that we have started take away a homework assignment for the first week – to keep a food chart. The purpose of this chart is to sort out some of the themes that continually reappear for you when you find yourself going towards food when you know you are not physically hungry.

TIME & DAY	WHAT I ATE	WAS I HUNGRY BEFORE EATING?	DID FOOD SATISFY ME OR NOT?	FEELINGS PRIOR TO EATING

Keep a record along these lines for the first week. The point of the chart is to *observe* how you eat and not to judge it. Through the entries on the chart you can begin to get a sense of what kind of eating patterns emerge for you. Do you experience yourself eating chaotically or with some consistency? Did any foods taste particularly satisfying? How does it feel to realise that your food intake is so circumscribed by 'shoulds'? Wasn't the chocolate cake and ice cream at three o'clock in the morning much tastier than the spinach and fish at regulation suppertime? Come on, wasn't it really a drag to eat that hamburger and salad in order to get to the ice-cream sundae you really wanted?

In addition to discovering what the chart reveals about actual food intake, it is also helpful to look at the circumstances in which you habitually eat. Do you eat alone? in hiding? never making dates to see people around traditional mealtimes? or do you eat with 'eating friends' in restaurants? or at home at a table? or at home walking around your house or apartment, half in the refrigerator? or in bed? or watching television? Observe when, how and what you eat, and when, how and what you enjoy the most. It may be that you will find that eating alone so absorbs you that it is nicest to sit yourself down at a beautifully set table, or you may find that you like a multi-media show with book open, music playing and the food in the middle.

Notice too the entries under 'Feelings prior to eating'. Is there any consistency in what triggers the eating when you are not particularly hungry? Can you pinpoint specific emotions which you find hard to cope with that drive you towards the refrigerator? In our groups many women mention boredom, anger, feelings of emptiness, disappointment, and loneliness as triggers. For others, the eating is like a punctuation point between various activities with the food marking the beginning and end of different phases of the day. Other women notice that they eat to give themselves a treat. The food provides – albeit fleetingly – an oasis of pleasure in an otherwise difficult day. As Isabel put it, 'If I didn't know I was going to have a few cream donuts during the day I couldn't see how I'd get access to pleasure.' In exploring this remark of hers, she dealt with several issues. Why was her life structured in such a way as to preclude other 'accesses to pleasure'? What does pleasure mean to her? Is she entitled to it? If she waits for others to give to her is she risking not getting? Must she therefore control it to ensure that she gets it? What other things would she enjoy as much? Does she always want cream donuts when she is hungry for pleasure or are there other pleasure-giving activities as well? These questions are raised in the service of examination. Isabel is not encouraged to give up her cream donuts. Quite the contrary, the aim of the group is to help her to enjoy her food more consistently so that every time she eats she is having a treat – it is a waste of an eating experience not to eat something really tasty. Isabel is encouraged by the group to think about her concept of pleasure and the immutability of her belief that no one but herself could possibly please her. This behaviour, while essential to her, was also a protection against her fear that others would inevitably disappoint her – let her down. Providing her own treats made her less vulnerable while she imagined that her fat kept the world away. This difficulty over pleasure is a familiar one for many women and speaks poignantly to the pain with receiving that they experience.

It is on this level that questions need to be raised. In the first few sessions, as you are getting to know each other, gentle inquiries will help elicit useful information both about group members' behaviour and the motivations behind it. Apart from discussing the food chart at the second meeting (and incidentally the chart can be used from time to time to help you check in with what you have been eating and how), you might start to go around the room and share your weight histories with each other. What is important here is not how many pounds you were at a particular point but the circumstances of your life through various weight changes. Notice any particular periods when your weight increased, using a family photo album to jog your memory if you find that helpful. Most likely, your group will include people with a range of stages in weight gain, including childhood, adolescence, leaving home, marriage, divorce, pregnancy or when the kids leave home. Leave yourself plenty of time to go through these histories, extending them over several sessions if necessary, so that you capture both the details and the quality of your own past relationship to your body and food. Make sure that you discuss your family's involvement with your food intake. Did/does anybody else in the family have an eating problem? What were the unspoken rules and regulations about food? What was the significance of mealtimes in your family? Were meals a harmonious time or very strained? Was there enough food in the house or were certain foods banned and only eaten away from home? Did your mother help you to diet or did she discourage your attempts? Did your husband egg you on to reduce or 'tempt' you with forbidden foods whenever you were actually dieting? Were there confusing messages from those close to you about how thin or fat you should be? Did you feel you had to be thin for someone else?

As the group continues and you become involved in trying to determine your own food intake, notice how the significant people in your life continue to play a role in relation to you and food. You may notice that your preoccupation with food has extended to hooking them into your eating behaviour so that they either actually are judges or you imagine them to be so. It will be very important for you to be the only one in charge of your eating from now on. This will mean:

1. Disentangling yourself from when and what others wish to eat.

2. Daring to believe that you can begin to take care of your own eating.

3. Getting rid of the person to whom you designated the role of judge.

If your lover has been roped into helping you not to eat 'bad foods' in the past and when you have sat down for supper together, his or her presence has stopped you gorging, reclaim that power for yourself but this time not in order to keep you away from the dangerous activity of eating but in the interest of helping you discriminate and select the foods you really enjoy.

Many people I have worked with have realised that their husbands have encouraged them to eat a lot while at the same time proclaiming their interest in slim, trim bodies. This was not dissimilar to their mothers' attitudes – an insistent 'Eat, eat, child', or 'A spoonful for Auntie Jane,' or 'Just one more bite for the poor starving kids in Africa!' These phrases were uttered with such pity and urgency that rejection was almost impossible even though the children were ready to gag. Rejection of the food felt like the rejection of mother. At other times, the same mothers beseeched their daughters to watch what they were eating lest their figures be ruined, or attempted to limit the food when they were larger than the 'acceptable' size.

Pull out as much information as possible about past eating patterns and how they relate to your present experiences with food. For those women who were *schtupped* (over-fed) by their mothers, consider what goes through your mind when you feel too full to have another mouthful but still cram in extra food. What would it mean to you to stop at the point of fullness? As you meander back and forth between your own past and present experiences with food, bear in mind that we are trying to challenge the idea that the compulsive eater is not entitled to food. Our view is that compulsive eaters are terrified of food (once having invested it with magical properties – for instance, comfort against loneliness, boredom, anger or depression – it is hard to see it as just food, a source of nourishment) and are constantly eating or avoiding eating in response to this terror. Just because you feel out of control when near food does not mean you are not entitled to eat.

Many women say that being in charge of their own food strikes them as particularly difficult because although they have been responsible for feeding others they feel that in the one area in which they could take responsibility for themselves they have abdicated it. They are worried that they will not dare or even know how to be that self-concerned. It is important to remember that while compulsive eating feels like an abdication it is, nevertheless, a definite act for which one has been responsible. The meanings behind the compulsive eating may be unclear so that you are left with feelings of being out of control or at the mercy of the food, but this is the conscious experience and at the unconscious level the activity has a purpose. If you can think of converting that responsibility for your food into a concerted effort to notice when you are hungry and what kinds of foods you are wanting, you will be able to approach many social situations which involve food with more confidence. Some common fears that come up in the groups involve practical issues, for instance, how to ensure your own food supply when living with others. In the group, it will be useful to explore the actual situation. Is it a family group, a commune, or roommates? Is food bought and eaten together, is suppertime the only time the household congregates? From this kind of information, alternatives will come. These may include keeping a shelf in the refrigerator of foods just for yourself and asking other household members to replace immediately any foods they take; withdrawing from the communal shop or allowing yourself a certain amount of money each week for food over the household budget so that you ensure you are getting what *you* want; explaining to household members that you have had a painful time around food and are trying to learn your body's real needs. Consequently, you may eat in a rather unorthodox way and would they please refrain from comments and cajoling. Another situation which frequently crops up is going to someone's house for supper. Group members often express alarm at this situation. We suggest several possible strategies: not to make social engagements at mealtimes for a while where you cannot choose what food is available; if it is a close friend the odds are that she or he has lived through several diets with you and been subjected to your instructions about permissible foods before. If this is the case you will benefit by telling your friend that your new interest in food may lead you to not eat everything on your plate and you hope they will understand. If you get hungry an hour or so before it is time to go, eat just a little to respond to it. That way the hunger will still be available to you an hour later. Above all, remember that you are entitled to eat, however awful you feel about yourself and your body. Just because you have used food for other than physiological reasons in the past, it does not mean you are to deprive yourself from here on.

As the group progresses you will want to incorporate the various exercises that are sewn through the body of this book.

1. Mirror work – in which you are trying to build a centre that includes the fat, pages 341–342.

2. Dressing for now – not waiting until you are thin to express yourself, pages 79–80.

3. Leaving food on your plate, pages 217–219.

4. Make your kitchen a supermarket, pages 353–355.

The above exercises will heighten your awareness of your body and help towards a self-acceptance. As I have stressed before, ownership of your whole body, including the fat, is a crucial factor in preparing you for a life at a lower weight. It will be very important for you to feel that your body has power at whatever size and that you can communicate through how you use it. An issue raised frequently throughout this book is how women imagine that their fat keeps people away. It is almost as though their fat is walking in front of them announcing their self-loathing to the world. We are aiming to build confidence to keep people away (if that is what is wanted) which rests on a self-acceptance rather than a self-disgust. The more you are your body, the more you can say 'no' with the whole of you. The fat then loses one of its functions as the ability to fend people off gets attributed to *you* and not solely to the fat. To help increase your acceptance and knowledge of your body you might begin to think of it as not simply a stomach or a mouth but an organic whole.

Try to experience the continuity in your body; feel it as one whole. You might try drawing unsigned pictures of yourselves within the group which can then be passed around for people to guess who is who. Since most group members will tend to represent themselves inaccurately, particularly in the early stages of the group, other members can provide help in correcting these perceptions by giving feedback about the poses, proportions and stances illustrated in the drawings. Polaroid photos can also be used to provide insight into how one projects oneself. As you become more and more familiar with your body you will be able to throw out your scales. The scales are yet another of those external measures of how well you are doing. Compulsive eaters are frequently hooked on scales. Every morning or night there is the ritual of evaluation; one finds out whether one has been 'good' or 'bad'. The pounds of wisdom have in the past given one the right either to binge or to starve. In general, for the compulsive eater, the scales are the real judge. If you have done well (lost weight) then the scales allow you to eat. If you have done badly (gained weight) the scales throw you into a depression only relieved by a binge or a plan to lose the weight yet again. So, instead of this twice-daily torture with its concomitant anxieties, we try to develop a familiarity with our bodies so that the feelings can come from the inside rather than the outside. The scales have become another outside evaluator which women can afford to do without.

The mirror exercise can help us move towards self-validation (a hard struggle indeed against the messages in women's magazines about how we should look, feel and weigh) and begin to rely on our own senses of self. For particular parts of your body that give you trouble try doing the fat/thin fantasy exercise focused on that specific area. For example, if you feel tremendous hatred towards your thighs, imagine yourself with fat thighs and then with ideal thighs and examine the meanings of the two different body states. One woman I worked with who longed for thinner thighs discovered in her fantasy that the fat around her thighs was like a house around her vagina. The concave thighs she yearned for actually made her feel vulnerable as though there was no protection against her sexuality. Through the fantasy work she was able to accept the 'hated thigh fat' and see it as one way she had coped with her sexuality. As she lost weight she began to find other ways to express her interest or lack of interest in sexual contact. For other women, full breasts or stomachs have symbolised one thing in conscious life but quite other meanings have been revealed by doing the fantasy exercises. The insights gained have empowered the women to review the limited ways in which they have communicated with their bodies. In the groups, or alone in front of a mirror, you can experiment with projecting different aspects of your personality through your stance. Try a variety of sexual expressions – project yourself as forceful, timid, retiring or active.

In preparing yourself for being thin without the thin meaning 'I must be wonderful, competent, beautiful, clever', spend a few minutes during every day on mundane tasks, imagining yourself thin while doing them. This could be the ride to work, social contact at work or home, going shopping or waking up feeling thin. Particularly watch for anything difficult about being thin in those daily routines. If you find things scary try and investigate just exactly what it is that is frightening and then discuss these experiences within the group. Then try feeling thin without associated elations and fears. Notice how you would walk, stand or sit when thin and try to incorporate those different poses into your body as you are now. If it is too long a jump, imagine yourself 10lb [4.5kg] lighter rather than dramatically thinner. This image may be more accessible and you may find less discrepancies in feeling the 10lb [4.5kg] difference. As this emerges it will mean that you are ready to lose some weight. Most likely, your body will indicate this by requiring less food. At these points, in particular, you will want to tighten up the process – being sure to eat exactly what you want and stopping precisely when you are full. Many compulsive eaters are unfamiliar with a full feeling that is not a bursting feeling. As an introduction to that bodily experience, eat several mouthfuls of whatever food you are wanting when you are hungry, being sure to taste them as they go down. Now leave the food for 15 minutes and involve yourself with some other activity. After a quarter of an hour see how your body feels. If it feels hungry and empty, continue to eat whatever food you think will fit that hunger. If it feels comfortable it means you are quite full and you can wait until the next hunger signals to eat again. If you are sure that you will allow yourself to eat whenever you feel hungry, and that you will give yourself whatever kind of food it is that you are wanting, you will find that it is less necessary to stuff yourself. When your body then indicates that it is not wanting much food, it means it is time for you to lose a little weight.

People vary enormously but it has been my observation that in the early stages of the group, members tend to stabilise or gain slightly. For those who do gain weight, this should not be a signal for alarm but an opportunity to experience what the fat is all about. It is a chance to embrace all the fat before a final goodbye. As you lose weight you will notice you may be inclined to lose a bit and then sit there for a while. It is as though your body is holding still while you do the next level of emotional work exploring fantasies such as 'Who will I be?' 'Who won't like it if I'm slimmer?' 'How will I protect myself if I am 10lb lighter?'

In the previous chapters I have suggested that fat has a lot to do with conflict about self-definition and assertion and that a worry associated with being thin is that one will be meek and mild and could be blown over. Body work as described above will, of course, help one live within one's body and thus use it more instrumentally in day-to-day living but additional homework exercises which strike at a woman's often-felt unentitlement will also prove helpful. These exercises are loosely grouped under an assertion heading and flow from attempts to define one's food intake.

Attempt to say 'yes' to something you want every single day. This could be something that only involves you, for example, taking a bubble bath, reading a book, going for a walk or writing a letter. As you learn to say 'yes' you will be fulfilling many things. Primary among these is saying that you are entitled to decide things for yourself. This in turn produces a certain amount of self-confidence and provides a chink in a self-image full of denial. As you are able to say 'yes' to a bath, so you will be able to say 'yes' to a snack when you want it. As you learn to say 'yes' you have the possibility of saying 'no'. Think of an incident in which you said 'yes' but really wanted to say 'no'. Replay that incident slowly in your mind's eye, only substituting 'no' and expressing the real feeling. Notice how that feels. What are you risking by saying 'no'? Now be conscious of the many times you are in this situation. Begin to say 'no' to things – even on what may seem like a minuscule level – as you begin to say 'yes' to others. Develop the sense of feeling more in charge. This will flow over to the food – being able to say 'yes' and to say 'no' and, perhaps more centrally, will provide you with a new way to use your mouth in expressing yourself.

The fat/thin fantasy on page 129 can be useful for discovering what different body sizes mean to individual group members in different circumstances. Topics you might find helpful to discuss are: What being fat and thin express for you living in this culture; what fat and thin have to do with sexuality, with anger, with competition, with your mother, with your father, or with your children. Add a specific person or situation to the one in the standard fantasy and draw out the issues as they occur for each person. For example, *'Get as comfortable as you can . . . imagine you are with your mother/father/husband . . . you are quite fat . . .'*

Now it may happen that in some groups only certain people talk or you may discover that the 'fat' is working in the group in some of the same ways in which it operates outside the group. If a particular member has experienced a week of bingeing, then she might feel she has more of a right to group time: 'If I am fatter, then I'm worse off than everyone else and I've a right to a lot of attention', or if a group member was consistently losing weight she might feel she does not have the right to group time: 'If I am thin, then I'm supposed to be perfect and not have any needs.' The woman losing weight might start to overeat in order to ensure her place in the group. If this situation crops up where those who have most difficulty that week get most time and those who have a relatively easy time with food are quiet, you might consider instituting a '12 minute rule', which means that each member is assured of 12 minutes of work time to discuss whatever she wishes in relation to food, fat or thin. This way you will be reinforcing neither fantasy – that thin, one has no needs and fat, one is insatiable.

In a self-help group, some people will play a more active role than others. However, it is the group as a whole that has responsibility for working together, selecting exercises, meeting places and times. You may find it helpful to rotate on a weekly basis so that a different person is in charge each time, preparing the exercises, keeping time and starting off the meetings. This is not essential, however, and every group develops its own patterns.

Self-help is an exciting concept in action. The potential to learn what is truly useful to you is enormous and, unhampered by preconceptions of what must or should happen, it opens the way for creative experimentation, evaluation and growth.

The guidelines above are to help you get going on the lines that our experience has shown to be useful, but they are in no sense intended to stifle the energy and imagination that you or your group feels to explore aspects of compulsive eating and self-image that are not addressed in detail here.

CHAPTER FIVE

Self-Starvation — Anorexia Nervosa

There is an elaborate and complicated eating condition closely related to compulsive eating called anorexia nervosa. It too, is characterised by self-imposed restrictions on food intake, a fear and terror of food and an obsessive — although secretive — interest in food. Unlike compulsive eaters, however, those who suffer from anorexia nervosa express their preoccupation with food by becoming very thin indeed — to the point of emaciation and sometimes even to the point of death through starvation. This extreme form of self-starvation is distinguished by a struggle to transcend hunger signals.

It often takes off from an exaggerated application of a diet, started because the potential anorectic feels fat. Like the compulsive eater, many anorectics engage in large-scale eating binges. The shame and self-disgust that follow propel an anorectic to fast, vomit or take laxatives — to purge her body of the food that has been taken in. When food is eaten again, feelings of bloatedness occur very quickly so food intake continues to be very minimal until another explosion of seemingly uncontrolled gorging occurs. Weight loss can be very dramatic and, in turn, creates a wide range of physical symptoms. Anorectics do not menstruate, often suffer from insomnia and constipation, hypersensitivity to hot and cold, excess hair growth on the body, changes in the colour and texture of existing hair, nails and skin, slow pulse rate and perspiration. These physical discomforts are endured in an attempt to reach the overriding aim – to become thin.

While the idea of an interest in becoming fat is difficult to grasp, few people would have difficulty in understanding this interest in becoming thin because it conforms to social expectations for women. It is also quite easy to understand that 90% of clinically diagnosed anorectics are women and that one of the workers in the field[1] argues that the definition of anorexia nervosa should be reserved for a special clinical syndrome occurring in pre-pubescent and pubescent girls.

It is the fact that anorexia nervosa is almost exclusively a woman's condition that ties it so closely to compulsive eating and obesity. For if men were to suffer from the same problem to a similar degree we should seek a different explanation. But the fear of obesity, the obsession with food, the hidden and furtive eating and the interest in feeding others, leads us to identify the behaviour as having origins in the social conditions of women in our society. *Anorexia nervosa is the other side of the coin of compulsive eating. In her rigorous avoidance of food, the anorectic is responding to the same oppressive conditions as compulsive eaters.*

It is important to note that while I have had little direct experience with anorectics, many women who suffer with this problem have sought me out because in reading of the Munter-Orbach view of compulsive eating they have found much with which to identify. Thus, what I have to say will be based on my reading of the works[2] on anorexia nervosa and discussions with women who have had anorexia, rather than on long-term clinical experience. My interest in touching on anorexia in this book is insofar as it sheds light on compulsive eating which is at the other end of the continuum. A feminist interpretation of anorexia confirms the approach used in compulsive eating.

Both anorectics and compulsive eaters binge and starve themselves. However, the anorectic starves for long periods subsisting on as little as an egg and a cookie a day and only occasionally bursting out into a binge which is then purified by even more rigorous fasting or cleansing by laxatives, vomiting or enemas. This bird-like eating is a reflection of a culture that praises thinness and fragility in women. Many women pinpoint the onset of their anorexia as an exaggerated response to dieting and teenage ideals of femininity. As with compulsive eaters, sensing something amiss at adolescence, they sought the answer in their individual biology. Their bodies were changing, becoming curvy and fuller, taking on the shape of a woman. They were changing in a way over which they had no control – they did not know whether they would be small breasted and large hipped or whether their bodies would eventually end up as the teenagers in teen magazines.

These upheavals rendered in these young women feelings of confusion, fear and powerlessness. Their changing bodies were associated with a changing position in their worlds at home, at school and with their friends. A curvy body meant the adoption of a teenage girl's sexual identity. This is the time for intense interest in appearance, the time when girls learn the tortuous lesson about not revealing their true selves to boys whether on the tennis court or in school, or in discussing affairs of the heart. These new rules and regulations governing behaviour, and

145

the explosive changes taking place are quite out of tune with what has previously been learned and the feelings they generate are enormously complicated. Several women have said on looking back on this time in their lives – a time when they were growing and yet effectively stopped eating – that they felt so out of phase with all that was going on that withdrawal from food was an immensely satisfying way to be in control of the situation. In transcending hunger pangs they were winning in one area of the struggle with their apparently independently developing bodies. They were attempting to gain control over their shapes and their physical needs. They felt their power in their ability to ignore their hunger.

But this power to overcome hunger results in a contradiction because in her very attempt to be strong, the anorectic becomes so weak that she becomes less independent, more dependent. She needs more care and concern from others because of her weakened physical state. This adaptation poses yet another dilemma. As Rosie Parker and Sarah Mauger write, 'For a great many women manipulation of their own bodies is too often their only means of gaining a sense of accomplishment. The link between social status and slimness is both real and imagined. It is real because fat people are discriminated against; it is imaginary because the thin, delicate ideal image of femininity only increases a person's sense of ineffectualness.'[3]

This latter point is, perhaps, the crux of the matter. Anorexia reflects an ambivalence about femininity, a rebellion against feminisation that in its particular form expresses both a rejection and an exaggeration of the image. The refusal of food which makes her extremely thin straightens out the girl's curves in a denial of her essential femaleness. At the same time, this thinness parodies feminine petiteness. It is as though the anorectic has a foot in both camps — the pre-adolescent boy-girl and the young attractive woman. This has its echoes too in compulsive eating. For some women who eat compulsively the excess weight is also an attempt to defeat the curviness of the female body which brings in its wake dreaded social consequences. Mary, who had a compulsive eating problem, started to overeat when she became a teenager and explained with hindsight that she was trying to smooth out her curves. The 'puppy fat' she acquired put her less in the girls' camp with the concomitant dating and beautifying rituals. She was able to see herself as one of the kids — rather than one of the potential dating partners. Pre-adolescence suggested a kind of equality to her, where kids were just kids and could do more or less the same things. Her fat was an unconscious attempt to hide her curves just as the starving anorectic attempts to disguise her form by ridding it of substance. In the ultra-feminine image of the petite woman that anorectics frequently project there is yet another parallel in the compulsive eater.

Some women's largeness conforms to another stereotype of woman, in this case the all-giving, nurturing, reliable, loving, caring, earth mother who excels in feminine skills of caretaking, food preparation and sensual hugs. This aspect of fat is for some women a relatively positive image to hold on to because it is at least an accepted image and smacks less of freakiness, but it is an image that in itself is problematic because it is the extension of the woman's reproductive capacity into the role of being mother to the world. Mothers of the world are forever feeding others and consequently get exceedingly hungry. Petite young ladies are admired and showered on — so goes the myth – and they do not need to take as much in, perhaps because they do not have to give so much out. Their success in womanhood lies in their being cared for and pampered by others and not in caring for and pampering others.

This attempt to balance both fronts, the ultrafemininity and rejection of femininity, is related to another aspect of the syndrome that has been given wide attention. This is the anorectic's intense energy and activity. This activity expresses itself in a compulsion to do well in school, excel at sports, and keep on the go at all costs. Many people will be familiar with the feeling of a second wind in the midst of an exhausting late night and the kind of tense energy this unleashes. It is a similar feeling to the hyperactivity that anorectics frequently feel for months and months on end. This rushing about is partly motivated by an over-powering desire to lose yet more weight by burning up as many calories as possible. A feminist viewpoint suggests an additional root cause. The young woman's attempt to be involved in as many activities as possible is a protection against the exclusion she anticipates on entering woman-hood because, in projecting into her future, she sees that the world is made up of men who are rewarded for being out in the world and women who are either excluded from activity in the world or, even more devious, included but not rewarded. In her frantic activities and involvements it would appear that she is trying to give herself a broader definition than her social role allows. She is striving to make an impact in a world hostile to her sex. This intense activity is painfully mirrored in the response of some anorectics whose fragile sense of self leads them to withdraw from the public world into their rooms, thereby highlighting women's invisibility. For the compulsive eater the reflection is reversed. The outwardly super-efficient, confident fixer and doer who can handle anything and carries the world on her shoulders is the exaggeration of woman as breast to the world. At the same time it underscores a woman's invisibility. The immovable blob — a common fantasy that compulsive eaters talk of — is analogous to the anorectic's intense activity and her experience of her self as ineffectual.

These converging images speak forcefully to a reconsideration of the origins of anorexia and as we have already seen, compulsive eating. Previous writers have emphasised some of the social factors. Mara Selvini Palazzoli[4] suggests that the change from an agrarian to an industrial society in Europe has had a profound effect on the stability of the patriarchal family and that the anorectic young woman is a challenge to its continuing conservatism. Hilde Bruch[5] addresses current social attitudes towards body size and considers the extent to which 'the concept of beauty in our society, and our preoccupation with appearance enter into the picture. The obsession of the Western world with slimness, the condemnation of any degree of overweight as undesirable and ugly, may well be considered a distorting of the body concept, but it dominates present day living.' Other social factors such as Peter Dally's[6] observation that the mothers of many anorectics were frustrated and hence ambitious for their daughters are described but their connection to the social situation of women in society is not explored.

The pinpointing of these factors is extremely helpful. However, there are still questions to be answered. That is, why does this happen? Why is it that some mothers are domineering? Why is Western society preoccupied with slimness? Why does the patriarchal family attempt to resist ange? What are the basic assumptions about our society that women with eating disorders are challenging? What in their abuse of the hunger mechanism and their body distortions are these women gagging to articulate how they feel? If this is a psychological state that affects women, what is an appropriate social response? Must not treatment include a recognition of the social factors that lead women to compulsive eating and anorexia nervosa?

As we have seen, modern Western societies place definite expectations and prohibitions on women's activities. Women are expected to be petite, demure, giving, passive, receptive in the home and, above all, attractive. Women are discouraged from being active, assertive, competitive, large and, above all, unattractive. To be unattractive is not to be a woman. In the case of compulsive eating, some women's strategy for dealing with these straitjacketed stereotypes is to become large to have bulk in the world; to become large to compensate for always giving out; to become large to avoid packaged sexuality. For the compulsive eater, food carries enormous symbolic meanings that reflect the problems women face in dealing with an oppressive social role. Even though anorectics have adopted the opposite strategy, self-starvation, the similarities to compulsive eating do not leave much doubt that the social position of women is as much reflected in the anorectic's behaviour as it is in that of the compulsive eater.

Anorectics share with compulsive eaters a conscious desire not to be noticed. They often feel nervous walking into a room at a party lest all the attention is focused on them. Instead of gaining weight to hide a real self underneath the layers, the anorectic literally becomes paper thin. But this paper thinness attracts more attention than does a 'normal'-sized woman. The crucial difference is that for emaciated (and overweight) women the interest they do attract is of a different nature than that which meets the woman of more 'normal' size. The quick 'once over' evaluation done by both men and women establishes the anorectic (and the obese woman) as outside the status of a sex object. Broadly, this means that men will dismiss her and other women will relax in her presence. The anorectic will be viewed as pathetic or regarded with sympathy, but in her seemingly narcissistic striving for ultra-femininity she curiously succeeds in desexualising herself. In addition, two related ways to understand this worry about being noticed suggest themselves. The first is reflected in the repeated theme of women's invisibility — wafer thinness is perhaps the quintessential expression of women's absence/presence. This forced invisibility leads in turn to a desire to be accepted and noticed for just being, rather than for having to look and be perfect and fulfil others' expectations. This desire, strongly felt and rarely satisfied, has little option but to be repressed, to be converted into its very opposite — a fear of being noticed which in its particular form makes the anorectic stand out.

This wish for acceptance stems, for many women, from a feeling of unwantedness and hence unworthiness. This may be either explicit: 'We really wanted a boy', or from a sensed disappointment the mother has in bringing a daughter into the world. Whether explicit or implicit, the fact is that many compulsive eaters and anorectics report feeling their mothers expressed enormous ambivalence about their very existence. To say we were hoping for a boy is to say to a daughter that she has let you down. It is a short step from feeling that one has fallen short of one's family's hope to feeling like a failure. In its turn, failure can bring feelings of non-entitlement. At

151

puberty where it becomes obvious that a girl is a girl, the feelings between mother and daughter may become so acute that two actions collide for the girl. She refuses food in an attempt to wither away, to not exist, to please her mother by disappearing. At the same time, the rage the daughter feels at not having been wanted for who she is, for not having had a mother with whom to identify – how can one identify with a mother who is self-rejecting without also adopting a rejecting self-image? – is expressed by a refusal to take in the one thing the mother consistently gives – food. In a mixture of rage and demureness, the adolescent girl gags on the first mouthful or is full after a few bites. She is rejecting what her mother gives and hurting her in the most powerful way she knows how while simultaneously carrying out what she imagines to be her mother's wish, which is for her to disappear.

The pressure that leads many parents to desire male babies is itself a consequence of living in a world that accords less social power to women. A tragic repercussion of women's inferior social position is that in the transmitting of culture from one generation to the next, the mother has the dreadful job of preparing her own daughter to accept a life built on second-class citizenship. It is in the learning of our gender identity – that is, what it means to be a girl and then a woman in this world – that we find our place in society. What defines this gender identity will vary widely in relation to class and cultural proscriptions so that what it means to be a woman factory worker in Bulgaria will be quite different than what it means to be a nurse in the United States but both these women will have become adults through conception of self, based on available models of feminine behaviour, assimilated first from their mothers. It is in the teaching of this gender identity that the tensions in the mother-daughter relationship explode and the confusing messages of female adulthood are incorporated by the young girl.

One aspect of this tension that seems especially pertinent to anorectics is the concern with having disappointed one's mother for having been a girl in the first place. The girl feels she is a shaky second best with a precarious right to survive. This worry about the right to exist is also linked to the academic excellence and performance aspects of anorexia. Many women have reported that their need to excel academically was a response to feeling that if they should fail they would disappoint their parents. If they did not disappoint their parents they might be accepted – as one woman who suffered from anorexia put it bitterly, 'I had to perform. I wasn't just accepted for who I was whereas my brother who was a delinquent was!' In this woman's life there was nothing explicitly stated about her not being desired or wanted, it was rather a feeling she picked up in relation to how she felt her brother was treated. That they were treated differently just because of their ages did not explain to her the feelings she had about herself and her mother's attitudes towards her. The only way she could understand this vast difference in treatment and her terribly painful feelings of being unaccepted was to see it as part of her parents' disappointment with her sex.

In the last 30 years, one of the most striking differences between the upbringing of girls and boys surfaced around adolescence when girls were supposed to be pure and boys were supposed to acquire sexual experience. Sex was definitely bad for girls and good for boys. To girls it seemed as though boys could only win at this game: they either succeeded and became experienced or were reassured that there was plenty of time. Indeed, there was even a special category of women who provided boys with this experience. For the girls there was no way to win. If you did 'it' you were bad, dirty, impure. Thinking about 'it' was not much better either. If you did not do 'it' boys would call you names, but if you did, you would get a bad reputation. You were preparing yourself for marriage many years hence and sexual activity up to that time was to be kept within definite limits. Against this background it is hardly surprising that young women are terribly confused about their sexuality, seeing it as evil, dangerous and explosive on the one hand and powerful, glorious and desirable on the other. Their sexuality becomes curiously disembodied from the person. It is an aspect of a young woman that in any event she must watch out for, almost as though it is some independent entity she must keep under control. This alienating view of sexuality from which women are now struggling to break free sheds much light on both the anorectic's and the compulsive eater's ambivalence about sexuality. The distortion of one basic body function gets carried over to another basic one, hunger. In the distortion of body size that follows, the manipulation of hunger feelings, the anorectic and the compulsive eater powerfully indict sexist culture. The young woman takes herself out of the only available sexual arena and worries that should she express her sexual feelings her whole world will crack.

In the retreat from a sexual identity the anorectic young woman is pointing to the difficulties of the various aspects of womanhood. Sexual identity is an aspect of gender identity so that in rejecting models of sexuality one is simultaneously rejecting models of femininity. This is the dilemma that faces many women and is expressed both through the symbolic meanings of being thin and food refusal for the anorectic.

For the anorectic then, the refusal of food is a way to say 'no', a way to reject. It is her way to show strength. Her thinness, on the other hand, also expresses her fragility and frailty, her confusion about sexuality and her interest in disappearing. For the compulsive eater the picture would seem to be reversed with the fat expressing rejection, protection and strength and the incessant consumption of food symbolising capitulation. In both these responses we see the adaptations to a female role which has quite limited parameters. Both syndromes express the tension about acceptance and rejection of the constraints of femininity.

What is interesting in comparing these two responses is to notice just where they converge and where they differ. One area of striking difference rests on the attitudes of those who suffer at either end of the continuum. For the anorectic, her problem is not a matter for public discussion. It is a very private issue which she does not acknowledge as a problem because she herself sees her refusal to eat as an attempt to control her situation, a control that feels precarious and that might be at risk if she were to discuss it. This is quite different from the experience of compulsive eaters who do not regard their overeating as an active state but rather something that happens only when they are out of control. They are quite happy to discuss this exterior, invading force and often initiate conversation about their 'problem'. This can partly be explained by the fact that the social pressure to be thin is so great that compulsive eaters feel they must offer an excuse for their size. The anorectic, however fat she sees herself, is, in fact, conforming to society's demand for women to be thin.

Paradoxically, the general public takes anorexia nervosa

quite seriously while viewing compulsive eating as the behaviour of an overindulgent, greedy person. As we have seen, however, both activities are extremely painful responses to which women may turn in their attempts to have some impact in their worlds.

CHAPTER SIX

Medical Issues

It is the thesis of this book that compulsive eating in women is a response to their social position. As such, it will continue to be an issue in women's lives as long as social conditions exist which create and encourage inequality of the sexes. Any treatment for overweight women must address this fact.

When a woman goes to see a general practitioner with a weight problem, the doctor will almost invariably tell her to go on a diet. In the doctor's eyes, it is clear that this patient eats too much and to lose weight she must eat less. This attitude is exactly the same as that implicit in all the diets thrown onto the market every day. The doctor has neither the time nor the interest to examine why this woman got fat in the first place. No dietary advice can help a woman lose weight permanently for the real reasons are not recognised and tackled.

Medical training today is becoming increasingly technical – high grades in scientific subjects have become essential to qualify for medical school and once there, the emphasis is on the technical approach to medicine. The human element of medicine is often lacking. This means that doctors are trained to make use of complex instruments and keep abreast of basic research. They do not acquire the sensitivity to recognise what is often troubling their patients. Therefore, many women are met with an unsympathetic face when they visit the doctor to lose weight. Doctors are no less susceptible than other people to cultural ideas about beauty and thinness and frequently feel entitled to comment on the size of their patient's body even when their medical problems are not related to it. As one woman put it, 'They always make me feel guilty, like a naughty girl for eating too much.' Clutching new diet sheets they are sent straight back to their homes and jobs and the problems they face there – the problems that were the main causes of their fatness in the first place.

But women come to know that diets and guilt do not work, whether they come from doctors or magazines. Some women may become desperate to find a physiological reason for their persisting fat. They may go further, to a specialist who deals with obesity and in whose interest it is to propose that there are biological factors which cause it. When a woman goes to a specialist she is seeking some further understanding; she may think, 'If there is a medical reason for my fat, then there is little I can do. I shall be fat but people should recognise that it is not my fault.'

In recent years there has been considerable medical research into the causes of obesity. While few of these theories have been wholly absorbed into the practice of the medical establishment, the publicity they have received and the hope that they instil in overweight people leads me to discuss the most favoured ones here.

Doctors and researchers with a mechanistic view of the human body picture it as an assembly of organs (liver, heart, brain), tissue (muscle, nervous tissue, bone), and cells (nerve cells, muscle cells and blood cells). Organs are composed of various kinds of cells, and the cells themselves are pictured as little biochemical factories that work to maintain the organism in good health. This perspective has allowed the development of a picture of obesity as a biological phenomenon. In the body there is tissue between organs like various muscle groups or bone and muscle, which is called connective tissue. This connective tissue has the capacity to accumulate fat that the body does not use. It is called adipose tissue and consists of cells which are called fat cells. It is in the pattern of accumulation of fat in the fat cells that has drawn the attention of many medical investigators.

THE FAT CELL THEORY Ten years ago Hirsch and Knittle[1] developed a method of counting the number and size of fat cells in a sample of adipose tissue. They suggested that obesity in childhood was accompanied by an increase in the number of fat cells in the body which are not reduced by dieting later in life. The cells themselves will reduce in size when a person loses weight but it is as though they are sitting waiting to be refilled. An extremely obese person can have as many as five times the normal number of fat cells. This theory is offered as an explanation for why some overweight people have difficulty keeping their weight down after dieting.

BIOCHEMICAL THEORIES The functioning of cells depends on the nature of chemical reactions which occur in them. All chemical reactions in the body – the conversion of food into energy, the expenditure of energy in exercise, indeed all human activity – depend on the presence of enzymes. Enzymes are protein molecules which assist the chemical reaction without being used up. Every chemical reaction in the body has an enzyme associated with it. Studies on bacteria have shown that the enzymes are made with the help of information stored in the genes. It is natural, therefore, from this perspective, to see a genetic explanation for obesity. Obese individuals are pictured as having slightly different genes from non-obese people. The different genes then result in slightly different enzymes. These enzymes are the ones that are involved in the chemical reactions related to the storage of fat in the body. The obese person is pictured as having different enzymes and hence their bodies respond to fat in a different way from the bodies of non-obese people.

GENETIC THEORIES   Related to biochemical approaches is the genetic approach. The general genetic approach does not specify necessarily where the genetic variation occurs but simply hypothesises that it exists, whether in the enzymes, the nervous system, or the hormonal system of the body. This approach leads to studies showing that 'obesity runs in families'.[2]

One genetic theory[3] suggests that fat people do not necessarily eat more than thin people. The argument runs that in subsistence agricultural societies, the pattern of eating is feast and fast and that those with the ability to store excess energy efficiently and release it for physical labour have a better chance of survival. In affluent societies where there is a regular and adequate food supply there is not the same need for the body to store and release energy. Furthermore, since we tend to be more sedentary we burn off less excess energy. Computer simulation runs of the pattern of lean and fat deposition in adults are offered as evidence for a biologically determinist view that whereas until recently it was functional to have an inherent tendency towards fatness, nowadays it is functional to have a predisposition to thinness.

INSULIN-RELATED THEORY When sugar and protein are eaten the islets of Langerhans, which are cell clusters in the pancreas, produce the hormone insulin. Insulin is a vital protein that is necessary for cells to take in and utilise sugar as an energy source. If there is an excess of glucose in the bloodstream it is converted into stored energy or fat. If a body does not produce enough insulin, the sugar and carbohydrates accumulate in the blood and do not provide energy to maintain bodily processes and growth. This is diabetes. Two thirds of diabetics are obese and this has led researchers to question whether there is a link between the two conditions. The theory of hyperinsulinism conjectures that the body produces too much insulin which may itself induce insensitivity to the hormone.[4] It is this latter view that has been popularised by Dr Atkins.[5] He calls insulin 'the fattening hormone' and suggests that excess presence stimulates a person to eat more to maintain the balance. He sees insulin as the crucial link between overweight, low blood sugar and diabetes.

NEURAL THEORY Simple neural theory looks at the body's system of regulation. A region of the brain, the hypothalamus, has been conjectured to be the location where the body's messages about hunger are processed. A satiation centre in the hypothalamus provides information on fullness. If there are lesions in this neural area, it is hypothesised, eating will continue beyond the normal stopping point. A study on rats with ventromedial hypothalamus lesions which raise the set point, delay the onset of satiation and cause obesity, reported various motivational deficits including rats' failure to hoard. This failure to hoard has led the researchers to see a parallel in human motivation and they suggest that obesity causes poverty.[6]

Other researchers see the hypothalamus as less central to the regulation of hunger. The basic principle, however, remains the same. A defect in the body's regulation of hunger is hypothesised as being the cause of overeating.

The shortcoming of some of these theories is that they do not offer a way to determine whether observed differences in human reactions between obese and non-obese persons cause the obesity or are due to the obesity. The fat cell theory has a limited use since a high proportion of fat cells in infancy occurs only with massive obesity. Treatment of adults who were obese as children does not prevent weight loss and stabilisation.[7] General genetic theories suffer because observed family similarity fits equally with an environmental model.[8] The evolutionary functional theory is weakened by the authors' underestimation of the allowable rates of genetic change in time.[9] The hypothalamus lesion theory first describes rat behaviour in human terms and in doing so falls into the trap of assuming that the observations of animal behaviour are analogous to those of human behaviour.[10]

What is most critical, however, are the treatment procedures which follow from these hypotheses. They offer the promise, through the understanding of human physiology of the development of a substance (a drug, for example), which can melt away excess fat cells, restore the satiation mechanism in the hypothalamus or permit the person's body to utilise more efficiently its fat and sugar intake. This attitude is to be seen in the treatment of diabetes. The body's inability to produce enough insulin is corrected by daily insulin injections. A similar treatment for compulsive eating or its usual effect – obesity – satisfies an often-expressed wish that the fat can be whisked away by a pill and we will be as thin as we like. The history of conflicting medical research into obesity for the last 103 years makes it unlikely that such a substance exists. Treatment that is often sought and used has commonly been focused on three major areas: drug therapy, surgical procedures, and diet therapy.

DRUG THERAPY   One approach to deal with obesity has been to prescribe thyroxine, a hormone that is secreted by the thyroid gland. Thyroxine is supposed to 'speed up metabolism' and in so doing causes the body to burn up food more rapidly. The long-term effects of this treatment are doubtful for it relies on very high dosages of the hormone. As such, it is potentially dangerous in that it can interfere with the body's normal thyroid functioning which is very delicate. Two other drugs are employed in the treatment of obesity. They are called anorectic agents. One class are appetite suppressants and known popularly as amphetamines or speed. The addictive and stimulative aspect of this drug has been well documented as has the patient's need for increased dosages to maintain a suppressed appetite. The other class are drugs such as Flen-fluramine which aim to produce feelings of fullness and inhibit the synthesis of triglycerides.

SURGICAL PROCEDURES   More frightening are treatment procedures which attempt to bypass the problem by surgery. A jejuno-ileal bypass is an operation in which part of the small intestine is inactivated so that food cannot be absorbed to the same extent. Normally performed in serious inflammatory diseases and cancer of the bowel, the bypass surgery has been performed for extreme obesity for the last 48 years. Its side effects have been extensively studied. Among the problems reported is psychological adjustment. In one follow-up study[11] 32 out of 40 people experienced distinct crises associated with weight loss. These include, not surprisingly, problems about self-assertion, loss of identity and loss of boundaries. Another researcher reports[12] persistent overestimation of body size by female subjects two years after their operations after an average weight loss of 100–112lb [45–50kg].

An even more direct mechanical approach is the surgical removal of fat cells. In one experiment,[13] three patients were placed on reducing diets and when 'normal' weight was achieved 47–60% of 'excess fat cells' were removed. One patient suffered a thrombosis, one patient regained 81.4lb [36kg] three years later and one patient keeps 'a rigorous diet and regularly pursues a strenuous physical exercise programme.'

DIET THERAPY The diet remains the major treatment prescribed by doctors. Medical researchers investigate the effect of the relationship of various foods and offer their dieting programmes accordingly. In comparison with the other treatments, dieting seems rather mild and harmless but it does not differ in principle from the more extreme drug or surgical therapies. It is as though the human body is the biological parallel of an automobile. Obesity is seen as a symptom of biological malfunction rather like a car's excess gas consumption. The human meanings of fat and thin and the social consequences and causes of compulsive eating have no place in this concept.

Although it is not my purpose to criticise those

practitioners who are committed to human welfare, it is important to note that the medical profession as a whole has an unfortunate history of direct involvement with the oppression of women in our society. The work of Barbara Ehrenreich and Deirdre English[14] has shown that the medical profession was established in the United States in the face of opposition from dedicated and informed lay healers, the majority of whom were women. Women's health groups – most notably the Boston Women's Health Book Collective[15] – have rethought medical issues from a feminist perspective and have been engaged in sharing and disseminating the kind of information women need to know about their bodies. The activities of some women's groups have met with opposition from the authorities. In one case, women involved in a self-help group in California[16] were prosecuted (albeit unsuccessfully) for illegal entry of the vagina.

What is distressing about the current medical perspective is its hegemony in such areas as compulsive eating where the root causes and problems have essential social aspects that must be understood for there to be effective treatment and interventions. Even overweight diabetic women can be compulsive eaters and this problem needs to be addressed in conjunction with medical issues.

In the last few decades we have seen a significant and increasing turn towards science and medicine to solve problems that are socially and economically based. Medicine is presented as the healer and science as the truth. A new religion reigns – the ideology of science.[17] This new ideology proposes that science is neutral and value free. White-coated men and women work away in laboratories seeking truth and progress. Medical researchers are not only truth seekers but humane too, since their work directly relates to human health. Few ask who funds the research and sets the priorities. Instead, the public are asked to embrace new technological fixes for human behaviour issues.

A glance through the medical journals reveals this attitude in another area. Typically, you see a picture of a distraught woman in her forties slumped over a table in a messy kitchen. The advertisement reads in bold type, 'X drug will help relieve the tension so she can cope better.' In smaller print the advertisement mentions the familiar situation of the depressed menopausal woman who feels lifeless, with no energy now that her children have flown the nest. It recommends X psychotropic drug to reduce the anxiety. Doctors, who are frequently male, overworked, untrained to see the social issues that have produced distress in their women patients and unlikely to face this kind of distress themselves, recommend tranquillisers and psycho-active drugs to lift the spirits of these women so that they can function well enough again to clean up their own kitchens and not be a nuisance to anyone. The underlying social cause of distress is not dealt with. Medication is offered, the women are drugged.

Compulsive eating is an individual protest against the inequality of the sexes. As such, medical interventions as detailed here are not part of a solution but are part of the problem. The situation requires a major reorientation of medical and scientific education, organisation and practice based on the demands of the women's health movement.

Notes

FIFI Today

1. Collins, L. Pixel Perfect *The New Yorker* 12 May 2008
2. www.hotgamesforgirls.com/plastic-surgery.html [correct at time of publication – link since removed]
3. Halliwell, E., Diedrichs, P. C., & Orbach. S (2014) *Costing the Invisible: A review of the evidence examining the links between body image, aspirations, education and workplace confidence.* University of the West of England, Bristol, UK www.eprints.uwe.ac.uk [correct at time of publication – link since removed]
4. http://www.berealcampaign.co.uk/blog/2015/10707/no-likesneeded-campaign/
5. Parenthetically, the vaginal microbial wash through the birth canal helps the baby develop immunity. Cho, C. E., *Am J Obstet Gynecol* (April 2013); 208(4): 249–54, 'Caeserian section and the development of the immune system in the offspring'
6. Orbach, S., & Rubin, H. (2014) *Two for the Price of One: The Impact of body image during pregnancy and after birth,* Government Equalities Office
7. See for example, Critser, G., (2003) *Fat Land,* Allen Lane, London
   Lawrence, F., (2008) *Eat Your Heart Out,* Penguin, London
   Schlosser, E., (2002) *Fast Food Nation,* Penguin, London
   Nestle, M., (2002) *Food Politics: How the Food Industry Influences Nutrition and Health,* University of California Press, Berkeley
   Pollen, M., (2006) *The Omnivores Dilemma: The Search for a Perfect Meal in a Fast Food World* Bloomsbury, London,
   Thompson, P. B., (2015) *From Field to Fork: Food Ethics for Everyone* Oxford University Press, Oxford
8. http://www.nytimes.com/2013/02/24/magazine/the-extraordinary-science-of-junk-food.html?_r=0
9. Spector, T., (2015), *The Diet Myth: The Real Science Behind What We Eat* Weidenfeld & Nicholson London
10. http://wphna.org/wp-content/uploads/2013/12/WN_13_04_08_618-644_BFW_Nutrition_and_Big_Food.pdf, http://articles.mercola.com/sites/articles/archive/2013/05/26/nutrition-professionals.aspx and see http://childhoodobesitynews.com/2014/06/06/michele-simon-and-the-academy-of-nutrition-and-dietetics/

11. http://www.eatdrinkpolitics.com/wp-content/uploads/AND_Corporate_Sponsorship_Report.pdf Simon, M., (2013) *And Now a Word from Our Sponsors . . . Are America's Nutrition Professionals in the Pocket of Big Food?*

12. Peretti, J. (2013) *The Men Who Made us Thin* BBC TV London Peretti, J (2014) *The Men Who Made us Fat* BBC TV London

13. See Critser above

14. See Spector p 204

15. Brown RE, et al. Secular differences in the association between caloric intake, macronutrient intake, and physical activity with obesity. Obes Res Clin Pract (2015),

16. Spector p 249

17. Interview with Rudolph Liebel, key theorist of set point theory in *Scientific American* 8th August 1996

18. Begum, G., Stevens, A., Smith, E.B., Connor, K, Challis, J.R.G., Bloomfield, F., White, A., Epigentic changes in fetal hypothalic ebergy regulating pathways are associated with maternal undernutrition and twinning, FASEB J. 2012 Apr;26(4):1694-703. doi: 10.1096/fj.11-198762. Epub 2012 Jan 5.

19. Salecl, R., (2011) *The Tyranny of Choice* Profile Books, London

20. Mann, T., Tomiyama, A. J., Westling, E., Lew, A. M., Samuels, B., & Chatman, J. Medicare's Search for Effective Obesity Treatments: Diets Are Not the Answer, *American Psychologist* Vol 62, Issue 3, April 2007, pp 220–233

W.C., Miller *How effective are traditional dietary and exercise interventions for weight loss?*

Med Sci Sports Exerc 1999, **31**:1129–1134.

21. Flegel, K. M., Graubard, B.I., Williamson, D. F., & Gail, M. H., (2005) Excess Deaths Associated with Underweight, Overweight and Obesity *Journal of the American Medical Association* Vol 293. Issue 15, pp 1861–7

22. Campos, P., (2004), *The Obesity Myth* Gotham Books, New York Oliver, J. E., (2005) *Fat Politics: The Real Story Behind America's Obesity Epidemic* Oxford University Press NY

23. Akerlof, G. A., & Shiller, R. J., (2015) *Phishing for Phools: The Economics of Manipulation and Deception* Princeton University Press, Princeton, New Jersey

24. Hoskins, T. E., (2014) *Stitched Up: The Anti-Capitalist Book of Fashion*, London

25. Becker, Anne E. The Body, Self and Society: The View from Fiji. Philadelphia: University of Pennsylvania Press, 1995.

(Thank you to Eileen Meidar for these references)

26. See the work of Centre for Appearance research, University of West England

27. http://nypost.com/2015/11/03/why-im-turning-my-back-on-instagram-fame-and-fortune/
http://nypost.com/2015/11/04/my-vegan-diet-almost-killed-me/
http://nypost.com/2015/10/11/our-double-lives-dark-realities-behind-perfect-online-profiles/
http://www.people.com/article/kate-winslet-bans-social-media-protect-kids-self-esteem

28. Ibid Mann, T.

29. Veenendaal, M.V.E., Painter, R. C., de Rooij, S. R., Bossuyt, P. M., van der Post, J. A. M., Gluckman, P. D., Hanson, M. A., Roseboom. T. J., Transgenerational effects of prenatal exposure to the 1944–45 Dutch famine, *BJOG: An International Journal of Obstetrics and Gynaecology*. Volume 120 Issue 5

30. The landmark book of the time was *Our Bodies Ourselves* by the Boston Women's Health Collective in 1971, The New England Free Press, Boston. The Vagina Monologues by Eve Ensler in 1996 was another landmark two decades later

31. Feeling fat is a shorthand for not feeling good, not feeling comfortable, not liking my body and so on. In 2015 www.endangeredbodies. org along with www.anybody.org and www.change.org rang a successful campaign to have the emoji removed from Facebook http://www. theguardian.com/technology/2015/mar/12/facebook-removes-feeling-fat-status-option-and-emoji-after-campaign

Prologue

1. See, for example:
G. Bychowski, 'Neurotic Obesity', *The Psychology of Obesity*, ed. N. Kiell (Springfield, Illinois, 1973). Ludwig Bingswanger, 'The Case of Ellen West,' *Existence*, ed. Rollo May (New York, 1958).

2. William Ryan, *Blame the Victim* (New York, 1971). This book shows how we come to blame the victims of oppression rather than its perpetrators.

3. Dorothy Griffiths and Esther Saraga, 'Sex Differences in a Sexist Society.' Paper read at the International Conference on Sex-role Stereotyping, British Psychological Society, Cardiff, Wales, July 1977.

4. John Berger et al., *Ways of Seeing* (London, 1972), p. 47.

5. Simone de Beauvoir, *The Second Sex* (London, 1968).

6. For discussion on this see:
Juliet Mitchell, *Psychoanalysis and Feminism* (New York, 1974). Phyllis Chesler, *Women and Madness* (New York, 1972).

7. D. Brunet and I. Lezine, 'I primi anni del bambino.' Cited in Elena Gianini Belotti, *Little Girls* (London, 1975), pp. 32–4. While this study took place in Europe it does not rule out its relevance in the American context. The book in which it is extensively quoted is one of the most

thoughtful descriptions of the socialisation of young girls and the significance of the early sex-linked feeding relationship.

8. Margaret Atwood, *Lady Oracle* (London, 1977), p. 88.

Chapter 2: What Is Thin About for the Compulsive Eater?

1. Sharon Rosenburg and Joan Weiner, *The Illustrated Hassle-Free Make Your Own Clothes Book* (San Francisco, 1971).

2. This is an Eastern European Jewish custom meant to bring colour to the cheeks.

Chapter 3: The Experience of Hunger for the Compulsive Eater

1. Diet organisations will not release figures on recidivism. However, various sources put it at 95%. See Aldebaran, 'Fat Liberation – A Luxury', *State and Mind* 5 (June-July 1977): 34.

2. Stanley Schachter, 'Obesity and Eating', *Science* 161 (1968): 751.

3. For a discussion of this see:

A. J. Stunkard and H. M. McClaren, 'The Results of Treatment for Obesity', *Archives of Internal Medicine* 103 (1959): 79.

Stanley Schachter, 'Some Extraordinary Facts About Obese Humans and Rats', *American Psychologist* 23 (1971): 129.

Stanley Schachter, 'Obesity and Eating', *Science* 161 (1968): 751.

4. Carol Bloom, 'Training Manual for the Treatment of Compulsive Eating and Fat', Master's thesis, State University of New York at Stony Brook (1976).

Chapter 5: Self-Starvation – Anorexia Nervosa

1. Mara Selvini Palazzoli, *Self Starvation* (London, 1974), pp. 24–5.

2. For useful discussions on anorexia nervosa see:

Rosie Parker and Sarah Mauger, 'Self Starvation', *Spare Rib* 28 (1976).

Marlene Boskind-Lodahl, 'Cinderella's Stepsisters: A Feminist Perspective on Anorexia Nervosa and Bulimia', *Signs* 2 (winter, 1976): 342–56.

Mara Selvini Palazzoli, *Self Starvation* (London, 1974).

Hilde Bruch, *Eating Disorders* (New York, 1973).

Peter Dally, *Anorexia Nervosa* (London, 1969).

Anna Freud, 'The Psychoanalytic Study of Infantile Feeding Disturbance', *The Psychoanalytic Study of the Child II* (London, 1946).

3. Parker and Mauger, 'Self Starvation'.

4. Palazzoli, *Self Starvation*, pp. 224–52.

5. Bruch, *Eating Disorders*, p. 88.

6. Dally, *Anorexia Nervosa*, pp. 93–4.

Chapter 6: Medical Issues

1. J. L., Hirsch and J. Knittle, 'Cellularity of Obese and Nonobese Adipose Tissue', *Federation Proceedings of the American Society for Experimental Biology* 29 (1970): 1516.

2. W. B. Kannel and T. Gordon, 'Some Determinants of Obesity and Its Impact as a Cardiovascular Risk Factor', in *Recent Advances in Obesity Research*, ed. Alan Howard (London, 1975), p. 14. (Hereafter cited as *Recent Advances.*)

3. H. E. Dugdale and P. R. Payne, 'The Pattern of Lean and Fat Deposition in Adults', *Nature* 266 (March, 1977): 349.

4. H. Keen, 'The Incomplete Story of Obesity and Diabetes', in Howard, *Recent Advances*.

5. R. C. Atkins, *Dr Atkins' Diet Revolution* (New York, 1972). '

6. L. J. Herberg, K. B.J. Franklin and D. N. Stephens, 'The Hypothalamic "Set Point" in Experimental Obesity', in Howard, *Recent Advances*.

7. Hilde Bruch, *Eating Disorders* (New York, 1973), p. 36.

8. Michael Schwartz and Joseph Schwartz, 'No Evidence for Heritability of Social Attitudes', *Nature* 255: 429.

9. A. Cooke et al., 'The New Synthesis Is an Old Story', *New Scientist* 70 (1976).

10. Ibid.

11. E. Espmark, 'Psychological Adjustment Before and After Bypass Surgery for Extreme Obesity, a Preliminary Report', in Howard, *Recent Advances*, p. 242.

12. R. C. Kalucy et al., 'Self Reports of Estimated Body Widths in Female Obese Subjects with Major Fat Loss Following Ileo-jejunal Bypass Surgery', in Howard, *Recent Advances*, p. 331.

13. J. G. Kral and L. V. Sjorstrom, 'Surgical Reduction of Adipose Tissue Hypercellularity', in Howard, *Recent Advances*, p. 327.

14. Barbara Ehrenreich and Deirdre English, *Witches, Midwives and Nurses* (New York, 1973).

15. The Boston Women's Health Book Collective, *Our Bodies, Ourselves* (New York, 1973).

16. *People v. Carolyn Aurillia Downer* LAMC 31426942 (1972).

17. R. M. Young. 'Science Is Social Relations,' *Radical Science Journal* 5 (1977): 65.

BOOK TWO

Conquering Compulsive Eating

To
Claire Chapman
and
the Spare Tyre Theatre Company

Contents

Introduction

Since *Fat Is a Feminist Issue* was published in the spring of 1978, I have received hundreds of letters from individual women about their eating problems. Many of these letters made it clear to me that women needed more detailed guidelines on how to translate the ideas in *Fat Is a Feminist Issue* into practice. Mira Dana, a student at the Women's Therapy Centre in London and I prepared a questionnaire designed to identify the specific difficulties individual women were experiencing and the obstacles that self-help groups might be encountering in attempting to apply the theories in *Fat Is a Feminist Issue*. The questionnaire was sent out to women who had attended introductory workshops that used the *Fat Is a Feminist Issue* method. This method looks at the meaning of food in a woman's life and the unconscious associations to body images of fat and thin. It offers a way out of the compulsive eating syndrome by showing how to distinguish between physiological hunger and emotional hunger, and how to respond to each appropriately. After analysing those answers and reflecting on the questions brought up most frequently by the group leaders I was training in this method, I decided it would be helpful to prepare *Fat Is a Feminist Issue II*, which is intended to be a very down-to-earth and practical guide to address the persistent bumps and barriers that many women experience in grappling with their eating problems.

Today several million people in America are on a diet or a weight-reduction scheme of one kind or another. Sadly we know that those methods work for very few people in the long run. 97% will regain the weight they worked so hard to lose, and the ones who didn't need to reduce their size in the first place will live in the grip of anxiety around food and will be constantly watching themselves. This book offers a different way to address the diet dilemma. It asks why we are fat and why we want to be thin, and it offers us a way to live more harmoniously in our bodies.

How to Use this Book

The main text and the psychological exercises in Part II of this book are meant to be used together. In Part I you will occasionally come across the symbol ★ which denotes the introduction of a psychological exercise. I suggest you read through the entire book once to get a sense of how it is organised and where the exercises fit in, and then work through section by section as each feels appropriate for you. The exercises will help you get in touch with emotional states you may not be aware of, that are connected to your feelings about your body and your eating.

Keeping a Journal

In all your work with compulsive eating – be it fantasising, answering the questions in the book, or in your day-to-day observations – you may find it useful to keep a diary or a notebook in which you jot down your reactions. Any insights you get can be written down immediately before you have time to 'forget' or unconsciously reject them. Those women working on their food problem on their own will find it particularly useful to keep such a diary and use it when they set out to do their daily or weekly sessions. In this way you will have a record of your development that you can refer to from time to time.

You will notice that some of the material in the later part of the book is especially directed at groups. Most of this, however, is equally relevant to individual women working on the problem of compulsive eating alone or in pairs. Some of the practical issues of group work will be less relevant to individuals, but the information given should be helpful in demonstrating how well a group might work for you.

Though *Fat Is a Feminist Issue II* stands on its own, I have not attempted to recapitulate in detail all the concepts I explored in *Fat Is a Feminist Issue.* You may want to turn to *Fat Is a Feminist Issue* for further discussion of particular theoretical areas. *Fat Is a Feminist Issue II* will spell out in more detail the kinds of practical interventions that can be helpful in working on a compulsive eating problem.

SUSIE ORBACH
New York, 1981

Part I

CHAPTER ONE

The Roots of the Problem

Habitual compulsive eating can become a painful and an engrossing problem, almost a way of life. People can get caught up in a syndrome in which they spend hours silently worrying and obsessing about what they should or should not be eating and, when they do allow themselves to eat, they end up not being able to really taste the food or gain much pleasure from it. Food and eating as a satisfying and unambivalent pleasure eludes the compulsive eater. Instead, food is used as a tool to help one cope – in the short term – with difficult feelings and emotional distress. Food then may become a narcotic, quelling the anxiety that unconfronted and unrecognised feelings raise. Compulsive eaters are out of touch with physiological cues that signal hunger or satisfaction. They look to food to meet all sorts of needs that may arise out of unconscious needs and conflicts. The activity of the eating and the preoccupation with food mask underlying problems.

Most treatment offered to those considered over- or underweight by doctors and dieticians focuses on manipulation of diet. In that treatment the strategy is to educate the patient, to get her or him to understand the rules of the body. The main point made is that you can't take in more than your body needs without gaining weight. If this educational approach doesn't work, and the patient doesn't follow instructions, she is scolded. And if this doesn't work a whole range of artificial 'fixes', from appetite depressants to wiring the jaws together, are available. But because compulsive eaters are psychologically addicted to food and patterns of bingeing and deprivation, such strategies rarely enable them to fundamentally change their eating patterns. Many people lose weight intermittently – some with ease, some with great difficulty – but they usually have a tremendously hard time maintaining that loss. The odds are that in a desperate search for a solution they will enroll at a diet clinic or return to the family doctor, or consult a specialist physician, or buy the latest best seller, and try to slim down again. *Their food problem hasn't been tackled.*

While the schemes offered by many diet books, doctors, and weight loss organisations seem on the surface quite sensible – a matter of getting the right fuel for a particular engine – few people can view food in that simple utilitarian way. The meaning of food for each individual must be looked at. The food we eat, how we eat and how we feel about food are a reflection of who we are. How and what we eat derives substantially from what we first learned in our families, how we felt around the family table and in the kitchen with Grandma, and so on. The family meal in itself was an expression of the social meaning of food. Mealtimes are rituals of family and friends getting together. Food is imbued with layers and layers of meaning.

Women as Nurturers

Food has special meanings in the lives of women. Traditionally women are intimately involved in choosing, buying and cooking food. They are responsible for making sure that the family's food needs are adequately met. They are expected to cope with providing breakfast, school lunches, supper and any specialised food requirements. They manipulate the family budget skillfully so that if economic circumstances worsen they will not suffer nutritionally or feel the lack of previously available favourite foods. In other words, women are at the centre of the household feeding pattern. On them rests basic responsibilities for the family's health and well-being. Because women of this generation were brought up to take on these responsibilities, such concerns may fall largely in their province even if they are in a non-traditional relationship or marriage. In fact, in a woman's psychology, an important aspect of her self-esteem derives from her ability to be a good nurturer – in perhaps a parallel sense the aspect of self-esteem that a man derives from his job and his capacity to be the economic provider.

If we take a look at almost any magazine that is directed at women whether aimed at the working-class woman, the housewife – low or middle income – or the professional and business woman, the magazine will be full of advertisements from food manufacturers accompanied by copy on how to serve the most economic, time-saving, natural, healthy, sexy or elegant meals. A woman is assaulted page after page with reminders about her responsibility to feed others. The assumption is that women are the right people, in an almost biologically divined sense, to be concerned about food delivery. (Just check your own reactions to a man who is a good cook. Don't you think he has something rather special.) At the same time, the not-so-subtle message of women's magazines and daytime television advertisements is that women cannot afford to rely on their judgment about what food is appropriate. They are deemed to need the constant guidance of 'experts'. Women are taught that, in this crucial area of their lives, they are always in danger of making mistakes. Libby's or Nestle knows best. At minimum the message is, there is always room for improvement in being a better provider.

Beyond getting the nutritional requirements right, the woman is encouraged to express her unique personality through the food she prepares. Food becomes a medium through which she communicates many feelings. It demonstrates her love, her caring and her concern for her family. A woman's value rises with her ability to produce prettier, more economic, more wholesome and at the same time delectable meals, snacks and picnics.

The woman's traditional role of service in the food arena is both a real and a symbolic reflection of women's relation to society and the family. The sexes are still legally, economically and sexually unequal. Women are still directed into one sphere of human activity and men into another, more highly valued sphere. This means that, when all is said and done, the home, the family, having babies and bringing them up, and looking after the husband's needs, washing, cleaning, feeding, nurturing and so on are *felt* as constituting the true realm for women's activity and satisfaction. The contemporary woman who has grown up with all these pressures and is now attempting to express herself more broadly through her work, her job, her career, is often subject to a complex of ambivalent feelings about herself and her body too. She may feel ill at ease if she 'sacrifices' a family for a career. She may find herself making a choice that is painful and limiting in another direction. She may feel resentful if she tries to juggle both roles, as those close to her often do not recognise the enormous demands she is trying to meet. Whichever way a woman tries to work out this dilemma, her struggle is set against an internal emotional background that nags at her, reminding her that, in order to be a 'proper' woman, she must have a man to share her life with. And, in order to 'catch and keep' a man, she must be attractive and appealing.

We are Alienated from Our Bodies

A woman's body, then, becomes for her an instrument, a commodity that she can and must use in our world in the pursuit of her personal attempt to find contentment and a place. And, a woman's body, we learn, is not a very good or safe environment to live inside. Rarely are our mothers and other female adults able to convey to a young woman that her body, whatever natural shape it has, is a source of pride and of beauty, since they themselves have not been able to feel that. We learn instead that our bodies are powerful in a negative sense, they can destabilise men and get us into trouble. It is no wonder then that we become frightened of our bodies and see them not as where we live but as a part of us that we must control, watch and direct.

Because of this we automatically see ourselves with a critical eye. A woman's body can always use improving; our legs, our hair, our bustline, our skin, our cellulite are all in danger of being unseemly unless attended to in a feminine way. Encouraged to see ourselves this way, it is not surprising that we grow up alienated and scared of our bodies. A woman's body is one of the few culturally accepted ways a woman has to express herself and yet the scope of this expression is limited by a contradiction: the pressure to look a certain way, to conform to today's slim image.

Food is for Others

A situation exists therefore where a woman's focuses on food and body image converge in a particularly intense way. In order to be feminine, she must present an attractive picture of herself, which today means a slender profile. Under this circumstance I think we can see just how significant food becomes in her life. Food is what she gives to *others* but must deprive herself of. Food is, if you like, good for *others* but somehow dangerous to the woman herself. Food is about health for *others*, but about beauty for herself. Food, it is alleged, does terrible things to women and one must be very careful approaching it. It can make you fat, spotty, ugly. It exposes your desires and your greed. Food, which is imbued with the spirit of giving when prepared for others, takes on a sinister face when women eat. A woman is meant to police her eating, to feel cautious of what she eats, to be constantly watching it. At the same time food is her way of caring for *others*. Food is her power in the family, it is a means by which she exerts incredible influence; she brings comfort, reward, reassurance through it.

For women food carries such complex meanings that it is nonsense to focus on calories or carbohydrate grams when working towards a plan to lose weight. The roots of compulsive eating in women stem from women's position in society – she feeds everyone else, but her needs are personally illegitimate. Food, therefore, can become a way to try to give to herself. Her fatness can become a way to express a protest at the definitions of her social role. Fatness, as an unspoken communication, can imply bigness, strength, motherliness, solidity; it can embrace any problem. Slimness equals beauty and attractiveness, and is elusive. For many women, fatness feels like a rejection of the packaged sexuality around us. We need to decipher the meaning of fatness to the individual, what it symbolises, to understand why a woman has expressed herself through food and body image. To focus on calories is unrealistic in such circumstances. The focus must be shifted to the *meaning* of food in people's lives so that distortions of very basic psychological cues can be understood and then corrected. When we think about the meaning of food in our lives for just a few minutes, we advance from calories and perhaps tap feelings of pleasure, connectedness, fear, love, and so on. It is coming to grips with these kinds of themes in relation to food and body image that can enable the compulsive eater to relate to food in a positive way.

A Note About Anorexia

Much of what I have written here and in FIFI applies only in a very particular way to those women whose compulsive eating problems express themselves through anorectic symptoms. Some of the most obvious differences lie around the issue of control and responsibility in relation to food. Any woman who has suffered with anorexia will clearly feel that her eating problems aren't quite accurately described. Her experience is of the need to be totally in control. The food is so terrifying that she will have developed schemes, perhaps hourly strategies, to control her desire to eat. She is persistently and painfully involved with thoughts about food and what it might do to her. Her needs in a group will be quite different than those of women whose compulsive eating problems predominately show up in patterns of bingeing, dieting and 'overweight' as opposed to bingeing, vomiting, starving and being painfully underweight. For this reason I am now inclined

that women who suffer from the anorectic side
drome would do best organised in groups specif-
igned for them. Just as a compulsive eater can find
roup provides the first place for honest sharing, so
too the anorectic woman can find safety and comfort in
revealing herself with others who have similar experience.
Anorexia involves hiding who you are, both from yourself
and from others. In the process you may also become
stealthy about what you do to protect yourself. In a group
with other women who've taken the same route, there is
the possibility of disclosing all the pain without fear of
judgment, or shocked reactions, and this is tremendously
important.

CHAPTER TWO

Slimness: The New God?

Women come in all shapes and sizes. Some of us are short, some of us are tall. We can have short legs, medium-length legs, long legs, big breasts, medium-size breasts, small breasts, standing up breasts, floppy breasts, large, medium or small hips; we can be pear-shaped, broad or rounded, have flat stomachs, full stomachs, even teeth, crooked teeth, large eyes, dimpled cheeks. But the extraordinary variety that is woman's body is systematically ignored in our culture. The richness of our different shapes is reduced to the overriding image of slimness. Advertisements for *women's* clothes feature pre-pubescent *girls* (especially in swimsuits), models with anorectic bodies display clothes designed to make women into objects, and shop mannequins are literally shaved down each year to present the newest fashions on figures that correspond to fewer and fewer bodies.

Meanwhile women, not surprisingly, feel 'oversized', too big in one part of their body or another, dissatisfied with particular features of their whole body as a 'package'. Bombarded by images of increasing slimness, women struggle to mirror the new image churned out seasonally. Trying on clothes in shop changing rooms, women judge themselves on how successfully they can reflect/reproduce the received images of femininity.

On one level it is a straight propaganda campaign coupled with the unavailability of stylish clothes in more than a few sizes – but the process is more insidious than that. Even women who have grown up with a reasonably healthy respect for their bodies (hard as this is to do in our culture) and who have not been previously preoccupied with body image are so assaulted with articles, advertisements, diet columns and advice on beauty matters that pedal thinness as a life solution that they find their confidence undermined. Feelings of dissatisfaction creep in, and few women under 45 would see themselves as slim enough or their bodies as satisfactory. What was 'acceptable' even ten years ago is now outsized. The Western obsession with slimness pushes women into a relentless struggle to press their bodies into smaller and smaller sizes. The beauty and variety of the female form are judged unacceptable, and instead slimness is promoted for profit and control.

As women are encouraged to become smaller and smaller and the Western obsession with health = slimness = happiness = diet intensifies, more and more books are rushed into the marketplace offering new, permanent weight-reduction schemes or advice on how to dress slim, minimise 'bad points' and project the perfect body. Slimness, first marketed as a way to emulate the international jet set, has developed a life of its own. Success, beauty, wealth, love, sexuality and happiness are promoted as attached to and depending on slimness. Slimness instantly conveys these qualities as though they automatically go together like salt and pepper, gin and tonic, Saturday night and Sunday morning. In other words, slimness is made into a fetish and abstracted from what it is – just one particular body shape. Slimness sells women's bodies back to them, promising in its wake the good life. Of course, none of these marketed attributes are remotely connected to slimness, which stripped bare is nothing more than a fashion, a current ideal promoted for a variety of reasons that seem to depend for their persistence on a pervasive fear of women and a desire to package them safely into commodities.

Selling body insecurity to women (and increasingly to men too) is a vicious phenomenon. It relies on the social practices that shape a girl's growing up to make her receptive. Little girls are cautioned against touching and investigating their bodies. Similarly they are discouraged from using their body strength to explore the world. Young ladies' bodies, we learn, are to be kept clean, hair is to be kept tidy, sexuality is to be hidden and poise must be developed. Much of a girl's childhood consists of injunctions against physical expression and exploration. Too much ballet produces big calf muscles and a Charlie Chaplin walk, too much tennis makes one breast bigger than the other. These so called 'wisdoms', transmitted from mothers to their daughters and from teenager to teenager, shape the way that girls feel about their bodies inside and out. They become inhibited and prey to the media persuasion that induces feelings of inadequacy at the same moment as it pretends to offer solutions.

This destabilising campaign takes its toll on the daily lives, activities and aspirations of women. Slimness is believed to be the answer to difficult social and personal circumstances. Many a woman has described the solution to an unfortunate encounter, a disappointing weekend, a job not secured, a lousy day with the kids, a squabble with her husband, a low exam result, in terms of 'if only I were slim' or 'I'm going to lose weight this week.' That women seek such a route is hardly surprising. That it is ineffective is a tragic comment on the complexities of how we are first robbed of our bodies and our access to many of life's activities and then thrust back on a narrow, individualistic non-solution – slimness.

Because of the pressure to be slim, many women who may not have had a history of eating problems in childhood or adolescence find themselves unwittingly interfering with the self-regulatory system that lets them know what, when and how much to eat. They disturb the mechanism of hunger and satisfaction signals and seek weight-loss schemes that actually initiate the diet-binge cycle. In moving away from internal cues to outside advice on diet, they inevitably try to reduce their food intake. This attempted reducing usually involves, in one scheme or another, the removal of certain types of foods from the woman's diet. In its place is put a scheme which depends on special food combinations of one kind or another.

There is always a new diet to try, always the possibility that *this* one will bring the accompaniments of happiness, success, love and health. But the schemes fail, for not only can't the diet deliver the goods, it becomes a jumping-off point for a cycle of deprivation that at some point – be it a day, a week, a month or even six months later – catapults into compulsive eating, bingeing and gorging.

Diets Turn Normal Eaters into People who are Afraid of Food

Diets rarely help a woman lose weight or reeducate her eating habits. Under the guise of control they bring havoc in the food area and frequently increased poundage. *Diets turn 'normal eaters' into people who are afraid of food.* Food takes on all the punishing and magical qualities that anguish the compulsive eater. Our cultural obsession with slimness creates a whole new grouping of women who are unnecessarily drawn into having a food problem. As the women attempt to get slimmer, the diet organisations, diet books, exercise programmes and so on get fatter and fatter on their pain.

This thin obsession that is inflicted on so many women makes it hard to resist the pressure to conform. Rebellion brings with it feelings of uneasiness and freakishness. It becomes quite difficult even to raise the question of *why* the massive variety that is woman's shape is systematically degraded; what is so awful and threatening about women's bodies at any size; why isn't fat considered attractive; why stature and fullness are devalued. Is the stigma that attaches to large or fat women not just another subtle way to divide one woman from another, thus promoting a false and individual solution to what should be at root a social concern – namely, the position of women in our society? Perhaps we can understand the impetus and energy behind the thinness campaign inflicted on so many women as a (possibly unconscious) skewed reaction to women's desires to be regarded seriously and take up more space.

Women look at each other and marvel at how older women manage to achieve 'the look', 'the face', 'the body' that gives them a place and an acceptability in the world. Beauty and attractiveness are forever being redefined, but there still exists no place in the current equation for substantial bodies to be considered beautiful. The driven, induced need to be slim diverts us from concerns that are more truly central to our experience of life. It absorbs an energy that could help us change the world, not just our bodies.

A few brave women in western Europe and the United States are now battling against the prevailing standards, challenging them, turning them upside down, demanding rights for women of all shapes and sizes, classes and colours. But it is an uphill struggle punctured at every point by the hidden (and not so hidden) persuaders, reminding us that slimness is essential and that women must not occupy more than a little space.

CHAPTER THREE

Food Awareness

What Is Compulsive Eating?

Compulsive eating means eating without regard to physical cues signalling hunger or satisfaction. It means, in fact, being so terribly out of touch with your body that these mechanisms are suppressed. Food is experienced as something almost magical, imbued with the power to make you feel better, to squash feelings, to provide comfort, to induce feelings of strength and so on. At the same time you may be fearful of food and what *it* can do, imagining that food is more powerful than the person who eats it, that it can do terrible things to you.

A compulsive eater feels out of control about what she eats. For some people that only happens at particular times, or comes and goes in waves. For other women, it is a constant battle. From time to time the compulsive eater will become inspired to 'do' something about 'it', by dieting, fasting, or trying to do away with the effects of the overeating by exercising, or taking diuretics and laxatives in large and dangerous quantities. Several times a week she will resolve to change the way she eats.

A woman frequently gets caught up in compulsive eating

199

in the first place out of a desire to change her size because she *feels* too large. This desire to get smaller, thinner or slimmer then leads her to attempt to reduce her food intake. For many many women this desire is the trigger to a seesaw of food deprivation and bingeing. The deprivation can be more or less stringent, the bingeing more or less frequent and 'extravagant'. Women express these conflicts in a variety of ways, but there are four definite group types that I have observed.

There are those women who have been large for many years, who feel themselves to be fat, although they frequently underestimate their size, and who are quite despairing about ever being able to lose weight. They are frequently unaware of how much food they do eat and experience their eating as somewhat chaotic. They discuss the topic quite openly and *feel that things would be a lot better for them if they were slim.*

The second group of women – by far the largest in number – are those who go up and down the scale (about a maximum range of 60lb [27kg]). They diet from time to time and binge irregularly, though they overeat fairly consistently. They are quite open about talking about their food problems and *feel that things would be a lot better for them if they were slim.*

The third group of women are often average size, but weekly, daily, sometimes hourly, they binge on substantial amounts of food, which they then bring up. The name for this particular pattern is *bulimorexia*. Very few women in this group feel comfortable talking about their way of coping. They are fearful that disclosing how they are with food will result in a loss of control, or that they will be forced to give up their method of coping. They are desperate because they feel purging after gorging is the only way they *can* stay slim.

The fourth group of women are anorectic. They try to avoid eating as far as possible, and devise various schemes and regulations to limit what they do eat and then to rid themselves of the caloric value they've taken in. They often have a distorted view of their bodies, not realising how very thin they are but instead seeing themselves as grotesque and enormous. Sometimes their control cracks and they binge (and sometimes bring it up). They tend to be extremely closemouthed about their own eating but observe others closely. *They feel that things would be a lot better for them if only they were slim*

When we look beneath the surface of these adaptations we can see that these ways of relating to food encompass much more than a desire to be slim. Their involvement with food stands for all sorts of communications that are unacknowledged. The way of being with food symbolises a way of being with self, for example, harsh, punitive, inconsistent, depriving, angry, rebellious. Much self-dislike is sifted into the compulsive eating. It becomes a conveyor belt for the digestion, or rather indigestion, of uncomfortable emotional issues. In a broad sense a woman eating compulsively is absorbing the message of the culture and mirroring its relation to her. The world tells her she is unentitled and second class. She must love and nurture others with food but not herself. She develops a distorted relationship to food and her body. At the same time she is, in a painful and very personal way, using the food and her body to make a statement in the world. She is crying out for the kind of attention she knows so well how to give to others. She is trying to make a personal peace with the pressure to look a certain way. A confrontation is in process around food.

The Goal

The aim of this approach is to break the addiction to compulsive eating – to transform eating and mealtimes into pleasurable experiences that we can look forward to. This transformation can occur only if we move out of the torture and complications of the cycle of dieting, revolting against the diet, bingeing, intermittent overeating, feeling out of control around food and then taking ourselves by the scruff of the neck and recommitting ourselves to the deprived structure of the diet until once again we break it.

The method starts from the following points:

1. Compulsive eating is motivated by emotional factors.

2. Overeating occurs when a person feels unentitled to food and consequently is always trying to stop herself from eating. This self-denial goes hand in hand with its opposite, which is bingeing.

3. Compulsive eating and compulsive dieting are two sides of the same coin. The abstinence of one state explodes into the seeming chaos of the other. Dieting is *not* control: it is a stricture from outside imposed on the self. The control is vested outside us. Compulsive eating *feels* out of control, but in fact it originates inside us. For this reason, understanding unconscious processes can lead to greater harmony with our emotional needs.

4. Compulsive eating and compulsive dieting can be understood as addictions. They are serious problems requiring thoughtful interventions.

5. The psychological factors in compulsive eating relate to conscious and unconscious ideas of body image, i.e., 'Who will I be slim?' 'Who will I be fat?'

6. Compulsive eaters are out of tune with the body signals signifying hunger and satisfaction.

7. Women have a particularly complicated relationship to food because of the social meanings of food, feeding, fatness, thinness, dieting and femininity.

8. Compulsive eating and compulsive dieting are not disabling for life. They are not a chronic, incurable condition. They are an understandable response to psychological and social pressures.

How to Achieve the Goal: First Steps

Many women have found that the way out of the diet-binge cycle is to *stop dieting*. Review your eating/dieting history and see what your experience has been. Take time to do this, using a journal to write down what you find out about yourself. You may well discover that dieting did not work for you either as a way to 'control' your appetite on a long-term basis, or to break your compulsive eating patterns, or to help you stabilise at a weight that you want to be. You may come to the conclusion that dieting, rather than solving your food problems, added to them. Though a diet may often have looked like a good solution, perhaps it never actually worked out as it promised to. Now may be the time to take a leap of faith and stop dieting.

This can sound like an alarming idea, but consider it carefully. How many diets and weight-reducing schemes have you embarked on in your life? Is one diet really that different from any other? Don't they all lead eventually to your breaking the diet and eating in an out-of-control fashion, trying to make up for the period of forced deprivation? *Diets do not help you learn about your own bodily needs. They don't alert you to hunger and satisfaction; they don't break the compulsive eating pattern.*

Identify Your Hunger

If you can give up the strictures of a diet, you can begin to approach your eating more sensitively. *Discover your times of hunger and what exactly you are hungry for.* Try to ignore all your mental restrictions on what you should and should not eat. Don't avoid foods you've always considered 'bad' – junk food, desserts, chocolate, biscuits, potatoes or whatever. Focus instead on what you would most like to eat. Have it, taste it. Eat it slowly enough to taste it. See how much you want of it on this particular occasion. Now see if you can stop when you are satisfied. If you can develop a stance towards food that allows you to eat, you will more easily be able to stop when you've had enough. In other words, in giving up dieting and allowing yourself a free range of foods, you are opening yourself up to the possibility of *not* overeating.

Entitlement to Food

Because shame often accompanies being fat, and because in our culture there is so much pressure to deny ourselves food and become slim, many 'overweight' compulsive eaters feel nervous about exposing that they want to eat. As a result, such women may often feel guilty about wanting to eat and may prefer to do so in private. Alternatively, they might try to conceal the kinds of foods they are eating so they don't experience the negative judgments of others. But this scheme rarely works out, since the woman feels such anxiety around food that she isn't really selecting carefully either when or what she wishes to eat. What *does* work is daring to break the taboo. Just because you're fat doesn't mean you have less right to food – or to anything else, for that matter – than other people.

Building Up Confidence

As you engage in this new process you will be building up a confidence that comes from satisfying yourself with food. You will be able to experience the sensation of hunger signals, and from that choose – without worrying about calorific values – the absolutely right food and drink that will meet whatever your particular appetite is at that time.

There are no recipes in this book, no menu suggestions, and no prescriptions as to when, what or how much to eat. Nobody can know better than you what feels and tastes right, what quantities match your appetite, what flavours will satisfy you.

Your eating behaviour may seem somewhat strange as you try to be precise in meeting your physical desires. You may want little bits of food every few hours; you may discover that a variety of foods appeal to you and that you go through food phases; you may discover that your hunger corresponds to designated mealtimes. In all this you are the one who knows best what is right for you. Listen to your needs and then stick up for them by responding appropriately and without interference from 'shoulds' or 'must nots', good or bad foods.

As you eat the food you have chosen you will be able to enjoy it unambiguously – that is, without guilt or judgments. Because you have let yourself eat absolutely what you are wanting – and you know that this will be one of many, many such experiences with food, from now on – you will be able to stop when you are satisfied and afterwards feel the contentment that comes from looking after yourself with food in a precise way. For so many women with eating problems, guilt, physical discomfort, feelings of self-loathing, disrespect and recriminations are automatic accompaniments to any eating experience or even thoughts about wanted food. It is important to remember that in this therapeutic approach we are trying to break the compulsive eating pattern so that food and meals are transformed from painful experiences into reliably satisfying ones.

You may wish to turn now to two exercises designed to help you find out more about your own psychological food constraints and aid you in trying to break through them. These are the 'Ideal Kitchen' (page 330) and the 'Supermarket Fantasy' (page 359). Allow yourself a good half an hour to do each exercise and then refer to the questions which follow it. You may wish to jot down your responses in your journal.

A Step at a Time

There can be infinite interruptions to the process of transforming food from a painful into a satisfying experience. Women eat compulsively for so many different reasons that, in the course of exploring why you do, there will doubtless be occasions when you find yourself eating more than you are wanting, grabbing for food or having mini-binges. These episodes do not mean the approach is not working, nor do they prove that you don't 'deserve' to eat what you want any more. Each of these possibly upsetting experiences is in fact useful as a *clue* to help you unravel the mystery of your own particular eating pattern. Remember that you can use these experiences to help rather than punish yourself. The more you discover about yourself, the more possibilities there will be for you to intervene on your own behalf in a way that makes sense to you. Your various unconscious reasons for compulsive eating – or wanting to go back to dieting – will eventually come to light as you examine these kinds of incidents.

For example, Sara found that she frequently overate, just that little bit, whenever she had French toast. She enjoyed it so much that she couldn't stop herself. When she delved into why, she realised that she only made French toast once in a while and she was packing it in because she didn't know when she would be tasting it again. In a mini-version, she had set up a feast and famine relationship to the French toast. Once she saw what was going on she decided to make it more frequently. The result was that she didn't feel the urge to eat it so voraciously. She could stop when she was comfortably full, secure in the knowledge that she might make some again in a few days.

From Relaxation to Awareness

The aim of this approach is to encourage guilt-free eating so that you can really listen to what your body is wanting and give it the right kind and amount of food. However, I have learned from many women that what can happen initially is that the relief of being able to consider eating and food in a guilt-free way can be so enormous it can blind them to other aspects of their eating. In the effort not to judge every morsel that passes their lips, an amnesiac relaxation can occur when they eat. The permission to eat is translated into not knowing why or what they are eating. This may feel a lot different from the terrorising voices that can accompany compulsive eating (as indeed it is), but if it continues for too long it can bring its own despair.

Often women tell me that they feel more relaxed around food but don't notice much change in their eating habits. What we then work on is how they can become more aware of what, when and how they are eating. Sometimes it can feel like a burden to have to concentrate on food, especially when you are trying to get away from being so obsessively involved, but in fact the only way to get through the obsession is to use it. Use it to observe your eating, gather as much information as you can, and then allow yourself to intervene differently. I am often pressed to remind women that the goal is to eat comfortably and with their hunger. The first step is to remove the guilt that surrounds all eating, but the next steps require more active engagement with the part of you that is struggling to eat in the new way. So from removal or reduction of guilt we move on to observe all the details of our eating behaviours.

Keeping a food chart is one way to find out more about your individual eating patterns. That food chart (on page 356) can be useful when you notice that you are somewhat glazed over about what your actual food intake has been and what the associated events, feelings and aftermath of eating experiences were like.

Observe in Detail

As you continue to observe your food intake you will probably notice that patterns emerge for you. For example, Clare noticed that she was really only comfortable when she was eating with her boyfriend or alone. When she wrote down her observations about having meals with others, she saw that she felt tense in a variety of ways. If it was a Chinese meal in which she was to share each dish with many people, she felt a certain anxiety that she would not be able to get what she wanted; either she would show herself to be greedy or she would hold back and feel deprived. This was in stark contrast to eating with her boyfriend Adam, with whom she could share quite comfortably. What she noticed was that with Adam she felt a confidence and security that she could have whatever she wanted. As happens with many couples, she went out of her way to give him the best of whatever was at the table and he went out of his way to give her the best. It wasn't that each was entitled to half — rather that in their relationship the meals expressed how they felt about each other, and since their concern for each other was in this case mutual, Clare could relax and feel reasonably sure that whatever she wanted she could have. There was never a hint of deprivation or worrying about appearing greedy. When Clare observed how she ate with other friends, where the sharing was based on an unspoken assumption of equal portions for each person, she noticed that the defined limit brought out her deprived feelings, and she felt she had to watch out that she didn't expose what felt to her like a desperation.

Clare decided to intervene and use this self-observation to explore the roots of her anxiety about eating with others. She began by choosing a restaurant where it was possible for her to have her own self-contained meal. This would allow her to eat with her friends without being under the pressure to share. In this way she might have more of a chance to find out what some of the underlying psychological reasons were for her desires to grab, without feeling she was acting them out in what felt to her like a humiliating way.

What she had to remember in the experiment was that when she was eating with Adam she ate with relish – and she usually ate less than at any other time. Clare needed to find out why this experience eluded her with others. She felt it must have something to do with emotional safety. What she discovered during the experiment was that when eating with friends she did not feel that they were really with her. Their attention was not focused on her but on the conversation or whatever else was happening. When it was focused on their interaction with her, Clare's eating was free of tension and she was able to eat leisurely and with enormous pleasure.

The issue that Clare had to confront for herself was: How could she help herself not to see others' actions as having directly to do with her? Why did she jump to the conclusion that something was being done to her (when people weren't riveted on her) rather than that she was affected by others whether their intentions were specifically focused on her or not?

When she looked back over her history she realised that when she was a little girl her mother was often distracted and only infrequently in Clare's memory did her mother pay specific attention to her around food. Of course, this information had long been obscured because so many of Clare's remembrances of her mother related to food and food preparation. Clare's mother, like most women of her generation, was responsible for feeding the family and spent much of her time in the kitchen and shopping for food. But she did not do this without having extremely complicated feelings. Some of these she hid from herself, because the times were such that it was hard for a woman to protest that aspect of her social role, but the impact of this forced service in the food arena meant that some of her ambivalent feelings spilled over into how she related to her daughter around food.

What had happened, from Clare's point of view, was that she did not have a secure sense of her mother's presence with her when she was eating. Because feeding is such an intimate communication in infancy and early childhood (since a child's survival is so dependent upon it), tremendous anxiety can arise when the child experiences her feeder as distanced or inconsistent. This is the memory that Clare had. She felt a richly secure and nourishing ambience with her mother but at other times felt a panic and fear that her mother was not attending.

This staccato pattern in her early relationship to food was psychologically jangling, and it was being replayed in her adult life in a more elaborated form. She had, unbeknownst to her conscious mind, projected on to Adam and her eating times with him that aspect of her mother that comforted and warmed her; on to her friends she had projected the distanced or withdrawn aspects of her mother, which induced anxiety in her.

With this insight Clare was able to take more responsibility for what she was actually doing. She could see that she grafted on to real situations emotional memories from her past. She struggled to trust that she could indeed allow *herself* to be engaged with herself when she was eating. She could be her own companion in that sense. She tried to sort through her feelings of insecurity and to acknowledge them more straightforwardly so that she need not express this issue through her food.

In fact, the painstaking psychological work she did in order to pinpoint what was going on for her not only freed her to work at the issues behind the eating – it also gave her a way to feel more secure within herself. Clare began to be able to see that as she allowed herself to pay more attention to her eating, she relaxed and enjoyed it. The good feelings she had experienced with Adam could now be taken into other settings. Unexpectedly, the new benefits regarding food made her realise how deeply tied she was to her mother and the never-ending conflicts that lived in that relationship. She began to feel an energy to work on their relationship unfettered by fears of food. This detailed analysis helped Clare find a new solution.

See if you can't piece together your own food pattern in a way that can open up new responses for you. Such observations may serve as a reminder to you that your compulsive eating has roots in your personal history. As you begin to understand those roots, remember that *each eating experience is a chance to change*. This means that every single day you will have one, two, three, five chances to intervene and not necessarily repeat that personal history.

Breaking the Binge Cycle

One of the dreaded aspects of bingeing is its cyclical nature. It starts with what feels like a mindless, driven stuffing down of food. This is followed by a feeling of being blotted out, stoned. The next morning, or a few hours later, when you have regained awareness and are perhaps feeling physically bloated, you are troubled by recriminations and you hope for the energy to make a new start.

Bingeing inevitably makes you feel you've blown it, and it takes a while until you feel able to put back on the straitjacket of the diet or whatever is your current regime for losing weight. Usually what follows is eventually another and yet another binge.

Giving up dieting does not mean that bingeing

automatically disappears. It may well decrease and occur only sporadically, seemingly rearing its insistent desire out of nowhere. It may occur on specific occasions, around menstruation or when you feel particularly tense or disappointed. While you are working on the psychological motivations of your bingeing, you will need some practical down-to-earth steps with which to intervene in the binge cycle. Try following these the next time you are in a compulsive eating situation:

1. Sit down, slow down and take a moment to register that you are bingeing. Accept that you are bingeing – don't fight the impulse. Do you always go for a specific food during a binge? Are you tasting the food? Enjoying the food? If not, stop and ask yourself whether it is the right food. What do you *want* to eat?

2. Identify the feeling that led you to eat. What would be so terrible about having the feelings? Think about the emotional state you wish to achieve by eating. Is it oblivion? What do you want as an end result to the binge? What is your eating trying to express? What is your fat trying to tell people? What would be so difficult about facing these emotions if you were thin?

3. What will happen if you sit with your feelings? What are you exposing about yourself? Why is that so shameful?

4. See if you can experience your feelings directly, even if only for a minute or two.

Focusing in on your feelings, allowing yourself the breathing space to see what you really want, puts you in touch with your own power. It reminds you that *you*, not some outside or superimposed authority, are going to help yourself out. For a compulsive eater, the only way out of the pattern is to get inside yourself – to trust that there is a voice, a part of yourself, that can inform you about what you want emotionally and what you want from the food. This voice will tell you about a way to eat that will be uniquely yours. It will have specific aspects in common with other people's eating, but at its foundation it will depend on your own body's needs. Remember, nobody else can tell you what is right for you; nobody else can feel what is right for you. When you feel distraught after a binge, remind yourself to wait until you feel hungry before eating again and when that time comes listen hard, feed yourself and reflect on how that all felt. Feel the relief of being able to nourish yourself.

Sometimes it is impossible to intervene in a binge – you just can't tear yourself away from it, you are stuck on gorging and at the same time feeling upset by your actions. However, some relief may come from knowing that you can either break that particular binge or intervene in a future one. The very next time you experience hunger offers you the option of making a choice based on that hunger specifically.

★ If you are in the grip of a binge-hunger now, you may wish to turn to page 328 and see if the exercise on 'Breaking into a Binge' can be helpful.

How to Stop at Fullness

Knowing what fullness is and stopping at that point are often quite difficult for someone who has a long history of relying either on diets to guide her about quantities of food or on blow-up binges that have a final resting point. The satiation mechanism is a delicate one and, if it is abused continuously, may not be able to respond appropriately at first to the body cues signalling that you are full. Once food and eating become overloaded with emotional meaning, you may be out of touch with the body processes signalling satisfaction. The end of the cake may be where you stop habitually, rather than at the right amount for *your* body.

A good way to start to intervene is by pausing – that is, simply interrupting the sort of mindless overeating that seems to occur out of habit. If you can check in with yourself during every mealtime or snack, when you are halfway through whatever portion you have designated yourself, you can painlessly give yourself a rest and a chance to see whether indeed you wish to continue to eat. Often you will, especially if you aren't giving yourself portions that are consistently more than you are wanting. But you may discover that your body needs much less food than you ever imagined and that a full dinner is too much food if you are trying to be really in tune with your hunger.

You don't need to pause for a long time – perhaps just for a minute while you put down your knife and fork or spoon, or the chocolate bar, and reflect on whether you are beginning to feel satisfied and full. As long as this interruption is backed up by the right to continue to eat if you so wish, you may be able to get in tune with your body's wants.

Bear in mind that food takes an awfully long time to be digested. What you are searching for is a sensation in your stomach that, if you would but hear it, says: 'Enough.' Enough doesn't mean stuffed, it means walking away from the table contented, perhaps with room for 'a little something else'. It means sitting with *that feeling* for a while after finishing whatever you're eating, and checking

20 minutes or so later whether you might be wanting some more food or whether food per se has in fact slipped your mind.

Often just stopping requires a tremendous effort. You can be caught in the grip of an almost excruciating tension when you interrupt un-thought-out eating. When you make the decision to stop at a point when you feel full but still feel driven to go on eating, you may indeed experience a few agonising moments of internal struggle. There is an intensity in that confrontation with yourself. The reassuring thing that you have to look forward to after those few minutes and that emotional hiccup have passed is the deeply satisfying feeling that comes from seeing yourself exert control rather than feeling controlled by the food.

Learning to recognise fullness is no mysterious process. At first you will need to be alert to the cues that your body sends out, but in time, after you have built up a repertoire of satisfying eating experiences, you will be able to stop as automatically as you did before you ever had a compulsive eating problem. Trust your body to let you know when to start and when to stop.

It is much more difficult to stop eating if you aren't hungry for food when you start to eat. Your body will be incapable of giving you clues about satisfaction, only about bloatedness or discomfort, and you will find yourself frantically trying to limit yourself to 'just one more slice', 'just one half a portion', and having very little success. Nothing can be more unpredictable than the point at which a compulsive eater will stop eating if she isn't hungry when she starts.

Try to avoid this situation as much as possible by saying no to food when you aren't hungry. Don't be over-concerned about offending others. Switch your concern to where it belongs – your own food needs. Saying no to foods when you aren't hungry and not retreating from that decision can give you a tremendous sense of well-being. It is a mark of the fact that you are more consciously in harmony with your body. Every such experience builds up a memory of positive interaction with food. It shows you that *you can be appropriate* in this area *without depriving yourself.*

Some of the difficulty of breaking food addiction comes from not feeling confident that you can make lasting changes that will be more nurturing than eating compulsively. Since your goal is to develop a relaxed relationship to food, reminding yourself of how destabilising it is to eat when you aren't hungry can help you make the choice *not* to do so, *not* to reiterate and act out the deep fear that you will never get through your food problem.

Leaving Food Over

As you tune in precisely with your bodily needs you are bound to have to confront the situation of leaving food on your plate at your own home, a friend's or in a restaurant. This can be extremely difficult, even when you are utterly full and you know that finishing everything is going to leave you feeling uncomfortable and stuffed, or not especially enjoying the food. These facts speak to how many emotional issues are tied up in eating, for if we just ate for enjoyment and the satisfaction of our physical needs, this dilemma would not arise. We would not experience conflict over refusing food or leaving some on the plate, or even turning it away.

Think about why this is so difficult in your case. Try, in different settings, leaving food over when you feel physically satisfied: first at home, then at a freind's, then in a restaurant. If it feels almost impossible, you might ask your-self the following questions (be sure to give yourself time to answer them):

1. Were you allowed to leave food on your plate as a child? If not, do you remember wanting to?

2. Do you feel you are offending someone by leaving food on your plate? Who will be offended?

3. Do you feel that this food is your last chance to eat?

Notice your feeling at the beginning of the exercise at the point when you are satisfied and are trying to leave whatever is left over on your plate. Get into the tension, experience its intensity and try to dissect it.

Try and sort out whether you feel you are offending others or whether you would feel too deprived yourself if you left it over. If it's a case of offending others, are you sure you really would be? Is it *everyone* you might offend, including the waiter or waitress, or is it just specific people, such as your mother, mother-in-law or a friend? Are you sure they still expect you, a grown woman, to finish everything on your plate? Perhaps your mother's attitude has changed now that she's seen you survive so well. Perhaps it would be okay not to eat everything she prepared for you.

If you imagine that you would feel deprived, are you sure that in fact you would? If you've enjoyed the food, you could choose to have the same again another time. What exactly would you be missing out on if you didn't finish the food? What are you frightened of not getting? Perhaps you could get what you really want from the situ-ation or the other people without having to stuff down all the food.

Observe other people's eating habits. Look around you in cafes and restaurants and you will see how routinely people leave food on their plates. Nothing terrible happens to them. They survive till the next time they eat (and they do eat again!) and nobody else is really bothered one way or the other if there are leftovers.

If it feels more emotionally loaded than I have described (and I know this issue can be a very difficult one for many people), try and feel through what it is you think you are refusing in leaving food on your plate. Are you being rejecting? Do you feel disloyal? Are you expressing ingratitude? Are you wasteful? Are you spoiled? Try and pinpoint the feelings that are involved in this involuntary ingestion of food you really don't want, and see if the knowledge you gain doesn't help you break this pattern.

Risk Not Eating When You're Not Hungry

Related to being able to leave food on your plate is the ability to say no to food when you are not hungry for it. There are two different kinds of situations that can create a desire to eat when you are not hungry and, for those struggling to get over eating compulsively, special attentiveness and awareness is needed so that you can respond creatively. One type of situation occurs when you (or someone else) have been cooking: it's time to sit down for a meal and you have no appetite. The other situation is where we find ourselves going towards food – out of habit – when we aren't actually hungry.

In both these circumstances there will be times when you can intervene and not eat and other times when circumstances will make it very hard to do so. You may feel it necessary to explain to whomever has cooked for you that you just aren't hungry at that time, but that you are happy to sit with them while they eat. See if you can stay with the person or people and hold on to your decision. If you are about to eat out of habit, try putting off eating for a while. Not eating in these circumstances and observing your reactions will help you in the long run. Again, it will only be possible to do this without discomfort as long as you can be counted on to feed yourself exactly what you are wanting when you *are* hungry. Otherwise, passing up food will feel too much like deprivation.

Because these situations can crop up so frequently, I have designed an exercise especially to help you *not* eat when you aren't hungry. It's called 'Increasing Your Food Awareness', and it begins on page 330. You may use it as often as necessary to help you increase your food awareness, clarify your emotional state and gain insight into your habitual eating patterns.

Theory into Practice

Some women have told me that they reach a certain level of understanding about their relationship to food and body image but do not find it easy to integrate their intellectual perspectives in such a way that it allows them to eat with more satisfaction. They may go through short periods of non-compulsive eating and then be even more disheartened when they find that they still go towards food when they aren't physically hungry. The question is often asked: How do I translate the theory into everyday practice?

My answer is as follows: eating is something we have an urge to do several times a day, and we have urges to eat for all sorts of reasons. Some stem from emotional needs that can't be met by the food and others arise when our body needs nourishment. At each desire to eat, we have a chance to put theory into practice – this means that several times a day we have the possibility of intervening in a creative way in relation to food. But it requires commitment, concentration and effort. It doesn't just happen.

When you notice that you want to eat, you can put theory into practice by *slowing down* and considering what and why you are wanting. Are you hungry? If so, what would you really like to eat? Is it available? How could you make it available? How much do you want? How is it tasting? Does it hit the spot? Stop and see whether it is as satisfying as you had anticipated. If not, think again. Perhaps you aren't really hungry. Perhaps the environment isn't quite right. *Check your reactions, slow down and give yourself the space to intervene.*

If you aren't hungry, what do you want? Stop and let yourself notice for a few minutes before you stuff down the response. Remember, this is a chance for you to understand something about yourself. *Don't expect this understanding to come without your attention.* Use the exercises on 'Increasing Your Food Awareness' and on 'Breaking into a Binge' (pages 330 and 328, respectively).

Take a breather from your routine of feeling that *it* isn't working. See if you can remind yourself that you aren't physically hungry, and that therefore you might be able to go without food on this occasion. That doesn't mean you are depriving yourself. You are intervening in a new way, gradually putting theory into practice.

The experience will be stored in your memory and, if it is pleasant, you will be able to draw on it in a reassuring way in the future. If it is unpleasant you will need to go a step further and investigate what need you are asking the food to fill. What are you really hungry for? What kind of nourishment do you crave?

If you focus on this next level of questioning, you will develop new resources to use as part of the process of change. Be persistent in your attempts if you feel the understanding is there but the doing is terribly far away. It will come eventually.

But don't rush to make an insight happen. You may be forcing things too fast. Your fat and eating behaviour are there for good reasons. They took years to cultivate. You may need time to assimilate new concepts and new possibilities. Don't berate yourself. Try to accept where you are right now. Above all, avoid the tendency to 'victimise yourself' with 'it doesn't work' or 'it doesn't do it for me'. Appreciate that you are involved in a struggle and that you need to find a balance within it.

This new approach may require a good deal of energy and this in itself may be irritating, for part of the attraction of this method is that it frees you of the obsessiveness associated with food and body image. This may present you with a short-term dilemma, but it will be in the service of your having a new and ultimately more satisfactory and relaxed relationship to food. Remember, you are working towards enjoying food and away from being so scared of it that you have to control or block yourself every time you eat.

CHAPTER FOUR

Food and Emotional Hungers

Individual Commitment

When you decide to work purposefully on your compulsive eating problem, by yourself or in a group, you will need to make a commitment to yourself that is flexible enough to encompass the various moods, disappointments, and ups and downs you will go through during the process. You may feel exhilarated on first thinking about food, fatness and thinness in this new way. You will perhaps have an initial surge of energy and feel as though you are ready to conquer the problem once and for all. Experiences of non-compulsive eating will encourage this enthusiasm, so it may come as quite a letdown to discover that the problem does not disappear overnight or work itself out as easily as you may have hoped. You may feel discouraged just as you have in the past when another diet didn't work. You may often feel bored.

It is important to pay attention to this attitude and try to take a different stance towards it by making a different type of commitment to yourself. *It* won't work. *It* isn't an it. *It* isn't magic. *It* isn't even a dramatic solution. What you have is a compulsive eating problem.

You can tackle your problem by engaging with it actively, by taking responsibility for yourself, your food struggles, your reactions to your body and your eating behaviour. The problem rarely disappears on its own. Nobody else can solve it for you. If you are in a group with a leader, the leader cannot do it for you. *You have to do it yourself.* You can get help, assistance and support, but that is crucially different from hoping that others will take the responsibility for you.

You will need to do a certain kind of emotional work. This can be wide-ranging, including promising yourself to observe and identify the particular issues that are especially hard for you; weathering the rough patches when it feels as though nothing is changing; asking for things you think might be helpful to you from the people around you; reminding yourself that there are bound to be times when you take three steps forwards and two steps back; being generous to yourself if you have a particular difficulty, without feeling as though you are being overindulgent or not engaging it; and so on.

Respect your own pace. Remember that you are seeking a fundamental change. Certain feelings or ideas that you hold as precious may shift, and that may be disconcerting, but allow yourself space to explore and work them through. At all costs, *don't expect to dispense with the problem in an inspired insight.* It might happen that way, but it most probably won't.

Be generous. You will be learning many important things about yourself during this process. One is that you *can* tolerate working things through. In your approach to this problem you don't have to reiterate the drama of success and failure, bingeing and dieting. You needn't be evangelical, just struggle to stay focused on your own issues.

Defining Oneself

Many women experience a fear of being defined, of drawing boundaries round themselves that then determine where they end and the rest of the world begins. We have grown up with the idea that our role is to be supportive, to help and give to others unselfishly. This requires that we ignore, suppress or sacrifice our own feelings and needs in the interests of those around us, particularly our families. Compulsive eating can often be a way of 'blurring the edges' of our personalities, and being fat is often linked to feeling 'big enough' to enclose and obliterate our own needs while still having extra capacity for meeting other people's emotional demands.

Behind these feelings of concern for others may lie a sense of desperation that our own needs are bound to be overlooked and would be impossible to meet in any case. For many women both the actual and the imagined responsibilities we take on for others cut us off from our own deeply felt needs. At the same time, they can prevent us from taking a certain kind of responsibility for *ourselves*.

This dilemma needs to be grappled with, for it can be tremendously fulfilling to follow through a commitment to be responsible for ourselves in the area of food. Redrawing the boundaries is a step towards empowering ourselves. It fills us up in a nourishing way.

Being Opened Up to New Emotions

When you decide to look into your problems around eating and body image, you will be opening yourself up to a different relationship to your emotional life. You will be exploring issues that you may have wanted to avoid –

indeed, the very point of the compulsive eating may have been to mask the issues or obscure the basis of any particular distress. For example, you may discover that you often find yourself eating compulsively when you are faced with a difficult decision – one that involves conflict. On your own or in a group you will be working towards understanding why decision-making and coping with conflict are so difficult for you.

Joan was the only daughter in a family of five sons. Her brothers had each gone to college, pursued the careers they wanted and married. She was the only unmarried child and had taken upon herself the responsibility for looking after her father when he was widowed. She spent much of her twenties making her life decisions based on his needs. As she approached her thirtieth birthday, she felt a tremendous urge to give up her well-paid job in advertising – for which she had just won an award – to take up a two-year course in creative writing at Iowa, 600 miles [966km] away from where she and her family lived. She felt very guilty and confused about whether she should be applying for the course, given her responsibility for her father; at the same time she felt in her heart of hearts it was the right thing for her. Her friends talked with her about her dilemma but it did not alleviate the guilt thinking about herself produced. She decided to let 'fate' decide for her. She would apply for a scholarship. If she got it, she would then face the issue of whether or not to go, how to leave her job and what to do about her father.

Throughout this hiatus period, she was eating compulsively. She was scared to face decisions that might bring change and upset. She wanted to suppress all the disagreeable feelings that making a new decision stirred up in her. It turned out that her compulsive eating had the function of drawing

226

her attention away from what she felt uneasy about – namely, facing making a decision – and diverted her attention instead into a familiar and somewhat more comfortable focus – food, fat and thinness. Joan brought up her eating problem in a compulsive eating group and was surprised to discover that she actually had a problem with making a decision when it involved conflicting needs. She understood why she was eating in an 'unthinking' way and her eating problem didn't feel so hopeless or incurable. She resolved to try and struggle with her newly discovered problem.

In order to have a new way to deal with this problem, you may find it helpful to remind yourself that you are embarked on an exploration. You will be engaging with aspects of yourself in a way that is new to you. It will inevitably stir up complicated feelings – many of them painful. It will help enormously if you can adopt an attitude of self-acceptance. Changing a deeply entrenched way of relating to yourself requires tenderness and compassion. You have been eating compulsively for substantial reasons. It won't just go away – you need to uncover its basis and then work towards finding a new solution.

Recognising a difficulty such as that in Joan's case is in itself an important step towards breaking the pattern, for it is often the case that much of our energy is bound up in *masking* the difficulty. There may be shame, confusion, rage and upset associated with why decision-making involving conflict is such a problem. Once the allied feelings have a place to be expressed directly, they can lessen and give precedence to the critical issue that is there to be worked through. Realising that you feel awful about being able to make a decision and that you often cope by eating compulsively begins to break the chain. The chain works as follows:

A difficult emotion occurs. This leads to some reaction of denial or repression that you come to feel bad about. In an attempt to stave off both the original difficult feeling and the associated feelings it throws up, you eat compulsively. This then leads to feelings of low self-esteem, anger, despair and so on about the compulsive eating. The original feeling that started the chain is displaced and seemingly uncontactable. You feel pain and alienation.

This confrontation with self is a critical feature of each person's work on compulsive eating. It is what will enable a separation to occur between difficult feelings and the usual response of eating. It won't be necessary to resolve the problem – in this case, the difficulty of making decisions that involve conflict – in order to stop eating compulsively, but it is crucial that the problem not be obscured and distorted in the process. If you are in a group, the group can help you hold and contain the problem, rather than hide it away.

I mention this particular example because it has come up so often. Many women experience tremendous difficulty facing conflict, whether it is in their job, community or relationships. It is part of our psychological development that we may experience conflict as so unbearable that actually living within the conflict seems an impossible option. Many women have discussed how they respond to this difficulty in two ways – either by not feeling able to be active at all in relation to an issue of conflict and being wracked by feelings of immobility; or by attempting to deny the conflict they feel inside by making a decision that does not feel right either. They have to deny the complexities of their reactions with a resolute stance because they experience the internal conflict as too painful. In other words, they draw a black-and-white picture and obscure the grey.

The activity of compulsive eating serves to stuff down and temporarily assuage difficult feelings. Now you will be working towards short-circuiting this pattern by looking behind the behaviour to see what feelings are hiding. This process will require patience and sensitivity, for each person has a different pace and it is important to pay attention to your own emotional rhythm and allow it to emerge.

How to Sit with Emotional Issues

One of the most difficult issues each woman with a compulsive eating problem may have to face in order to change the way she eats lies in how she relates to her emotional life. It may seem surprising to the compulsive eater that this is a problem at all, as she may experience herself as being emotionally expressive and open. But often the compulsive eating activity itself is a response to and a substitute for all sorts of emotions. Compulsive eating may be hiding a painful store of emotions that a woman finds hard to accept in herself.

It may be that the compulsive eating exists to mask these emotions, that it acts as a stopper and stuffs feelings down. Or it may be that uncomfortable feelings become transformed in the course of compulsive eating so that whatever unpleasant emotions are experienced take the form of berating yourself for having overeaten.

In any work on emotions that you do, either on your own or in a group, it will be important to concentrate on emotional issues in a different way. Throughout our lives we receive specific injunctions about having or expressing particular feelings. For example, many women grow up with a taboo against showing anger. The taboo doesn't, however, successfully do away with angry feelings. Instead, such feelings become transported into more culturally acceptable forms such as women feeling depressed, or engaging in 'nagging', or withdrawing, and so on. When we delve into some of the symbolic meanings of fat for individual women, we discover that it is frequently a way of showing anger.* The anger cannot be expressed directly and the woman unconsciously shows it through her body – she attempts to have the fat speak for her. At the same time she may stuff food down in a race to prevent the angry feelings from bursting out. If she weren't to eat compulsively when she experienced anger, she might feel overwhelmed with the unfamiliar feelings – that they will not stop, that they will propel her like the motor force behind a binge. Therefore an essential part of working through compulsive eating problems involves building a new way of relating to emotional issues.

Distortion of painful emotions most often stems from the following three circumstances in our backgrounds:

1. We may have received injunctions against showing particular emotions.

2. We may have been discouraged from engaging in certain activities, e.g., initiating ones.

3. We may have felt emotionally rejected or misunderstood.

---

* For further discussion of anger and fat, you may want to refer to *Fat Is a Feminist Issue*, pp. 38–46.

Throughout the time we are growing up we pick up strong signals about what is acceptable. In order to fit in we eventually hide away the feelings that others find unacceptable. But this can lead to an incredible confusion and discomfort about such feelings, so that when they are touched they can be extremely raw and painful. This is often the process behind compulsive eating.

Linda has throughout her life received messages that her sad feelings aren't really to be shown to others. She walks around unaware of the fact that she, like everyone else, is subject to sad feelings. She knows she likes to go to a film and have a good cry over some sentimental plot, but in her everyday life she is cut off from her feelings of sadness.

However, Linda does eat compulsively, and when she gave herself some breathing space to explore the emotional issues behind several of her compulsive eating episodes, she noticed (and indeed felt somewhat overwhelmed by) feelings of sadness. Preceding each compulsive-eating experience were sad things that touched her momentarily. Not knowing how to cope with these feelings, she converted them into eating compulsively and then felt awful about that. She moved rapidly away from one feeling into another more familiar one. She used the food as the mechanism, although logically the food couldn't possibly know what feeling it was supposed to take away. It couldn't know that its job was to prevent Linda from feeling sad.

The more she was able to break into her pattern of overeating and bingeing, the more space Linda was able to give herself to find out about her sad feelings. As she experienced them more they became less overwhelming. *They were experienced and then they passed.*

Food Cannot Banish Feelings

Linda discovered that in allowing herself to feel the sadness, she was filled up from the inside with something very real. She didn't feel hungry for food to fill a hole or a yearning that could never be satisfied. And this is perhaps the central point to grapple with in relationship to foods and moods: *food is incapable of making feelings go away; it cannot make things better, it cannot fill up whatever emptiness there is inside.*

All the involvement with food can do is to mask the processes of your inner life. At the end of each compulsive eating experience you are still faced with whatever emotional turmoil existed to propel you into the eating. Feelings don't live in food. Food can provide *temporary* relief, and *that's all*. Compulsive eaters suffer because, instead of digesting an emotional experience and thereby integrating it, they interrupt the experience with eating and are left with undigested feelings.

Making Space for Feelings

Linda used the information she gained to try to intercept a binge while it was happening. In order to do this she gave herself several options. First she decided to stop eating. She then tried to locate anything that might have led her to feel sad. Sometimes she was able to contact those feelings and sometimes she wasn't.

On those occasions when she was able to pinpoint an incident that brought up sad feelings in her, she then had a further choice. She could either give herself some space to experience the feelings and to work out what pained her, or she could decide to ignore the feelings.

Ignoring them did not mean resuming eating compulsively. It meant identifying the feeling that was leading her to eat. This kind of intervention allowed a shift in the way she ate. She might find herself eating compulsively, but she had a choice whether to continue.

Why One Binges

Eating compulsively and then obsessing about it has a function. It removes you from the immediate confrontation with whatever is causing you so much pain. Although the obsession cannot solve the problem but only postpones an honest look at what is going on, it can provide relief in a short-term way by removing you from the source of the pain. A binge is predictable. You are familiar with the course it takes. It leads you through a pattern of emotional responses that you have come to know, and it allows you to temporarily absent yourself from what is going on in your environment that is causing the distress. Difficult emotions can be postponed and transformed into a form that is knowable — a binge. There are few surprises in a binge, as they almost always follow the same pattern for each individual (although the pattern varies from individual to individual).

If you are anguished about not having a close personal relationship, you might find yourself having a binge. In the course of overeating, you will make the food and your fat the reason why you aren't having the kind of intimate relationship you long for. As the binge continues the food provides a bit of comfort while your mind proceeds along the following lines: if I weren't bingeing, if I weren't fat, I could be in a relationship. As it is, I'm not and I feel bad about it, but it is in my power to change the circumstances if I were just to stop eating.

Now of course this reasoning has both some truth to

it and some falseness. We cannot control very much outside of ourselves. We can't as individuals make the world turn out the way we want it to. But this is a humbling idea that most of us, because of the way we have been raised, find hard to accept. We want to be able to have a decisive impact – we want to be able to make things happen. Giving yourself a reason that you seemingly have control over is an attempt to justify things to yourself internally.

The tragedy lies in the fact that the obsession can take up the energy that you might use to affect things in so far as you *are* able. Obviously all of the reasons do not lie in your hands as to whether or not you have a close relationship, but some of them do. Looking at what you can actually do to affect things means living with a kind of uncertainty and risk-taking. Choosing overeating and obsessing as an option can feel safer.

The problem is that this doesn't address the anguish that we carry around inside. It substitutes a self-contained obsession for an engagement with the problem. Moreover, no particular food can respond precisely enough. It cannot meet the feelings appropriately. It doesn't know what to give you. The food doesn't know whether to quash anger or hurt, disappointment, sadness, conflict, fear, insecurity, guilt or whatever. A person who is engaged in compulsive eating is actually giving the food the power that they themselves own to suppress uncomfortable emotion. The Mars bar does not have written on it: this will make Sally feel less angry; this will make Jane feel less guilty; this will make Sandra feel less chaotic.

★ Emotions such as these, that trigger the compulsive eating, *are* ultimately knowable. At first they may seem mysterious, perhaps even ridiculous, but as you devote more energy to exploring them you will come up with emotional explanations for your compulsive eating that make sense in your guts. The exercises on 'Exploring Your Feelings' and on 'Expressing Your Feelings', which you will find on page 335, and on page 333, will help you explore, acknowledge and express your uncomfortable feelings. Use them as often as you wish.

If you feel incapable of coping with such emotional turmoil, remember this simple point: you are already cutting off the feeling. The food isn't doing it for you. Therefore you don't need the food to do it. The food is just a conveyor belt, from you to you, that allows you to cut off the feeling. You could eliminate the taking in of the food without eliminating its purpose.

If you don't feel at a particular moment that you can cope with a distressing feeling, it is all right not to. Ask the Mars bar what kind of feeling you were wanting it to suppress. Inquire of it what kind of feeling you were wanting it to give you. Then see if you can reach that state without it. If you are trying to break through your food obsession, you may not feel comfortable being flooded by so many emotions. You can certainly control the flow. Sometimes try to experience the feelings directly, at other times acknowledge that they are there but do not allow yourself to be swamped by them.

Feelings Are there to be Experienced – Not Solved

Many women say that once they discover they are eating compulsively for emotional reasons they then don't know what to do about the emotions they are uncovering. But there isn't anything to *do* about emotions, except to recognise them. They aren't objects or monsters – they are part of you, even the dreadfully painful ones. But they can feel *not* part of you if they have been hidden away and denied for years. They can feel unmanageable and disruptive. In fact you have been carrying them around in a distorted form and thus they have rarely had a chance to come to the surface, be experienced and find their own level.

If, for example, you discover that you eat compulsively to cover terrible hurts that you don't want to look at, it may come as something of a relief to experience the hurts rather than being bound up in suppressing them. They are past hurts that you unconsciously pushed aside because you didn't have the resources to deal with them when they occurred. But you aren't in the same kind of vulnerable position now that you were in when you were very young. You don't need to rely on others in exactly the same way that you once did. If you allow the feelings to come to the surface and perhaps find yourself tearful, you are not likely to be scolded for being silly. You may not feel sufficiently understood if you try to explain what you are experiencing to someone else, but you will not be humiliated in the same way that you were when the original hurt occurred.

We can't help but project on to our present the emotional melodies of our past, but it is important to remember that we will not necessarily be met with the same kinds of responses. Our vulnerable areas may not upset those we are close to now in the same way they affected those we were close to when we were little. If you tell a friend you are miserable, she may be more likely to listen or perhaps try to cheer you up than were your parents, who felt more identified with you and subsequently were often less able to hear your pain.

Parents and children are often entwined with one another in such a way that the parent can feel guilty or upset on the child's behalf rather than giving her the space to live through her own upset. Friends are not merged in the same way. They can feel an empathy that does not necessarily bring up feelings that either it is their fault or they must do something to make you feel better immediately.

Feelings aren't there to be solved, but to be experienced. As you can allow yourself to have your feelings, they will become less frightening. You will be developing confidence that you can have more direct contact with your inner life and not have to cut it off by obsessing about other things or by eating compulsively.

CHAPTER FIVE

Body Image

How to Improve Your Self-Image

In our work on compulsive eating we take as a starting point the assumption that most women feel uncomfortable with and in their bodies, whatever their size and weight. Women feel insecure and frequently reach out to body transformation as a cure-all for other issues. The perpetual enticements of the 'slim body' merchants mean that tremendous strength must be exercised in order to look afresh at our bodies and try to see them for what they are.

If they are fat, that may well be a statement of self-dislike, a desire to be distinguished from the crowd, a test, a rebellion. It is not just one thing and it isn't the same for everyone. It may be that feeling or being fat so upsets us that we hate our bodies and feel despair about taking care of them.

Finding out for yourself what your 'fat' is expressing – need? anger? loneliness? emotional hunger? protection? substance? – allows a new relationship to your body. As you can understand its language you can get a better sense of it. You may be able to notice what you really look like

238

rather than living in a condemned cell flooded with seemingly relentless negative self-judgments.

★ The 'Fat/Thin' exercise on pages 337–340 is designed to elicit the many feelings and associations we attach to body size. Don't be surprised if you find contradictory or negative associations emerging. You may discover that fatness is not only felt as negative, but also has positive connotations. You may contact feelings about the 'thin' you that are unpleasant, as well as those that are pleasant. It is important that these ideas – which you hold preconsciously and are not generally aware of – are brought out into the open so that you can explore them and grapple with their meanings.

In *Fat Is a Feminist Issue* I discussed the importance of familiarising yourself with the conflicts and symbolic meanings that are part and parcel of body-image states. The more you get to know about who you are and what you are asking the various body states to convey for you, the quicker you will be able to work through the barriers that prevent you from being your ideal size.

So many times when a woman looks at herself, it is as though a tape full of self-denigration is turned on. She feels wrong. Her image in the mirror does not reflect what she would like. She doesn't look like Naomi Campbell, Kate Winslet, Jennifer Lopez and so on. Look again.

Try to open your eyes wide enough to see yourself, who *you* are. Imagine being more *you* than you are, rather than more somebody else. What would that mean? How would you look? How would you hold your body if you didn't disapprove of it? How would you walk? How might you sit? How would you stand? How might you dress? What would being comfortable in your body *feel* like? See if you can imagine it. Don't zoom to pictures of past or instant thinness. They could only have felt precarious in their own way.

Concentrate on yourself. What do you see? Look from the outside in and then try to feel your body from the inside out. Think of the functions of your different body parts. Are hands merely for decoration or are they moving, active parts of us? Are legs for adornment or do they serve important other functions? Try and see the wealth of activities that your body performs and is capable of; try and appreciate its physicality and adeptness.

Now think through how often you judge your body, censor yourself for what you put in it, thus creating a spiralling self-loathing. What pose do you slump into when you have these thoughts? Look at yourself and allow yourself the possibility of enjoying your body, of learning to appreciate it rather than castigating yourself. Be as *you* in your body as you can and try to project that feeling as you go about your daily life.

This is often difficult to do. However, it can be extremely useful for helping you move on from self-loathing to a more accepting attitude towards yourself. It is almost impossible to get rid of something you cannot bear to look at in the first place. You can't lose something that doesn't belong to you. Thus until you accept the way you look now, you won't be able to change.

★ To work on this aspect of body image, turn to the 'Mirror Work' exercise on pages 341–343. Put a chair in front of a full-length mirror, and make sure you won't be disturbed for 20 minutes or so.

First Thing in the Morning

Often our dreadful feelings about our bodies come over us almost from the moment we wake up. Before we have had a chance to approach the day, we are disabled by self-loathing. To try to break into this painful pattern, imagine as you are waking up that you have a body worthy of respect and appreciation. For just a moment give yourself a breather from the judgments. Lie back in bed and look down at your toes, your feet and your ankles, gradually working your way up as far as you can see, and then feel your head perched on your shoulders. Now instruct yourself to imagine that you are contented with your body. Lie back, close your eyes and think about your activities over the next half hour. Plan what you will do: shower? dress? breakfast? Bear in mind your newfound pleasure in your body.

Now get up and involve yourself in these selected activities, all the while holding on to the idea that you like your body. Soap it with affection, dress it with care, feed it with just what it is wanting. See what a difference having a positive self-image makes. Stay with these good feelings for as long as you can during the day. Make a plan to remind yourself every hour of your experiment. It is very easy to fall back into a sort of mindless self-disapproval, but for one day try and take a different view towards yourself.

Experiencing yourself in new ways will provide you with a break in your routine of self-judging. At first, experiments like this may feel somewhat contrived and artificial, but their function is to provide stepping stones to a more harmonious self-image. You are bound to stumble on important insights that you can use as you make the journey towards greater self-acceptance. As with all that I suggest in this book, approach yourself with compassion and tenderness in order to build your self-esteem.

Fear of Being Your Ideal Size

One of the problems that can come up when you increase your awareness about food is the need to recognise the conflict you feel about being your fantasised ideal size. I have noticed during the course of therapy, as some women begin to eat in a more truly nourishing way, that, although they are initially delighted at their capacity to eat in this new way, they suddenly find themselves becoming preoccupied with how they look and their body size, and they can feel as desperate as ever about wanting to lose weight.

When we explore what is going on more deeply, we often discover that the worry about size is acting as a sort of bludgeon – almost as though it is preventing the new changes that are occurring from being consolidated. It's like a needle of insecurity that serves to undermine the good feelings that were building up from the positive eating experiences. It is terribly distressing to the woman involved but it can be an important message to her too, alerting her to look into aspects of her relationship to food, fatness and thinness with which she hasn't yet come to grips. Jessica came to therapy when she was 22 years old, having felt herself to be out of control around food and full of upset about her body size since puberty. When I met her she wanted to learn how to eat differently and to reach a size that she felt more truly expressed who she was. This was a size she had dieted to many times before, lived at for a week or two and then retreated from.

After several months of therapy she was having continuous experiences of feeling comfortable around food. Released from dieting and deprivation, she rarely binged and found that, as she was tasting food rather than shovelling it in, she was much more selective about what appealed to her. Her eating became a source of pleasure and a time to give herself a particularly nice kind of attention.

However, Jessica found that she was eating just that bit more than she really wanted on every occasion when she sat down to a meal. She had lost the food obsession per se but was caught in a tug of war trying to reach her goal size and continually retreating from it. As the pattern persisted it became obvious that the focus of the psychological work she needed to do should be on the meaning of her desire to reach her ideal size and the fact of her clinging on to a larger one. The actual weight difference in her case was not very marked (10–15lb [4.5–6.8kg]), but the fear associated with being her ideal size served to make her feel uncomfortable and rejecting of who she was on a daily basis.

She then concentrated on what thinness and non-thinness meant to her. She reviewed in detail her previous experiences of changes in body size. She discovered in herself feelings of precariousness and frailty when she felt herself to be slim. She felt diminished and scared that she would have achieved something she had to keep up. She realised that her current size somehow gave her the leeway to be more herself – she didn't always feel on top of things, she felt comfortable with a certain fuzziness around the edges, she felt she was somewhat scatty and liked that about herself. She felt that her ideal size presented her as more angular and purposeful than she felt herself to be. She had enormous difficulty detaching these emotional issues from the body states she had assigned to them and would frequently interpret situations in such a way that body image became an explanation and a vehicle for emotional expression.

At that time Jessica became ill with pneumonia and her

dilemma about body size was dramatically back on her agenda. As part of her illness she lost weight and became frail, weak and vulnerable. The very feelings that she had feared emerged in the illness, but with a result that perhaps she would not have anticipated. Recovering from the pneumonia and getting her strength back showed her that she could be slim and survive. She did not undergo a personality change through being physically weak or because she lost weight. She was every bit herself and just as reassuringly scatty.

Jessica reached her slim state by a rather unfortunate route, but once having reached it she demystified it for herself. It is my belief that with or without the pneumonia she would have in time risked being at her idealised size to find out what it actually held for her. She could then have worked through which size felt more comfortable when all was said and done.

If your experience of teetering between two body images is similar, you might try following the steps that Jessica took and use her experience to learn and experiment with yourself. Obviously you do not need to become ill in order to stabilise – even if just for the course of the experiment – at a lower weight.

★ Do the exercise on 'Fat/Thin' (pages 337–340) and try to specify what various body images mean to you.

1. Try to detach the body states from the emotional issues.

2. Explore the emotional issues in their own right.

3. Experiment with the different sizes. Do they actually conform to what you imagined?

If slimness is what you desperately feel you want, then eat with close attention, allow yourself to reach that size and see how it feels. If you don't like it, try and pinpoint why. If it feels not like you and not like a you that you will get accustomed to, you can always allow a truer size for you to emerge. Just because you experiment with slimness doesn't mean you have to stay in it if it doesn't feel good. Doing the 'Fat/Thin' exercise on a regular basis is extremely useful. You will discover that slimness means different things to you from the vantage points of different actual body weights. Remember, slimness is not a panacea, it was just sold to you as such, and once having succeeded in becoming slim you may feel able to reject it with strength rather than out of feelings of inadequacy.

Living in the Here and Now

Many women have faced the problem of feeling impatience that their body is not changing as fast as they would like it to. They resent that this method involves a process instead of producing instant change. While the slowness of this method does have significant advantages in that it allows you to explore the feelings that accompany different body sizes, the way down or the ups and downs in size that can occur can be frustrating. As comfort I can only say that perseverance does pay off. Experiencing different body sizes and getting used to them will be useful in the long run. The body size you decide to stabilise at will have more certainty in it and you will have developed confidence and self-acceptance in the process.

Each body size has something to teach you and has a validity of its own. Self-acceptance, a key goal, can be achieved if you can give yourself the permission to live in the here and now at whatever size you are. Just because you desire to change your body size should not preclude you from treating yourself well whatever your current size. Living in the present and inside your body means ceasing to torture yourself, making the effort to be as imaginative with your clothes as you can be and not excluding yourself from activities because you are 'too big'.

Largeness should not exclude you from loving, eating, dancing, swimming, running or involving yourself in the millions of activities you have put on the back burner until the slim you arrives. Life doesn't start with slimness or stop at anything larger. Life is for living with as few personal impediments as possible.

Goodness knows we are channelled into one route or another in hundreds of different ways because of the rules of the society we grew up and live in. The external constrictions can get under our skins in extremely complicated ways, and we may choose to use our energy to try to change the conditions of our lives that oppress us. But a part of that struggle involves being able to maximise the power we have in shaping aspects of our lives at a very personal level.

For a woman to take pride in her body for herself, rather than as an instrument or as an object, is a radical act. For women to proclaim that comfort and pride at whatever size they may be creates a chink in the armour of a patriarchal order. Taking this stance is difficult and hard to do on our own. But as more women reject the stereotype of driven slimness and exhibit a pleasure in women's physical variety, individual women can draw on that collective strength to build acceptance and confidence.

Self-hatred focused on body image is both painful and in the end dysfunctional. It rarely motivates anyone to change permanently, to lose weight and feel good. If your particular wish is to become smaller, start off with where you are now. Give yourself a bit of a breather. Direct the energy that is harnessed in self-loathing in a new direction. Try accepting who you are at this very moment, not who you will be ten, twenty, thirty, forty or fifty pounds from now. Life does not have to be postponed until the day slimness arrives. It can be engaged with actively right now, whatever size you are.

If you can follow this prescription, the odds of your reaching the right size for you and staying there are measurably increased. If you are living for now every day and not postponing or restricting activities to when you plan to be slim, you will feel less precarious when your thin self emerges. It won't be a big unknown, a body size all tangled up with complex emotions. It will just be a new body size that you've been preparing for and that is organically you.

★ Beyond feeling too large or too fat in general, almost every woman has a part of her body that she is prone to focus on, seeing it as too fat or otherwise unacceptable in one way or another. If you do the exercise on page 344, entitled 'Part of the Body', you may gain some insight into the various emotional issues that you've invested in a particular body part. You may be able to determine any distortions you have and thus feel some relief. If there are several parts of your body that especially bother you – let's say you've deemed your thighs and your breasts unacceptable – do the exercise twice, focusing first on one part and then on the other.

Pregnancy and a New Infant

For women who are struggling to find a comfortable relationship with their bodies, pregnancy can be a time of continuing shifts in how they relate to themselves. Some women enter pregnancy with their food problems mostly worked through but with twinges about how their new state might affect their eating and body image. Others become pregnant before their compulsive eating problem is resolved and have to cope with complicated feelings of lack and loss of control of their bodies.

Many women have observed how being pregnant forced them to focus on their bodies in new and exciting ways. The changes that each trimester brought, the daily changes and new physical sensations and emotional states coupled with the desire to provide the healthiest possible environment for the baby growing inside of them, produced a heightened awareness of what they were eating and how they were holding their bodies.

Many women have reported that, after the initial confusion during the first three months as to what their food needs were, they settled into a pattern of feeding themselves and caring for themselves that felt easy and good. Their bodies were changing beyond their control but in reliably predictable ways. They were feeling good within themselves and were the recipients of much attention, concern and approval from others for being in the pregnant state. Having a tummy was for the first time legitimate and praised. People used different words to describe these body changes than those associated with fatness. They effortlessly found ways to compliment the new growth, thus giving the lie to the 'fact' that only slimness can be beautiful. So for many women the experience of pregnancy brought unexpected side benefits.

The arrival of the new infant, and the profound changes this event ushered in, affected women whom I've worked with in different ways. For some, the experience of mothering in a supportive environment, their enchantment with the child and their pleasure in the intimacy shared in the feeding relationship allowed the women to enjoy the postpartum changes in their bodies and to settle at a size that felt comfortable and right. The importance of responding appropriately to the new infant's food needs spilled over into a consciousness of their own food requirements.

For others, the loss of the foetus inside of them and the reality of what it meant to be with a baby, with all the attention now riveted on the new arrival, brought up in them feelings of loss of identity, confusion about boundaries and of being somehow cast aside. They experienced others' concern for them mingled with a focus on when they 'would get their bodies back'. The sheer exhaustion of being up all night with a newborn, providing so much nurturance and having little sense of separation, led them to eat when not hungry in an attempt to give something to themselves. In moments of frustration, when perhaps what they needed was a rant or a hug, food was accessible and comforting.

Still other women found the shift from breast- or bottle-feeding to spoon-feeding difficult. In bottle- or breast-feeding they had found that their babies could send out cues that they were physically satisfied, and the infants could perhaps rest at the breast, not requiring food but enjoying the comfort. Spoon-feeding removed the give and take somewhat and provided for less discreet discerning on the mother's part. Feeding times became more tense and mothers found themselves agitated over whether the baby was getting enough food, only to find they were no longer being as self-discriminating about their *own* food as they desired. If pre-pregnancy clothes did not fit, some women found it hard to take the time or the money to find comfortable alternatives. They became involved in a process of ignoring their own needs and by so doing effectively disowning their bodies. In those instances where regular sexual relations for one reason or another had not resumed after the arrival of the baby, the feelings of being distanced from their bodies were reinforced.

As these different dynamics – and of course, as people are individuals there are as many variations on them as there are mothers – were recognised, the women felt strengthened in their attempts to reintroduce themselves to their bodies. One working woman was pleased to return to her job and the identity and purpose it gave her. She felt that professionally people were relating to her almost as they had before. People valued her for her accomplishments, not only in terms of her mothering qualities. She appreciated the division between her home life and her work life, and this separation helped her become more defining again in regard to her body.

As babies become toddlers and begin to show more independence, that too can bring up changes in how a woman expresses her body image. If her child's passage through early childhood evokes in the mother echoes of her own early life, she may find herself over-identifying with the child, psychologically merged so to speak, and expressing this through a body change that indicates her lack of boundaries and self-definition.

The cyclical nature of the mother-daughter relationship, through which, in turn, the girl grows up to be a woman like her mother, can trigger off in the mother extraordinarily complex feelings. Women have talked about how their adolescent daughters' developing sexuality stirred up feelings in them they found hard to handle, and how in some cases they almost abdicated their own sexuality to become the protectors of their daughters. Previously modish women have been startled to find themselves 'spreading' and dressing in a matronly fashion, or conversely competing quite unconsciously with their daughters and losing a sense of their own age, shape and appropriate body image. This is not to alarm those embarked on motherhood but to alert the readers to the kinds of issues I have come across and the vulnerability that can create difficulties for women at different stages of their lives in relation to body image.

Only 20 years ago, mothers of teenagers looked like 'mothers', middle-aged and somewhat straitlaced. A flashy mother was exceptional and attracted comment. But with today's stress on 'youthful' images, which means slimness and fashion consciousness for all, women's bodies do not necessarily go into hiding after the age of 40, and the old rules now conflict with expectations. Motherhood can thus be an extremely confusing time for women, and this can be expressed through their self-image.

CHAPTER SIX

Exploring Your Problem

Helping Yourself

Self-help is a challenge. It is uncharted territory for everyone, and whatever happens for you as an individual (or as part of a group) will be unique. Many people are awed by the idea of self-help therapy. They may worry that, without therapy skills or a leader, they will do the wrong thing. People often feel hesitant about knowing how to help themselves or each other and may feel unsure about any interventions they might make. These concerns are understandable because obviously it feels hard to ask yourself, or someone else, the very questions you might have been running away from about your relationship to food, fatness and thinness.

However, this is also precisely the strength of the method, whether you are trying to sort through your compulsive eating on your own, as a pair or in a small group. For the questions you are afraid to ask may also be the ones that are most helpful. Once having given yourself permission to focus in on this area in a new way, you are already on the road to engaging with those very questions.

Choose a pace that feels right for you. In setting aside

time to look at the issues involved in your compulsive eating, the possibility opens up that understanding, thinking, feeling and being compassionate towards yourself can give you more than dieting and deprivation. So often for compulsive eaters the first and virtually automatic response to a feeling or an event is to eat. Here we are clearing space for a special time to explore those impulses and to find new ways of coping with them.

Before working on the psychological level, many practical issues must be sorted out. If you are thinking of starting or joining a group, please refer to Chapter 7, 'Organising a Compulsive Eating Group', before plunging in here. In *Fat Is a Feminist Issue* (pages 119–150) I discussed how I thought it was helpful to structure a compulsive-eaters group. In this section I will also suggest ways of working alone or in pairs that will help you explore your feelings within a safe and supportive framework.

First, however, it must be acknowledged that it is hard for many of us to take the time on a regular basis actually to focus on our own needs. You can have all sorts of good intentions that you'll go swimming each week, keep your room tidy or answer letters promptly, or whatever. Sooner or later these schemes break down and it can be ages before you are able to make a new resolution. In working with yourself on your compulsive eating, you will probably find it quite easy to start off with energy and enthusiasm while at the back of your mind you still feel wary about when you will let yourself down again. I think it is quite important to recognise this dynamic so that you can take it into account and not be depressed by it.

If it is realistic to spend ten minutes a day reflecting on your food problem, do it that way. Use five minutes to review your eating and another five to think through the difficult emotional issues that came up for you. If it is more realistic to spend an hour every four days reflecting on these themes, then choose that method. Using the exercises can help to focus your mind and energies, so allow time to do them *and* to note your responses. Be as flexible as you can, knowing who you are and what is likely to work for you. If you find you are not scheduling special time to think things through, then apportion a little time after each meal to digest not just the food, but your emotional relationship to it.

But *don't be totally casual about this time*. However and whenever you plan it, make sure you have quiet space to yourself. Take the telephone off the receiver or settle the children down to bed first if that is what it takes to guarantee that you are not interrupted. Have a notebook handy to jot down your thoughts, or speak aloud into a tape recorder and listen back to yourself. Take yourself and your work on compulsive eating seriously and make sure you spend purposeful time with yourself. Allow yourself the time and space to come to grips with the problem. As I have said before, this method depends entirely on *your* willingness to allow it to work for you. The way to start, after having assured yourself of some uninterrupted time, is by thinking, feeling, talking things out and reviewing your experiences of eating in a purposeful way.

Co-counselling: Learning to Listen and Learning to Talk

Co-counselling is a good vehicle for talking in pairs about emotional issues. In this method, two women take turns talking and listening to each other for a set period of time. The idea is to offer each other reciprocal help. The talker, who sits facing the listener, is aiming to say what is on her mind. The job of the listener is to *be attentive* – not to intervene – to listen to what the talker is saying and allow herself to feel with the talker the incidents and feelings she is describing. After an agreed amount of time (usually between seven and fifteen minutes) the talker and listener exchange roles for an equal length of time.

You decide what you want to work on, and how. You might find yourself talking about your current difficulty around eating, or how hard it was for you to attend your session because you were feeling discouraged. If you are in a compulsive-eaters group, you might use a short co-counselling exercise to sort through what you will eventually discuss during your time in the group. Often what is uppermost in our minds turns out to be less important to us than we think it is, and by talking we discover that our immediate concerns mask something more central to us.

It could also be that simply being able to say what is on our mind resonates and makes us realise just how important that particular issue is. In fact, you can use co-counselling to learn how to talk in a very different way for – unlike conversation in which people agree, disagree, interrupt, intervene, encourage and so on – you will be on your own, having to tap into what is really central for you using whatever words express what you really feel.

As you are talking you will be developing a new voice, a voice that is authentic. Because there will be space around your words, you will simultaneously be able to be reflective. This is quite a unique experience. Even if you are working on your own, you can adapt this method by speaking into a tape recorder and listening to yourself attentively afterwards.

For the listener, too, this will be a new experience. For in that capacity, you will be developing your skills as a listener; learning to give attention to another person without interrupting her space; learning to understand things from the other person's point of view; learning to get inside her experience and out of your own. This listening skill is of enormous importance if you join a group, where you will be trying to pay special attention to the words, feelings and interactions of other group members.

After a period in which you have each had a chance to talk and a chance to be listened to, I suggest you sit silently for a minute or so to reflect on what you have noticed. Then give each other feedback about your experience of yourselves and of each other. If you try a short period of co-counselling in pairs at the beginning of a larger group meeting, use the time to find out what you want to work on later, and how you're feeling. Often what you will be confronting in these co-counselling sessions are difficult, painful, confusing and sometimes incomprehensible feelings. Listen to yourself with the same caring attention you give to your partner.

Facing Feelings, Facing Defences

★ Often in the course of a session someone discovers that she has angry feelings towards her mother, father, lover, husband, child or friend. It must be pointed out that these are not the *only* feelings she has towards them, but that they *are* strong feelings in conflict with other feelings and, unless they are acknowledged by the person, they will come out in indirect ways, such as compulsive eating. If the woman tries to hide the 'negative' feelings from herself, they will interfere with the relationship in confusing and

256

destructive ways that she will neither understand nor control. (The two exercises on pages 333–335 on expressing and exploring feelings are useful for dealing with this dilemma.)

It is important to remember that we all have a right to our own feelings, whatever they are (and they change). How we understand and act on them depends on our accepting the feelings in the first place. We have all become used to ignoring our feelings, either by stuffing them down before they have a chance to fully emerge or by transforming them into something else (for example, feeling miserable about being fat rather than exploring the miserable feelings in the first place). We may feel somewhat scared of experiencing them now, and may unintentionally use many different props to protect ourselves from them.

These defences are so much a part of each person's psychological make-up that when we encounter them, we must be extremely sensitive. *Trying to bash down a defence only makes it more resilient.* This is important to remember, both in terms of how we relate to our own feelings and how we relate to others. In a group situation it may often be very easy to tell that someone is being defensive – that they seem to be erecting a wall around some inner piece of themselves. You may feel tempted to try to break the wall down, but if the person resists, respect their right to do so. We do this for good reasons. Defences develop because we have not felt understood.

How Defences Evolve

During early childhood all of us at one time or another have had the experience of feeling misunderstood, rejected, ridiculed or dismissed. I'm not referring to major traumatic events, but to the complex texture of ordinary communication in which our needs, desires and our feelings as children are sometimes misinterpreted by those on whom we depend. In fact, the most painful experiences can arise from surprisingly minor, everyday conversations and events that are not 'outstanding' enough to be impressed on our conscious minds. The response we get leads to our feeling ashamed of these needs, desires and feelings, so we unconsciously lock them away deep inside us. We then develop defences to protect ourselves against anticipated future hurts.

By being hidden away, our feelings are in a sense protected from dismissal or belittlement by others, but they are also not easy for us to re-examine and re-experience, and they can remain distorted and confused. Here is an example.

Mara moved from York, in the north of England, to London when she was 7 years old. At her eighth birthday party she was looking a bit miserable, and her father asked warmly what was wrong. She replied, 'I miss my friends from York.' Her father said, 'Don't be silly, dear. You have lots of lovely new friends here today.'

This interaction, which on the surface was quite unremarkable, actually cut Mara to the quick. She walked away from the encounter feeling confused, terribly hurt and dreadfully ashamed. Her feeling of being miserable had not been acknowledged and thereby validated; instead, it was dismissed. Her father had indicated to her (out of his own desire to cheer her up and take away her bad feelings) that she had no reason to feel sad. Inside her, this transaction translated as follows:

1. Mara is feeling upset.

2. She is asked why.

3. She reveals her vulnerability.

4. She hears father telling her not to feel that way.

5. She feels ángry at her father for not understanding her.

6. She feels nervous about her anger towards her father.

7. She feels ashamed about wanting to have been understood.

8. She wonders whether she isn't silly, wrong, to have strong feelings of missing people.

9. She sees that these feelings are not acceptable, so she knows she had better not show them again.

10. She buries them.

Hidden away and so often accompanied by shame, the feelings in a distorted form continue to affect Mara. Other incidents like this contribute to Mara's psychological development. They are like terrible sores that are re-infected because of something someone says or because current emotional pictures reproduce the past.

For instance, Mara grows up feeling that both her sad feelings and her feelings of wanting to be understood are wrong. So, in the course of growing up, she develops defences that keep this part of her hidden. While it is hidden away from the world, it is also hidden from herself. Once she joins a group or works on her problem herself, Mara's dilemma needs to be recognised.

Her dilemma is that she would like to get beneath her defences but does not know how. If this can be acknowledged, then Mara will be able to feel the kind of safety that will allow her to peek beneath the defence and feel the feelings. A helpful intervention when observing defen-siveness in another person might be to share with them that you have noticed their nervousness about looking into their feelings. Often by acknowledging your under-standing of their fear and their need to be protective of themselves, you can create a comfortable space for them to relax such a tight grip. Bear in mind that your own defences, and the defences of others, are not intentional; they will best dissolve when you feel sufficient empathy to work them through.

Fat itself can be a defence. We use fatness in a protec-tive way and an important step in coming to terms with our body image and compulsive eating problem depends on being able to make a shift in how we relate to the fat. You are trying to develop an understanding and a relation-ship to it, rather than attacking yourself for being fat. In other words, *get to know your fat; don't distance yourself from it; don't pretend it isn't you.*

Your fat is a part of you; it is there (or has been) for good reason. Beating up on yourself about it doesn't give you a new solution. Try to accept it. The more you under-stand about your fat and the more you can accept how it expresses aspects of you, the more of its meaning you can integrate into yourself. In turn, this integration opens up the way for you to give up your need for the fat. Once the parts of you that it was protecting or representing don't have to be compartmentalised, but can be owned, you can then let go of the fat as a defence.

Group Work

The work that goes on within established compulsive-eaters groups set up along the lines discussed in *Fat Is a Feminist*

Issue is also extremely relevant to women working on the problem alone or with a friend. The types of issues that come up, the ways that can be tackled and the need for self-acceptance are common to all compulsive eaters. Looking at one self-help group in action could give you greater insights into your own eating patterns and problems with body image, regardless of whether or not you are a member of a group.

The group we are going to look at has been meeting for six months at the point we've chosen to observe a session. There are six women in the group:

PAMELA is 32, a schoolteacher, married, feels herself to be 20lb [9kg] overweight.

JENNIFER is 34, married, has an 8 year-old daughter, does knitting design. Sees herself as about 30lb [14kg] overweight.

BELINDA is 26, an architect. Not overweight, but compulsive about food.

JUDY is 48, a music teacher, divorced with two children who have left home. Sees herself as slightly overweight.

KATHY is 31, has one child, is living with partner, not working outside home at present, was a nurse, feels 10lb [4.5kg] overweight.

CAROL is 43, married, a housewife, has three children, 21, 19, and 16. Writes poetry in her spare time. Sees herself as 35lb [16kg] overweight.

Of the six women, Judy has been in individual psychotherapy and Kathy has worked in psychiatric nursing.

There are no other group members with a therapy background. Jennifer is the first to take her turn at this meeting.

JENNIFER: Well, I think I'd like to talk about this weekend when I went home to visit my parents and I had a really difficult time with food – as per usual. And I would really like Pamela to listen especially carefully and help me out if necessary. Is that okay with everyone?

PAMELA: It's fine with me.

GROUP: Sounds okay. I'm sure we will all be able to identify with what it's like to go home.

JENNIFER: Isn't it strange that we call it home, even when in my case I've had my own home for 15 years. Anyway, I'd decided to visit my parents. Bob couldn't come, so I went for the day with Rachel *[her daughter]*, as I thought she would enjoy being able to run around helping my parents around the garden.

So we arrived about 11:30a.m., and Rachel and my father went into the garden. My mother was waiting for us, but didn't, as per usual, express any real enthusiasm about seeing either of us. She just sort of sat there in the way I've described before, waiting for me to make all the effort, entertain her, tell her things she could talk to her friends about, and never asking me anything real, and so on. At least now I can feel my fury mounting inside of me over the whole set-up.

Anyway, I just had to hold it all in and remind myself that I was only there for a few hours. But, of course, that didn't exactly work because *[cries and is clenching her fists]* when it came time to sit down for lunch, I knew I was going to overeat and I did. I didn't eat exactly compulsively, but I did feel that I ate more than I wanted and that I got up from the table feeling physically uncomfortable. Then when I was clearing off the table and doing the dishes, I just sort of scoffed the leftovers – I mean, can you imagine – the leftovers in my mother's house – *[Cries.]* – Oh, I feel so frustrated and angry – *[Silence for about three minutes, then Jennifer looks over at Pam.]*

PAMELA: Would it help to try and go through some of those heavy emotions with a bit of breathing space here?

JENNIFER: Yeah, but I don't know how to.

PAMELA: Well, I noticed that you said you had to hold your fury and upset; perhaps you could try to feel it here now in the group –

JENNIFER: I don't know what to do to feel it.

PAMELA: Well, let's focus on what you were feeling when you were on your way to your mother's.

JENNIFER: Well, as usual when I made the plan, it was done out of guilt, not to disappoint her, done because I feel Rachel's entitled to have grandparents. So I suppose I felt at first I was doing my duty. Then on the way out there, I got my usual pangs of wanting it to be nice – which is so stupid of me. I'm really wrong for wanting something from her. So, of course I'm sure I arrived in a state of wanting – I know I did. Rachel ran out of the car to greet my parents; they kissed me lightly on the cheek. I suppose I felt a bit ignored. *[Sighs.]* I definitely felt ignored, passed over, not seen. *[Weeps.]* Oh, God. I feel so over-whelmed with that feeling now, but guess what I did. It's so uncanny. Automatically I found myself in the refrigerator – searching for God knows what. *[Laughs.]* Oh, to enter that house without having to open that fridge door – it's so bare anyway; nothing nice in it. *[Sits quietly for about three minutes.]* I feel that day is such a microcosm of my problem. I don't feel seen as myself; I feel my mom taking things from me, and then it's like I stealthily take from her.

PAMELA: Does it help clarify anything to look at the act of overeating in terms of the message you might be asking your 'fat' to convey to her?

JENNIFER: Yes, you're right. I feel she can't ignore me. She hates fat, my mother does, being a dieter all her life, so she'll – or rather I think I'm trying to say to her, 'Hey, you don't ignore me – look at me, see –' Also, I'm somewhat desperate and I think it's maybe a way to show her how angry I am. *[Sits quietly.]* If I feel it in terms of the emotions my overeating is expressing, I'd say anger over not being given to. *[Cries and bangs on the floor with her right foot.]* I feel I've got to allow these emotions to come up a bit more as they have been recently and not convert them into silent, aggressive fat –

Thanks, I feel I've had enough time.

PAMELA: Are you sure?

JENNIFER: Yes.

KATHY: Can I ask something, Jennifer?

JENNIFER: Sure.

KATHY: Well, something occurred to me when you were talking when you first described going to your mom's. You said you were stupid for still wanting things from her, and I heard you being *so* self-punishing with yourself. I do that to myself all the time. I want something from my mother, and she can't give it and then I blame myself for wanting. Somehow, hearing you say it clarified something for me, and I wondered if we all take out on ourselves others' inadequacies. I mean, it's not your fault your mother is a bit cold, nor that mine is overbearing, and yet we both think it is.

JENNIFER: If only I could feel that.

TIMEKEEPER: It's getting close to the end of your time. What would you like to do now?

JENNIFER: Does anyone else know what I'm on about it?

GROUP: Absolutely.

JENNIFER: It's such a relief to know I'm not totally isolated in these kinds of dilemmas. Thanks for all your attention; I really appreciate it.

TIMEKEEPER: Before we move on to the next person, perhaps we should each take a minute to think quietly to ourselves about how we were all affected by the things Jennifer experienced.

This gives group members a chance to be in contact with whatever feelings were triggered off for them. This minimises the chance that people will then ask questions out of their own needs, rather than in the explicit interest of the member who is presenting her problem. The more the group can design intervals for silent reflection, to allow each member to see what is going on inside herself, the easier it will be to minimise the difficulties that can arise over misidentification.

Jennifer's story about her visit with her mother stirred

up, in other group members, similar feelings of disappointment, wanting and anger towards their families. Some members felt temporarily confused about what they wanted to work on in their time that session. Giving members a chance to reflect on their own experiences provides a certain breathing space in which each can see what is most important for her to discuss that night. It may be what each one had in mind originally, or it may be something akin to Jennifer's experience.

TIMEKEEPER: Okay, who would like to talk next?

JUDY: Well, I've got something on my mind. I've really noticed that for the last month or so, since my weight has been lower and I'm looking closer to what I really want – in fact I'm at my imagined slim size – I take almost every opportunity to just slightly overeat. It's almost as though I can't just accept my success. I'm defeating myself or playing games with myself. It's so upsetting, because in one way I feel I have really understood so much and put it into practice, and here I'm almost deliberately sabotaging myself.

BELINDA: Are you scared of being your ideal size?

PAMELA: Do you think you could be worried about being slim?

JUDY: Hang on – one at a time.

It is important in the group to agree that the person whose time it is has as much say over what happens in that time as possible. So, for example, if group members ask a lot of questions simultaneously, or fire off too many questions so that it makes it hard to assimilate them and use them usefully, the person who is on can and should say, 'Back off' or 'Stop' or 'No more questions please.' She should feel free to direct others' interventions in ways that make more sense and are truly helpful to her.

JUDY: What did you ask, Belinda?

BELINDA: I was wondering whether you were worried about having actually achieved your ideal size.

JUDY: Well, I must be because I seem to be quite preoccupied with the whole thing. It really does feel almost deliberate and a bit self-destructive, like I'm not allowed to enjoy what's going on for me.

PAMELA: Suppose you were your ideal size and it wasn't a precarious state of affairs –

JUDY: I can't really feel that. Maybe if I just think of being more relaxed around food. I think I get scared that I won't know what to do with all that time I spend preoccupied with food and weight – Sometimes I realise I haven't been that obsessed for a day or so, but I have felt a bit anxious and I don't know why – a sort of general anxiety and fragility. I can feel it now, just talking about it, and I feel like shuddering away from. There obviously is some major reason why I'm scared to be slim. *[Looks scared.]* Partly it feels like it has to do with envy and not having a place – My younger sister was always slim and very pretty, and I feel she gets so much attention from everyone in the family. Everybody sort of clucks over her and I suppose I've always felt outside of the competition, like I wasn't – *[Cries.]* I feel I'm not good enough and that she gets it all and I've always had an excuse for that for myself. I've been that fat, reliable, older sister who stood in for Mom – I think I'm really scared of renouncing that role and asking to be seen in another way. It makes me feel all queasy inside.

BELINDA: In a way, that sounds really good, like you are having the feelings you often run away from.

JUDY: But it is scary to think of competing with my sister, or even just changing my self-image and not being the dependable one in the background. I mean, that is so much a part of the way I've seen myself – I want to change. I want to bring other parts of me forwards, although I do feel a bit ashamed of the attention-seeking me. But I know I have to try because the queasy feelings won't go away unless I do – I feel I've sort of cheated myself for a long time. I'm not sure what is at the other side of the attention, but I think I want to find out. You know, I think behind my fat was a very energetic me trying to get out.

[sits quietly reflecting]

Would someone please come to my house and help me fling out my clothes, or at least sort them out? I might be too scared to part with them immediately. I feel most of the things I wear don't really express who I feel I am; they are so dowdy.

GROUP: Maybe we could go shopping with you. You wouldn't necessarily have to buy, but you could try on various styles and experiment.

JUDY: That would be great. Who could come to my house on Tuesday or Thursday?

PAMELA: I can come tomorrow.

JUDY: Great.

TIMEKEEPER: Do you want to arrange a shopping trip, too?

JUDY: I think I need to do the cleaning out first. Maybe next week I could take some of my time to report in on that experience and then see whether I would like some help trying out new styles. At any rate, I feel I've had enough time for today.

TIMEKEEPER: Does anyone identify with Judy? Think about what might have been set off in you when she was talking. Let's sit for a minute and think about it.

KATHY: I really identify with the part about feeling frumpish, but for me it's more to do with my mother. Shall I go on? I could use my time to work on it.

CAROL: Well, I identify, too, but differently because my sister was the one with the 'brains' and I was the pretty one with the personality. It's so ridiculous because we both suffered from being seen that way. She never felt really adequate, and was always scared of talking, and I've never really felt okay in my body – but why don't you talk now, Kathy?

KATHY: Well, you know how I've said my mother always takes such incredible care of herself. If she wasn't my mother, I think I'd think she was horribly vain, but because she is my mother, I feel, or at any rate I've always felt, thoroughly infuriated by her bottles of perfume, creams, lipsticks, her dresses and shoes. I can remember so well when I was little watching her getting ready to go out. She'd be wrapped in a sort of magic aura – queenlike to me – it was lovely. But I suppose although all of that was so close; it was also not for me in some profound way. And

I think in some very private place I've thought of it as a vanity that is allowed to beautiful women, but not to plain ones like me. So it's sort of okay that she primped herself, but it would be obscene if I did.

CAROL: But why do you think you are plain? You are anything but dowdy, although it is true you don't project all that you could. I think you are really attractive. You've got a really nice body, and you are very attractive. You've always seemed so nonchalant to me about it. In fact, I've thought of you as someone who sort of took the fact of their being good-looking for granted and was at ease with it all.

KATHY: But I don't feel that way at all. I feel awkward and not very clear how I look or how I'd like to look, and sort of ashamed of being interested in the whole topic in the first place. Recently I've been looking in magazines and at people on the street and wondering how they put their images together and being almost intrigued like a little girl at a magic show.

PAMELA: But isn't that the thing we were all talking about a few sessions ago when we were saying we were never shown how to be women? We felt no one, especially not our mothers, had helped us learn how to dress or appreciate our bodies.

KATHY: It's true, and it seems to go so deep. I even feel that, beyond not getting help from my mother, I was even discouraged from seeing my feminine side, if you know what I mean. I remember all the no's and don't's about being a girl, but I can't remember any of the things I imagine other girls had – touching, shopping, talking about appearance. Maybe nobody did get it, but I feel anyway as a result that part of me feels very inadequate at all the feminine stuff and a bit ashamed of being inadequate.

JENNIFER: This might not be the right thing to say just now, but I was wondering if you couldn't use the group to get just that kind of attention – I mean, we all think you are lovely, obviously, and we understand that you can't exactly feel that, but I'd be very happy to help sort through things about image and femininity here.

KATHY: I feel I've got such an awful self-image really, and I even feel talking here that I don't know if you do all feel that accepting, but I know that is *my* problem, and yes I would like to do more about it.

PAMELA: Well, maybe you could do something now that might help, which would be to think of one of those images you noticed and liked and then try to put it on yourself. Do you understand?

KATHY: Feels a bit phony, taking something that isn't me and putting it on –

PAMELA: Well, it is. But it's more like trying things out that you might have wanted to try before but haven't felt it's okay to do. I agree it isn't integrated, but it is a start.

KATHY: Well, if I can get past all the rubbish, there is a look I go for. I suppose it's what's describable as sort of a sixties' look – I don't know – sort of elegant bohemian, a bit like how you dress, Belinda. Nice lines – but I suppose you know how to do that, because you have a good sense of design. If I could dress like that, I might project myself better.

JENNIFER: Well, why don't you imagine you are dressed

like that – head to toe, you know – bag, jewellery, the whole thing – and just see what happens.

[A big smile comes over Kathy's face.]

In this interaction, the group is in effect providing the looking after, and giving Kathy the permission she feels she's never had from adult women to explore and express what she would like to do with her body.

[Kathy straightens her body, changes her seating position and sees how that feels.]

BELINDA: We're near enough the same size. Would you like to try some of my things on?

KATHY: Well, I've always wanted to wear a shirt and jacket like you do.

BELINDA: Here. *[She takes them off.]* Try them on.

[Kathy puts them on but resumes her old posture.]

JENNIFER: Now, why don't you try sitting or standing in a way that goes with that look for you?

KATHY: It feels really nice. Can I go look in the mirror? *[She goes to the mirror.]* Well, now I know what feels so hard about all this. I look a lot like my aunt, my dad's sister, who was sort of described as a tough woman but with a bit of a wink. I always got the impression that my mother didn't approve of her because she was single and had lovers and was risqué in her day. It's hard to hold myself this way, because I'm so habituated to looking frumpish, but this does feel a bit more like the me I wouldn't mind being.

BELINDA: When you started to talk, you said you didn't really feel you knew what you would like to project, but maybe you do. It doesn't seem all so elusive – or maybe you want to experiment more with other looks?

KATHY: What feels important out of this is it just being okay to even think about these things.

BELINDA: Maybe we should spend a whole session discussing this. I'd like to bring in clothes to try on that I feel I can't wear out of the house, although I bought them. I feel I could get some accurate feedback here about whether I look ridiculous in them.

GROUP: I think that's a good idea, because we all seem so confused by this stuff.

CAROL: I don't even know what images I like – that's how cut off I am! I think it will be great.

PAMELA: Maybe we could also think of it in terms of women in our family and how their images affect us.

This is an aspect of self-image you may want to explore on your own. Consider how all the women in your family may have affected your image of yourself. Were they fat or thin? What was each one's role within the family group – was she admired, loved, feared, hated, resented, exploited, crushed, ostracised, imitated? Explore the unspoken judgments that rush into your mind if you see yourself looking a certain way. Whom do you remind yourself of? Allow yourself time to notice what feelings come up for you, and try giving yourself permission to have the feelings and still dress that way.

As this session continued, Pamela discussed an aspect of body image that was important for her – dislike of her large breasts. She discussed how she has never really enjoyed her body because of them and that she stays away from slimness because she doesn't have a perfect body. This way, she doesn't have to cope with that fact. If she were slim, she thinks, she would feel just as dissatisfied with her body and her breasts would seem proportionately bigger. She's scared of getting pregnant because her breasts would be so large that she'd look like only breasts and stomach.

Other members of the group responded in several ways. First, they pointed out that she had a distorted view of her body – when she looked in the mirror, she only saw breasts, but when they looked at her, they saw a whole body. They also pointed out that she was usually hunched over, which emphasised rather than hid her breasts. They also commented that, as her size had been gradually changing since she'd joined the group, so too had her breasts. They hadn't stayed exactly the same, but had decreased in proportion. Pamela began to focus her attention on the feelings of loathing she had towards her body – when they began and what was beneath them.

Belinda talked about how she was beginning to realise that she was fearful of success, both in terms of her work as an architect and in accepting her body and her looks. She noticed that she undermined herself constantly without even knowing it until the end of the day when she reviewed her food intake and noticed the many self-defeating ways in which she had acted. It emerged that she was frightened of the independence her work success was enabling her to achieve and having difficulty accepting the gulf she felt it opened up between her and other people. She found this feeling most unsettling.

The group worked with her to see where her compulsive eating fit into this, and she thought that it might be that the compulsive eating was a way in which she was blurring the edges and expressing her fear of being defined. She also thought that she might be focusing on her food as a way to avoid confronting the much harder conflict that was emerging for her around work.

Carol talked about how upset she felt about her sexuality and her relationship with her husband. She felt her fat was keeping her in the marriage, and that she couldn't afford to lose weight because then she would have to face how much she desired the sexual and emotional contact that she felt was lacking in the marriage. She didn't feel her marriage could improve in the ways she would like, but at the same time, she was scared of separation. Since joining the group, she had been very attracted to another man, and they had discussed having a love affair. But she felt she couldn't be unfaithful to her husband. She was afraid that if she could attract and be attracted to a man at her current size, it meant her sexuality was almost uncontrollable and could create more serious problems if she were slimmer. In the group, she tried to begin to sort through the confusions about sexuality, size, attraction. There was no resolution, but she came away thinking about how strongly sexual she felt and how she might express it.

In this particular session, then, themes emerged that are extremely common in women with compulsive eating problems. In each case, the women were not able to feel comfortable around food or in their bodies. Each woman had fantasies about who she might be (different from who she currently was), if she were to feel or project slimness.

For Carol, slimness was linked with sexuality; for Belinda, slimness meant being separate and independent; for Pamela, slimness meant she would have to accept herself – as long as she wasn't slim, she could blame her imperfections on her fatness; for Kathy, slimness meant allowing herself to look somewhat dashing; for Judy, slimness meant getting attention in a different, unfamiliar way; for Jennifer, slimness stirred up worries that she wouldn't be seen.

These concerns are intertwined with unconscious fantasies about the symbolic meanings of fatness and what fat is expressing for the individual woman. After more than six months of meeting as a group, these women all gained sufficient understanding of their inner processes to realise slimness had eluded them for 'good reason', that they weren't just lacking in self-control and will-power but that their compulsive eating was a reactive and protective mechanism that they employed when they could not cope with underlying conflicts in a more direct way.

How to Ask Questions

If we review this session, we can see that, by sticking to very simple questions and being disciplined about leaving time for those questions to filter through to the member they were directed at, individuals in the group can 'work' effectively at a psychological level together. It is especially important to be careful, as this group was, not to plunge in or bombard each other with queries. Help each other pursue the feelings that are behind the compulsive eating and the symbolic meaning of fat and thin for each of you.

When you ask questions of each other, be sure to leave time for the answer to stir up something inside rather than to provoke a quick intellectual reply. Don't push hard on the questions; that isn't the point. Offer them and if they aren't useful, think again and see if you can get inside the other person's shoes momentarily to see what they might be experiencing.

There are an almost infinite number of questions that

might be helpful. The point isn't to show how well one can ask questions, but to do so in a way that both strikes a core issue and gives the other person the chance to respond. For example, the possible questions that might have been useful to Jennifer (the first woman who spoke in the group session just described) to help her break her automatic walk to the refrigerator in her mother's house include the following:

1. Can you say what you were looking for?

2. What are you looking to find out?

3. How old do you feel at the refrigerator door?

4. What would you like to find when you open the refrigerator door?

5. What are the feelings you are rushing to cover up by eating?

6. What would happen if you didn't go straight to the fridge?

Another possible intervention would have been to focus on any aspect of the day that Jennifer had described, linking it to her longings, her feeling of not being noticed, her desire to 'over' eat and her wish to get something from her mother. For example, Jennifer might have found it helpful to talk about the meal itself, in which case the following line of questioning could have been useful to her:

1. Do you know what you were feeling when you sat down at the table?

2. What was your mother serving?

3. Did the food have any particular meaning for you?

4. What were mealtimes like for you when you lived at home?

5. What was the atmosphere at the table?

6. Did you play a particular role at the table?

7. Do you know what you were feeling at the precise moment when you crossed the line from eating comfortably to eating more than you wanted?

When asking questions, it is important to bear in mind several points:

1. Ask questions one by one, leaving plenty of time for the person to digest each question and respond to it (or reject it as unhelpful).

2. Ask questions from a perspective that is sympathetic to each woman's dilemma. Try to think about where she is stuck and then ask your question with the intention of helping to open up the stuck area.

3. Ask questions which elicit feelings, not concepts or impersonal abstractions. The point is not to satisfy your curiosity or clear up your own confusion.

4. If you aren't sure why you want to ask any particular question, ask it of yourself first. It may have more to do with you. Then reconsider whether it would be helpful to the other person.

5. Remember that you offer a question as an aid to the other person. Try not to feel rejected if she doesn't find it useful.

It is *not* useful or appropriate to tell the speaker if you find yourself feeling bored while she is working. This is much more likely to be a clue to what is happening for *you* than for her. Look inside yourself to check whether you might be withdrawing your attention in order to stop your own painful or unpleasant feelings from coming up, or if the boredom could be part of an unresolved conflict that already exists between you and the speaker.

★ Difficulties around food are often particularly noticeable in family situations. Childhood experiences of eating with parents can be very important in understanding present-day compulsive eating patterns, even if these now occur in many other settings as well as at home. To explore the links between your own early food history and your current eating behaviour, turn to the exercise 'The Family Meal', on page 353.

Replaying Difficult Times

★ Another type of intervention that might have been useful to Jennifer would have been to suggest that she reenact the scene at her parents' house, but this time to see if she could *not* overeat at lunch, and instead allow those feelings that she was stuffing down through food to rise to the surface. (The exercise 'Increasing Your Food Awareness', which you'll find on page 330 could be helpful for this.)

Jennifer would thus remember back to the meal itself and all her associated feelings. She would allow the scene to play through her mind briefly, focusing in on the point when she continued to eat even though she wasn't physically hungry. Stopping at this point, Jennifer would try to feel what had been going on inside her. She might notice feelings of anger towards her mother. She might feel very troubled by such feelings, and rather scared of them.

A good way for Jennifer to explore and discharge such angry feelings would be to ask one of the other group members to play act being Jennifer's mother so that Jennifer could tell her mother what angered and upset her. By doing this, she might be able to get the feelings off her chest in a safe place without fearing her mother's real reaction, and she might discover that her feelings were in fact less overwhelming than she had imagined. Through this preparatory method Jennifer could see what it was like to acknowledge that she did indeed have angry feelings towards her mother. She could then decide what to do about them in reality. *(The exercise on expressing feelings, on page 333, could also be useful for this.)

Ending a Group Meeting

After the last person in a group has finished speaking, it is a good idea to allow fifteen minutes or so for the group to discuss what you might like to do at your next session. This might mean selecting an exercise together and having the timekeeper for the next week's meeting take responsibility for bringing a prerecorded tape of the chosen exercise.

Then, to end the meeting, the current week's timekeeper could ask all the group members to sit quietly for a minute or two to think about what each of them would be taking away from the session. This time to refocus attention on yourself also allows an opportunity for anyone who may be in particular emotional discomfort and may feel loath to leave the group, or may feel the need to get something off her chest, to have her need acknowledged before she leaves. So, at the very end of the session, you may decide to build in the option for people to say how they are feeling.

Here is what the members voiced at the end of the meeting we've been observing:

PAMELA: I feel so much better now, although I certainly do have a lot to think about. Thanks so much all of you for being so understanding and helpful.

BELINDA: I feel a bit nervous with what I talked about, like the insight could just slip away or I could bury it under eating, so I could use some checking in with so that I don't.

GROUP: Well, we could check in with you next session but in the meantime maybe you should have a home-work assignment to write down what feelings you are trying to stuff down instead of eating them away, and see how difficult it is to actually hold on to them.

BELINDA: Thanks, that's a good idea, I'll try it.

CAROL: I feel so relieved to have talked about what I did but I also feel HELP! I'm scared!

GROUP: That is so understandable and also you must remember that you don't have to act on anything, you are just trying to sort things out for the present and you can fantasise leaving your husband or having affairs without doing anything until you feel comfortable.

JUDY: Well, I feel a lot better just saying what I did tonight.

KATHY: Me too and I'm always amazed about where this subject takes me. I start off on one thing and end up with such a bigger and more intense view of things.

JENNIFER: I know what you mean. I always feel worse and better at the end of a session. You know I'm determined to go to my mother's one day and not overeat!

Spending a Day Together

A day spent with other compulsive eaters can give you a chance to inject new energy into the work you're doing. You can do a variety of exercises together that will not only give you data to explore later, it will also give a group a cohesive feeling after having interacted together in a different way. If you would like to spend a day together, I suggest you make arrangements to be in a large, comfortable room, and to make sure that you won't be disturbed. Plan some of the day in advance and keep some of it open so that spontaneous happenings don't necessarily have to be nipped in the bud. If you feel you want to relax the equal-time rule that operates in most groups, do put in its place a carefully thought-out exercise or topic that makes sense for each person to concentrate on and which takes into account the different needs of each woman.

The compulsive eating group of six women that was described in the previous sections decided to meet from 10a.m. to 6p.m. on a Saturday. They agreed in advance that they would also use the time together to try eating when they were hungry and stopping when they were satisfied. To help this work, they decided to bring along a variety of food that they knew they liked to eat.

Each woman was to eat when she felt hungry. They did not make planned breaks for food, although there was a break in the middle of the day to talk conversationally, stretch, take a walk or, of course, eat if anyone was hungry. Each woman was to take responsibility for mentioning to the group when she had a desire to eat and was not phys-ically hungry, or when she had a desire to continue eating past the point of having satisfied her stomach hunger. In this way, she could do an on-the-spot investigation of what was motivating her compulsive eating at that time.

Choosing Exercises: Dress as Your Mother

With these minimum guidelines set, the group chose the following activities for the day. Kathy very much wanted to work on creating a self-image that felt right for her. She proposed an exercise that would go to the heart of what she thought was her problem: the confusion between her identity as a woman and the overwhelming picture of her mother's femininity. She thought that if she could try acting as her mother, she might be able to get the physical presence of her out of her system and in that way come to grips with her own physicalness. She suggested coming to the group dressed as her mother and seeing where that took her.

The other women were so taken by her idea that each decided to dress up as her own mother. As it turned out, the awkwardness, excitement and the different aspects of each personality that became emphasised made for a very energetic opening to the day. The women were all involved in a rather exposing activity together and were able to handle their complicated feelings about emulating their mothers directly and with warmth. Nearly everyone was shocked to realise how much like her mother she felt herself to be. This led to a major discussion about the role of their mothers in their conceptions of self.

In acting their mothers, this group of women found out where some of their internal judging voices came from.

For nearly all the group members, it was a revelation to discover that they looked at themselves with what felt like their mother's eyes. During the course of the exercise, they 'role-played', talking to their mothers about their figures and their food. The despair, judgments and hopes that their mothers seemed to have pinned on them were almost mirror reflections of their own views.

In realising how much of their picture of their mothers lived inside of each of them, the way was open to look into not so much the why of it all, but into what to do about it. Kathy, for instance, felt that her attachment to her mother in this way acted as a barrier to her being her own person. Once she had experienced that realisation in a very stark way, she needed to come to grips with not hiding herself behind her internal mother.

Jennifer realised that much of her strong feeling of wanting from her mother was an echo of the longing she felt her mother had wordlessly expressed to *her* throughout her childhood. She realised that the terribly disappointed feelings she always experienced around her mother and the bitterness that accompanied those feelings were similar to the attitude she experienced as emanating from her mother. Jennifer felt the weight of her mother's unsatisfied emotional life and saw that she was headed down the same path unless she actively intervened. She realised that, for her mother, nothing was ever good enough and that her mother often acted as though she were bound to get the raw end of any deal. Dressing up as her mother was a startling confrontation for Jennifer. She realised that the very aspects of her mother that distressed her were, in fact, a large part of how she experienced herself.

Pamela felt that this exercise provided her with a new experience regarding her breasts. Dressing and holding

284

herself as her mother, she realised that she felt her body to be very similar to her mother's — *except* for her large breasts. She remembered how ashamed she had felt when she first wanted a bra and there was nobody with whom she could talk about it. She had felt she couldn't turn to her mother, because her mother had still seen her as a little girl.

The re-experiencing of this incident, which she had thought about many times but had never really *felt*, released Pamela in some very important way. She described it as feeling the blood flow back into her chest. She tried to hold her back straight and really felt for the first time just how hunched over she was and how that had been a response to feeling uncomfortable with her developing breasts. Because she had been holding herself that way for so long, she decided to find out about exercises that would help her straighten up.

In this exercise, each woman was able to identify a part of herself with a part of how she saw her mother. This can be a very powerful experience as our ingrained habits of internal condemnation are shown for what they are — thereby becoming less automatic and inhibiting.

The Chinese Meal Exercise

★ Another exercise this group did focused on food. In it they imagined a birthday party for themselves at a Chinese restaurant. This exercise is aimed at opening up the following questions:

1. How do you feel about sharing your special day with others around food?

2. Who orders the food?

3. Does each guest, or does the birthday person or her partner do it?

4. Are you able to invite only the people you really want?

5. What are the conflicts, if any, at the table?

6. If there are any, how are they played out through the food?

★ If you would like to do this exercise for yourself, turn to page 350.

When this group did the exercise, all the women felt really good about having a meal for their birthday. As far as food ordering was concerned, three of them wanted the food to be a surprise and the others felt very strongly that they wanted to be sure of having their favourite dishes. Everyone felt they couldn't really invite only whom they wanted to their party; in each case there was an unwanted guest whom the birthday person felt she couldn't offend by not inviting. This realisation was quite important, because it expressed at a level other than food and fat the issue of feeling it was impossible to define or show themselves as they felt they were inside.

When each woman asked herself how coming up with a guest list that was absolutely right for her could affect how she felt at the party and in relation to the food, this seemed to raise a feeling that things would be 'too good.' They felt, in varying degrees, a certain anxiety if life turned out just as they wanted – either it was impossible or they didn't deserve it.

These responses, which at first glance may seem surprising, stem from our experiences of growing up female. If we are encouraged to devote our energies, concerns and hopes to others – especially our families –

we may experience an internal confusion, a wrench, once we begin to turn that attention towards ourselves and try to pursue what *we* would like. This kind of anxiety, which may be expressing a fear of 'getting too much', is a reaction that many women experience in the process of trying to be more self-determining. It is something you are quite likely to feel if you are trying to change the habit of repressing your own needs.

Body Image Exercises

Another exercise this group did focused on body image. They imagined that they were all as fat as they had ever feared, and they acted out being at a party and circulating with the other guests. They walked around the room and talked with each other, feeling how it was to be in that situation. Then they changed their posture and walked around, talking to each other as though they were all slim and their ideal size.

What is striking is the difference each time you do this exercise. You may be able to feel that a part of you is resisting slimness and, at the same time, be aware of the pain that goes along with being fat and feeling excluded and different. For most women, the pain is a definite step forwards from the blind self-hatred that once accompanied any recognition of their fat selves.

★ You can also re-use the 'Fat/Thin Fantasy' exercise on page 337 as often as you like, either on your own or in a group. It too will help you to experience whatever emotions are connected with fatness and thinness for you.

Often, like Pamela, we tend to focus our feelings of dislike for our bodies on to one particular body part. We can, as a result, develop a rather distorted view of that part. It can leap out at you whenever you look in the mirror and seem much more prominent than it really is. You may imagine that your problems would be solved *if only* your breasts/thighs/hips/legs/tummy weren't so . . . Similarly, you may fantasise that the shape of that part will change completely when you reach your ideal size. Regardless of whether this is always the same area of your body or a succession of different ones, such dissecting always leads to judging, which gets in the way of self-acceptance.

★ The 'Part of the Body' exercise can help you to explore the meaning of your distress about various body parts and to work through the barriers to feeling at ease in your body. The feelings we have about our bodies and various aspects of our bodies are constantly changing. By using the exercise from time to time, you will be able to experience that movement for yourself. After you do the 'Part of the Body' exercise, which is on page 344, refer to the questions below.

1. What kind of associations did you come up with to this part of your body?

2. Do any other members of your family share the same concern about this part of their body?

3. If so, how do you feel about that part of their body?

4. Now spend some time exploring the themes that came up for you when you were doing the fantasy. Think through in detail your first awareness of your discomfort with this part of your body. What kind of role does this discomfort play currently, and what are the emotional issues this discomfort is masking? Are you perhaps assigning it

more power than it has? Does being preoccupied with this part *help* you in any way?

5.   Why do you so dislike this part? Is it because it doesn't conform to a stereotype? If in the fantasy you superimposed someone else's body part on to yours, whose was it – and what does that mean for you? If you saw yourself younger, what was so special about that particular time?

6.   What is the actual bodily function of this part of your body? How well does it perform its physical function? How do you feel about its function?

Looking at Feelings

Another exercise this group did focused on whatever emotion each of them was having difficulty with at the time. In this they were touching on important issues that compulsive eaters have to grapple with because, as we have seen, so often compulsive eating serves to cover up or transform feelings. Carol, for instance, wanted a chance to look at her angry feelings – what was so awful about them that she felt she had to eat them away. Belinda felt she always ran away from feelings of sadness; Pamela wanted to see where her enthusiastic feelings had disappeared to; Judy and Kathy focused on their competitive feelings towards other women; Jennifer wanted to get more in touch with her guilt feelings.

This exercise was designed by Luise Eichenbaum and myself for many of the single-topic workshops, held at the Women's Therapy Centre in London, that are aimed at pinpointing key issues such as anger, jealousy, competition, giving and receiving, dependency and difficulty with power. You can do it equally well on your own at home. It gives you a chance to explore your feelings and reflect on them.

If you take your time over it, the exercise will also help you to sit with the uncomfortable feelings. This very process of giving yourself time may be a novel experience for you, because frequently compulsive eaters find that they only experience for a microsecond the feelings that cause them pain and upset. The feelings are then rapidly buried, either under an avalanche of food or because they have developed psychological mechanisms that cut them off. These inaccessible feelings often seem quite scary, but this exercise (which you can use frequently) can help you gently reacquaint yourself with your subterranean feelings. It can also provide valuable insights into why certain feelings cause you distress.

When we give ourselves the chance to explore a feeling, often we discover that another (perhaps more confusing) feeling lies behind it. This is another reason for pacing yourself so that you can catch hold of the nuances of the feelings and come to accept them. Often the reason the feeling causes so much upset is that you can't accept having the feeling, or else the feeling itself is masking another feeling that makes you even more uncomfortable.

* You may want to turn to page 335 now, and try the exercise 'Exploring Your Feelings'.

You may find that some of your reactions to the exercise mirror those of the women in this group. Judy, a music teacher, discovered that her competitive feelings were a lot more complicated than she had at first thought. She noticed that these very painful feelings came up a lot when she thought about her musical capabilities in relation to those of her most proficient students. At first, she condemned herself for even feeling competitive in the first place, but what emerged from behind the feelings of competition were deeper feelings of regret that she hadn't taken her desire for professional recognition more seriously.

Judy realised that her competitive feelings towards others functioned to stop the pain she felt about her own life. It wasn't that the people who brought out competitive feelings in her were necessarily competitive themselves, or especially blessed, or even that they could be blamed for stirring up these feelings in her. It was rather that her focus on her competitive feelings towards them acted as a blocking mechanism that was stopping her from looking at the real issues in her life. She was projecting her own internal conflicts around ambition onto others.

Kathy's competitive feelings arose from feelings of being inadequate and excluded by others. The competitive feelings she felt towards others in this case were more an expression of her internal feelings about not accepting herself and not feeling sure that she had a right to good things out of life. The competitive feelings were almost a psychological stick that she unwittingly beat herself with, reinforcing her underlying feelings of exclusion and inadequacy. She recognised this as another aspect of her struggle to feel valid and legitimate.

Pamela noticed that her feelings of enthusiasm drained out of her when her husband didn't relate to her as she wished he would. She sometimes felt that her husband didn't understand her and what she wanted. She longed for contact but it was almost as though her emotional engagement shut off, and in its place she had to face her feelings of disappointment and frustration.

Feelings and Femininity

As we allow ourselves to explore in more depth the feelings that caused us confusion and anguish, we often notice the internal taboos that operate against our feeling whole, that keep us from being in touch with and from expressing our emotions. In other words the social restrictions that all women grow up with are reflected at the psychological level. These social practices are enforced legally, economically, politically, ideologically and culturally, through our education in our families and at school and in the ways we come to experience ourselves from the inside in our emotional lives as somehow less than, not deserving – in short, as second class.

When we as women begin to review our experience of life, we are involved in the process both of transforming our way of seeing things and of changing what we can do. Consciousness-raising is a very powerful tool for opening up new territory at all levels. The aspects of ourselves that are touched at a personal level, however, can be as painful as they are exhilarating. I have noticed time and again in my practice how shocked we all are to discover that deep inside our emotional lives we are subject to a kind of internal policing that serves to keep us in our place. This makes tremendous sense, however, because one does not grow up female without absorbing powerful lessons about who one can and cannot be.

I can't stress how important it is to *be generous to yourself* when exploring these uncomfortable emotional revelations. Often you will discover feelings inside of you that may feel divergent from the new model of yourself that you would like to be. But don't shy away from coming to grips with these feelings. They tell us an enormous amount about who we are, our personal histories, and what we need to work on in order to move forwards.

Frequently, women in therapy have told me how uneasy they become when they contact their feelings of jealousy, envy or competition towards other women. They can feel so uncomfortable that they fear investigating them further, lest they uncover even more distressing things. The discovery of these complicated and sometimes disturbing feelings, however, can deepen our understanding not only of how we as individual women come to be who we are, but also of how deep are the psychological consequences of a society that denies us aspects of personhood on the basis of gender.

If we are trying to break out of the rigid sex roles in which we live, we need to have as much knowledge as possible about how they operate, both at the social and at the emotional level, so that when we try to change things we recognise the interrelationship between the personal and political world. Finding out that women carry deep feelings of inadequacy, isolation, unentitlement, inhibition, anger and rage strengthens our understanding of how the world operates and points to how seriously disabling women's oppression is.

Jennifer, for example, discovered that entwined with her guilt feelings were feelings of rebellion, bitterness and fear. She described an incident that involved her husband Bob, her daughter Rachel and the compulsive-eaters group. It was their accepted practice that Bob looked after Rachel on Tuesday evenings so that Jennifer could be free to do whatever she wanted. In fact, Tuesday came to be the night of her compulsive-eaters group, and she looked forward to getting out of the house, meeting a friend for a drink, and then going on to her meeting.

At lunchtime one Tuesday Bob was unexpectedly offered a ticket to see a play he was interested in. He wanted to go, but he did not make any alternative plans to have Rachel looked after. When he came home from work he just assumed that Jennifer would understand how important it was for him to see the play and that she would stand in for him this time. So at 6p.m., just as Jennifer was preparing to leave the house with her friend, Bob walked in and told her about the play.

Jennifer and her friend immediately rang the other group members and asked them to meet at her house that night. After the group left later that evening, Jennifer ate compulsively and was plagued by guilt feelings. One of the women hadn't been reached in time and had arrived at the original meeting place only to have to journey again to get to Jennifer's.

Jennifer realised that she had felt distracted during the whole evening and hadn't felt able to concentrate. Partly she was listening for Rachel, hoping that she wouldn't be disturbed or disturbing. Given the fact that she had psychologically absented herself from the group session, she felt very bad about having rearranged the meeting place in such short notice.

Before Jennifer did the exercise around looking at feelings, she had been aware of her uneasiness about being so demanding – not wanting to give up one of her meetings – and her guilt feelings for asking people to go out of their way for her. What emerged through the fantasy exercise, however, were a whole set of other feelings that were poised just behind her guilt.

Jennifer contacted her feelings of resentment towards Bob for leaving the arrangements in her hands. At first, she hadn't felt she had a right to be angry with him, because she hadn't protested against the situation in the first place. She felt she had colluded in a dynamic between them that rested on the (unstated) premise that she was the one who should be responsible for Rachel, and that Bob's activities had a right to take precedence over hers. The incident pinpointed both their roles in the set-up. If she didn't stand up for herself, Bob would act in an unthinking way; she would then sacrifice what she wanted and end up feeling guilty for wanting what was legitimately hers in the first place.

These kinds of feelings and the paths they travel will be part of what you will be exploring as you work on your compulsive eating problem. Coming in contact with your inner feelings can be an exciting, relieving, painful and reassuring process. It is always preferable to try to come to grips with your inner life, because feelings are insistent. If they are buried, as they are so frequently in compulsive eating, they can motivate us in ways of which we are unaware. We then find ourselves doing and saying things that seem inappropriate and confusing. As we begin to know more about our feelings, we can make more sense of who we are.

★ To work on expressing your feelings in appropriate, satisfying ways, turn to the exercise on page 333.

Coping with 'Difficult' People

It is inevitable that, within each group, the people will take on different roles and responsibilities, even in a situation where there is equality of experience. However much emphasis we put on structuring the group as an equal and safe environment, everyone is unique and the combination of each person's uniqueness shapes a group and gives it its particular flavour. Because you are embarked on an experiment to help you focus on aspects of what makes you tick, you will be using the group to explore your individuality, what makes you who you are, and the kinds of experiences that have led you (unconsciously) to eat compulsively as a way of coping and using your body size to express yourself. This is different from a consciousness-raising group, where the stress is on the similarity of women's experiences so as to pinpoint the ways society affects us all as women.

Tensions can arise in a group situation because of the gap between the type of person you are in the world – for example, spontaneous, passive, organising or whatever – and the part of you that needs to be explored in order for you to get over your compulsive eating problem. In a group you will need to call on a different part of yourself. You will be encouraging the reflective, patient and empathetic aspects of your personality to develop so that you can come in contact with the deep feelings that cause you to eat compulsively.

It may be that your group includes a member who has such difficulty finding this part of herself that she acts in ways that feel unproductive to the group. Some groups have consulted with me over what to do when they find one of their members is disruptive, domineering or bossy in the group.

This is an extremely difficult situation to face and you may find yourselves trying to ignore the problem or 'forgetting it', hoping that it will just go away or that the difficult person will leave town unexpectedly. It may take a while for these feelings to be verbalised among group members and, most often, these communications happen outside of group meetings while you are chatting on the way home in twos and threes.

The group already described contacted me for advice on just this problem. The matter had come to a head for them during one group session when Belinda was absent. The session proceeded very smoothly, and the last fifteen minutes or so people opened up to each other that they had felt particularly relaxed that evening and able to work together in a more trusting atmosphere than usual. Realising how comfortable they were with each other that evening, they were starkly confronted with the question of how much Belinda's presence contributed to the tension and occasional anger that ordinarily existed in the group.

Several women then mentioned that they had been thinking of leaving the group because they found her overbearing and somehow frightening. They felt extremely uncomfortable and somewhat guilty discussing this without Belinda, while realising that they never could have had the discussion in her presence. Before doing anything – saying anything to Belinda – they decided to see whether they weren't each individually making Belinda into a scapegoat for their own problems.

Being in a self-help group can be difficult because it is such a new experience and it can be as confusing as it is exciting. Everyone was very wary of casting Belinda in the role of the person who made the group difficult for them, because each member realised that she had to be responsible for trying to work on her compulsive eating problem as effectively as possible in the group setting. However, the relief that all of them felt on this occasion led them to ring me and ask for advice.

As I listened to two of them on the telephone, it sounded to me very much as if Belinda, very energetic but unable to work on her own eating problems, was transforming that energy into almost taking over others' problems, being over-involved with them, and being pushy with her own ideas about what they needed to do for themselves. It struck me that perhaps she was afraid of the things that were inside of her, of her emotional life, and that her dominating personality both covered her vulnerabilities and pushed the attention on to others' emotional problems and away from herself, while still keeping her in the picture.

The group decided that the best thing for them to do would be to try and talk through these issues with Belinda at the next session, and they decided to be open-minded about where that might take them. Their intention was to fill her in on what they had noticed about the group session without her. They were very gentle and not at all judgmental, taking on to themselves the responsibility for not having cut her off in the past when they had found her comments unhelpful. They shared with her how they felt – that she was charismatic and powerful, that it was partly their problem that they didn't intervene differently or relied too much on her energy, and that they felt they could hide their lack of therapy skills behind her knowledge.

Belinda was shaken by all of this but also relieved, because she recognised that she was acting in this group as she had in many other settings. She had a tendency to take over and people saw her as quite dazzling and strong, and yet she felt small inside – ineffectual and as though her own needs went unaddressed. She shared with the group just how vulnerable and hopeless she did feel, and she said she worried that if she exposed herself in the group she would make everyone else feel as helpless as she did.

For the first time, Belinda revealed the anguish that her complusive eating and her fat caused her. As she opened up to herself, her own pain, the rest of the group was overwhelmed by it as she had anticipated. But they were also moved and felt much closer to her, and they were able to reassure Belinda that they could understand *her* and help *her* too.

During the course of the evening they discussed the

ways Belinda avoided her own experience and jumped into someone else's, and how they might all together try to intervene in that process so that she could get more out of the group for herself without invading other people's space. They committed themselves to seeing how this would work for four sessions, and everyone agreed to be aware of the dynamic in which Belinda lunged with her energy into another person's problem, leaving that person feeling pushed out of shape.

Belinda's commitment was to notice when she felt inclined to do that and to intervene as soon as she could identify that she was doing it. Instead, she was to try and contact the part of her that was feeling vulnerable or identified with what another woman might be exposing about herself. The woman who felt invaded was to say so as soon as possible, so that she could ensure that her space was not taken up by Belinda's needs and could also alert Belinda to when she was being unhelpful.

In this group, an extremely good result emerged. The group was solid enough to handle Belinda's upset and give her a sense of the possibilities that lay in the group for her. But this is not always the case, and it may be that a group has to come to a more difficult decision that the members feel very tortured about.

My advice to groups which contain a member who is disliked or found difficult by other group members is as follows:

1. First examine why you find this member difficult. Is it her? Is she controlling? Bossy? Always inappropriate? Is she overbearing? Is it a case of identification? What are her problems with compulsive eating? Do they remind you of your own? Is she a scapegoat?

2. Can you think of how to change the dynamic? Will she benefit by your sharing your insights with her, or would it only be hurtful?

Set aside a time to be open with her, telling her of your experience of her. Perhaps she needs additional help such as one-to-one therapy. Perhaps she is very ambivalent about being part of the group at this stage. Perhaps she isn't ready to work on her compulsive eating problem. See if you can't all come up with a solution together that would make it possible for her to stay in the group and work with herself differently. If this is not possible, consider taking the hard step of asking her to leave. There is a real danger that an entire group will be worn away by frustration through trying to cope with such a difficult situation. But asking her to leave will be quite hard, and it may bring up complicated feelings for all the remaining members of the group.

It is important to talk these feelings out with each other should you face that decision, so that it can be a group responsibility. In most situations, while several group members may feel strongly about such a move there will also be several others who feel too uncomfortable to act on it. This can then produce a sort of no-go situation in which people are less conscientious about coming to the group, put less energy into it when they are there, and the group withers away through attrition. Several members may then regroup and start up again.

'Difficult' group members come in different personalities, and how they interact with other members can cause friction, upset and misunderstanding. One group may be quite comfortable with someone whom another group finds hard to integrate.

A group with one very reticent member who always talks

last and hopelessly, may find her 'difficult.' They may experience leaving meetings on a down note and feel as though they haven't been able to give anything to her. I would advise such a group to make an effort to help this person talk earlier on in the evening and encourage her to focus on why she feels it is so hard to be given to. Another group may become terribly irritated by a member who doesn't speak to the point, overruns her time and is generally unable to discipline herself.

To try to alleviate this and similar problems, I suggest building in regular assessments of the group process during which matters of timekeeping and general group functioning can be discussed. This doesn't have to take up more than, say, 20 minutes every six or eight sessions, but it is a way to air problems that are bound to come up in any compulsive-eaters group. It can also provide a space for group members to discuss worries and concerns that do not have a place in the regular work of the group. It is during these assessments that the discussions can cover plans for special group activities, the issue of bringing in new members, or complicated feelings between two group members that are not disruptive to the group as a whole but are painful for the individuals involved.

A self-help group works well on compulsive eating as long as it focuses on the topic at hand and each individual's relationship to compulsive eating. The group tends to be much less useful if it gets involved in the dynamics between group members, which usually means a turn away from the purpose of the group. To explore complicated group dynamics in this setting can serve the individual members as a defence against working on the issues at hand – compulsive eating, fatness and slimness. (If you are interested in exploring the dynamics that develop between group members, I suggest you join a general therapy group where such themes are the focus of the group.)

Intensity and Boredom

At times, like anyone else, whether in a group or working on your own, you will go through ups and downs, boredom, times of despair, and so on. Nor is every time you sit down to work going to be automatically exhilarating. In fact, there can be weeks on end when it just feels like hard work or doesn't seem to make much sense.

Almost everyone goes through periods of boredom when they feel discouraged and may even think of abandoning the approach or dropping out. Nothing seems to be happening, and you feel energyless. In itself, I don't think this phenomenon is entirely negative. For linked to the compulsive eating syndrome is an almost equally compulsive tendency to see things in extreme terms – either you are great or awful, either you are a star or buried deep within a crowd. Events are either smashing or terrible. In other words, life is experienced only with intensity; the texture of ordinariness is never investigated for what it might have to offer.

Curiously, this very intensity is a kind of deprivation, for it obliterates crucial dimensions of human experience. It is almost as though the person is not sure of her existence if she is neither suffering acutely nor ecstatically happy. This is reflected at the food level, where the compulsive eater is habituated to eating in dramatic ways, either bingeing or depriving herself.

Experiencing ordinariness, boredom, frustration and discouragement can be helpful. You are learning to tolerate these kinds of feelings without rushing away from them and drowning yourself in frantic activity, deep depression or filling the space by eating. In living through these feelings and accepting them, you can begin to have a sense of yourself as surviving and existing in an undramatic emotional environment. This begins to alleviate the need to be always intensely involved in a compulsive way. In accepting these moods, we can become less afraid of them and explore them for what they are. Often the psychological profile of a compulsive eater expresses a deep need to run away from the more pedestrian aspects of daily life. But these times have their own pleasures if we know how to listen for them, just as ripples in a sea have their own beauty distinct from the dramatic intensity of crashing waves.

When these unremarkable patches occur, it is useful to note your own reactions to them and to see how the situation affects you. It may be that you are learning to express a side of your personality that has long been buried, the side that is not always sparkling or interesting or making sure that everyone is all right; the side that is sitting quietly and going along with what is happening, not having to initiate action or whip up energy out of a fear of being with yourself.

This learning to sit with yourself and be inside your own skin in a calm way is not to be confused with another feeling that often can set in, which is a feeling of boredom or passivity when you don't feel you can risk really exploring what your food problems are about. It is important to remember, in these cases, that your boredom may well be a way of fending off the changes that might result from purposeful work on your food problem.

Creating Psychological Safety

Sometimes the energy flows out of the room and the atmosphere is one of depression and keeping things down. In other words, there is an almost tangible feeling of suppression, like the closeness of a humid day. This can happen when you and your partner or all the members of a group are so afraid of looking into your food problems that you park your energetic selves at the front door before you start a session, and you transmit to one another word-lessly a sort of 'keep-off' warning that is hard to break through. The best thing to do in those circumstances is to acknowledge that they exist. If the mood persists for several weeks and you don't seem able to generate any energy, then there may not be enough safety in the situation to open up.

This sometimes happens if you feel, even if you don't articulate it to yourself, that the hour or two that you have set aside each week for working on the problem isn't really enough. Opening up under such circumstances may make a person feel too vulnerable, especially if she feels that what she might have to expose about herself (and *to* herself) is her neediness. In many groups, women have found it helpful to make arrangements to have phone contact with each other between group sessions. In a group that starts off composed of strangers, this might need to be instituted, rather than hoping that it will just happen. If you're working on your own, perhaps you could invite a trusted friend to join you and support you in exploring your fears (it is much better if she also has a food problem).

For example, some women may not feel they can open up because they fear they will lose control. Such a woman may feel that her problem is so big that neither she nor anyone else can handle it. If she were to make arrange-ments to phone different friends or other group members each night of the week, say, and discuss with them how her day had gone in terms of her emotions and her eating, she might feel sufficiently supported to try new things out.

Most people would not consider such arrangements a burden and are happy to make themselves available to each other provided they feel clear about exactly what it is they are being asked to give.

Other strategies that can be useful for groups include planning special sessions to last five hours or more, in which everyone has much longer to work on her problems and to pursue issues that perhaps don't emerge in shorter weekly group sessions.

CHAPTER SEVEN

Organising a Compulsive Eating Group

Getting Started

There can be many stumbling blocks to overcome when grappling with compulsive eating problems. Partly this stems from a disbelief and despair that anything can change, partly from the difficulty of coping directly with a whole range of emotional issues and partly it is a reflection of a dynamic of the problem itself – namely, the difficulty with being persistent and openly responsible for our food intake.

For many women, getting involved in a compulsive-eaters group will be their first experience of therapy. They may have lots of ideas about such a group but feel hesitant about how to put the concepts in *Fat Is a Feminist Issue* into practice. These two issues – the compulsive eating problem itself and inexperience in therapy – can join together and translate into difficulties in organising groups. This section is an attempt to share the information we have been accumulating at The Women's Therapy Centre about compulsive-eaters groups so that you will have a chance to benefit from that experience and see if any of the difficulties you might be coming up against have been solved by other groups.

For some women, the problem starts with not knowing how to get in touch with a group; or how to get one going if there are none in their area. The first step is to go to your local women's centre and find out if a compulsive-eaters group already exists. There are so many groups now that the odds are you will be able to make contact this way. If you can't locate an existing group the next step may be to put up notices in obvious places – doctors' offices, colleges and in the local newspaper calling for a meeting at a specific time and place. This seems preferable to just giving a telephone number and collecting names, for several reasons. People are able to set aside a specific date to attend, you won't be juggling other people's schedules in your head, and it minimises the difficulties that may arise in relation to leadership of the group.

When you have come together for your first meeting you will want to explain to each other why you are interested in being involved in a group to tackle compulsive eating. Find out if there is indeed a common interest. You may want to share your own experience with food and discuss what appealed to you in this approach.

Depending on the group's familiarity with the ideas in *Fat Is a Feminist Issue*, you may be able to start your group therapy at the first meeting. If people are new to the ideas, it will make sense for them to first familiarise themselves with the book so that they can be sure they are committing themselves to something they want. This also helps keep the original organiser of the group from getting trapped into being a leader because she has more knowledge of the theories.

This is an important point, because it is quite hard to lead a group *and* be in it for yourself. An ex-compulsive eater can be enormously helpful in enabling a new group to get off the ground, but a person who wants a group so that she can work on her own problems with food and body image would be well-advised *not* to see herself as a leader just because she is an initiator. This is to be a self-help group, which means that you as a group will need to share the commitment for making it happen. It isn't helpful to rely on one person. So, at this first meeting, make it clear that you have organised the getting together but are not in a position to lead the group, and that as a group you will evolve a collective sense of responsibility and leadership.

Once you have assembled a group (5 to 10 members seem like the right number) you will find it helpful if you not only set a regular meeting time and place but also make an initial commitment of meeting weekly for six months. This time commitment will allay your fears of sharing intimate things about yourself one week and receiving no response or support the following week. It also forces the group to confront a perhaps uncomfortable fact. For most people this approach does not produce instant results. It takes time to eat differently and feel differently in your body. Don't underestimate it. Give yourself and the group a chance to be helpful for all of you.

When you make your six-month commitment, try to be there every time and make sure you contact someone if you have to miss a session unexpectedly. If you are having difficulty getting to the group or if you feel nervous about the issues that are coming up for you, see if you can share this with the group so that they can provide gentle support.

Finding a Place to Meet

There are so many unanticipated problems that can come up in this kind of experimental group that the more you can plan for, the better are your chances of group survival. So, for example, it's a good idea to set a regular meeting place; or, if that doesn't suit group members, plan in advance where the group will be meeting so that there is no anxiety about where the sessions will take place. It is best to work within a fairly small geographical area so that travelling distances don't become a reason not to make a group meeting when you are finding it hard for emotional reasons to get to the group.

Through the questionnaire sent out by The Women's Therapy Centre, we found that some women like to meet in each other's homes on a rotating basis; others like the anonymity of a room booked from a church hall or community centre. In groups that included several mothers, baby-sitting sometimes proves to be a problem, so those groups often met in the homes of those with young children. It is not important which system you choose, but it is important that the group members are comfortable with the system, know where the meetings are going to be, and make the commitment to start the meetings on time.

Planning the First Sessions

After you have set a time and a place, you will want to plan for your first few meetings. In these first weeks you will be feeling each other out, getting a sense of one another, a new sense of yourself and beginning the process of building sufficient safety and trust to open up the painful issues that are involved in your compulsive eating. In the chapter on self-help in *Fat Is a Feminist Issue* – which I recommend you all read before the second group meeting – I have laid out some exercises designed to help each person pinpoint underlying themes that are expressed in their eating.

* Two of these exercises are reproduced in the back of this book in slightly different forms. They are the 'Fat/Thin Fantasy' (page 337) and the 'Supermarket Fantasy' (page 353). As your group progresses, an almost infinite number of topics will evolve that you will want to discuss.

You may wish to start off your first group meeting by going round the room, with each person taking 10 to 15 minutes to introduce herself and share the history of her food problem. Of course, we could all talk for hours and hours about the ins and outs of our individual food histories, but here in this first exercise you should be trying to achieve certain things. One, you are presenting information about yourself in a selective and purposeful way – not rambling on, trying to find or avoid the point, but rather searching to put into words the painful story of your relationship to your body and your food over the years. Try to convey the feelings about how having a food problem affected you in the past and in the here and now. Try to sort out when you first noticed that you had a problem around food. How, or through whom, did you become aware of it? What was the extent of your family's involvement? Did food become a battleground at home? Was it a hidden problem? Did you have friends who had similar problems? Were you always dieting? Did you ever reach the weight you felt pleased about? What happened when you were your ideal weight? How did you feel climbing up the scale, and so on.

Secondly you are trying to see whether any patterns or insights emerge for you about yourself and your eating by looking over the long term. Thirdly, you are learning to talk in a supportive environment about issues that may be very hard for you to face. Everyone in the group has a difficult history with food and can therefore be understanding.

You will have some time to talk and to be listened to without interruption so that you will hear your words reverberate back and begin to notice what is significant for you.

As presenting your food problem will undoubtedly bring up much more than can be covered in 15 minutes, you may wish to carry on with this exercise at home. You may find it helpful to take another period of time, say up to an hour, when you are on your own to reflect on what meaning this history has for you. You may wish to talk into a tape recorder, and just meander leisurely back over your experiences, or you may want to write your observations down in a journal. The method you choose for work outside of the group should be one that suits you best.

After everyone has had a chance to talk, the group may wish to spend 10 to 15 minutes at the end of the group time sharing the common themes that emerged, identifying with each other, commenting on anything you noticed about each other's stories that might be insightful and helpful. You should then plan for who will tape the fantasy for next week. I suggest you start with the 'Fat/ Thin Fantasy', and then in your third week do the 'Supermarket Fantasy.'

When you come to the group meeting hungry for attention, it can be hard if your turn doesn't come up for some time. Or you may arrive feeling you have nothing to say, and this can be a form of resistance, often related to being scared of what is on your mind. If the group then goes on for an hour or so before your turn comes up, you could become even more withdrawn. In order to avoid these problems, I suggest starting each group session off so that each member has a chance to talk in the first fifteen minutes.

At the beginning of the meeting, decide on one person to be timekeeper for the session (this should be a revolving job). Divide up into pairs for a short period of co-counselling, which the timekeeper will direct by suggesting that those who talk first should tell the listeners what is on their minds about food and body image. When five or seven minutes is up, the timekeeper should tell you to swap roles. Having a chance to talk early on in the session can lessen problems of resistance, impatience, or not knowing what you want to talk about. It can also form a clear boundary between your activities of the day, including getting to the meeting, and the work you will be doing on compulsive eating.

After the 10 or 14 minutes is up and each person has had a chance to speak and a chance to listen, I suggest you sit silently for a minute or so to reflect on how you would like to use your time that evening. Would you like to pursue something that came up for you during the co-counselling, or are you aware that another theme is actually more pressing? Be clear what your intentions are for the session, and decide what makes most sense for you.

In the second part of the session the timekeeper might begin by asking who would like to talk first. In some groups, members find that choosing an order to go in ensures that everyone talks, including those who are shy. Some groups are especially sensitive to members who hold back and encourage them to speak early on in the session so that waiting doesn't build up extra nervousness. Other groups have found that acting spontaneously but keeping aware of who tends to talk at the beginning – and making sure the less assertive get their chance too – works well.

The aim is not to bludgeon members into baring their souls, but to make it safe and comfortable enough for everyone to talk freely about food, fatness and thinness. In order to create that space, it is helpful that each member's time be hers to be used as she wishes, rather than making her stick rigidly to a pre-arranged topic or activity unless it is relevant to everyone.

In structuring the sessions, I recommend dividing the time equally among group members. Sharing the time from the beginning can obviate some of the problems that have cropped up before in self-help groups. It minimises the possibility of some members dominating the others and provides a mechanism to cope with imbalance if it occurs. It also places the responsibility for the group – and hence individual progress – on each person, thus undercutting the problems that can arise when people seek or offer leadership.

Sometimes in a group it feels as though things would be smoother, sticky patches would be unstuck more easily, if there was a group leader to give guidance and direction. Unthinkingly, participants may transfer those leadership expectations to one or two group members, and, in each group, there may well be one or two women who accept that role. However, this is often not a useful development, especially for the designated 'leaders', because they may find themselves with skills that they can use with others without this attention being reciprocated. In addition, if a leadership expectation is set up, it will be very easy for group members to become disappointed when the unspoken leader lets them down.

In self-help you will be learning about yourselves and how to help others simultaneously. The group will be strengthened by each person developing a confidence that she could be a leader. To encourage this, you may wish as individuals or as group representatives to attend workshops on therapy skills and then bring them back to the group. You may wish to do some reading about self-help, and you will definitely find Sheila Ernst's and Lucy Goodison's book *In Our Own Hands: A Book of Self-Help Therapy* (Houghton Mifflin, Boston, 1981) very useful. It is full of suggestions and examples of how to do self-help therapy. However, bear in mind that yours is a focused group, and that you must not lose sight of your goals regarding food and body image.

What to Do When People Leave the Group

People leave a group for a variety of reasons. Some will leave because they feel they have conquered the problem; others will leave because they don't feel ready to engage with the problem at the level required; and some others will leave because they feel hopeless. It is a good idea when planning to leave a group to discuss your reasons with the group members to see if, having spoken aloud about it, you still feel the same way. You can also work out a timetable for leaving that seems appropriate. The person who is leaving may feel overjoyed, scared, grateful, disappointed, angry or discouraged. There are bound to be reactions stirred up in the remaining group members, which can range from abandonment or fear to relief or anger.

Because at such a moment in the life of the group there are so many feelings flying around, it is a good idea to set a time aside to express them. Those who leave because they have done well will want the group's support and blessing. Those who are left may want to discuss new issues that crop up for them, such as feeling over-responsible for the group, feeling that to question the workings of the group would jeopardise its very existence, or feeling pressure to produce interesting things to talk about each week in order to keep other people interested and so on. Make sure this extra time is added to each person's personal allocation so that it doesn't take away from the direct work on compulsive eating that needs to happen each week.

Closed or Open Group

Obviously there are two choices in relation to whether your group should have an open-door policy in regard to new members or whether the group should become closed after it has stabilised its membership. The crucial factor to be considered is what will most contribute to a feeling of safety so that people can openly talk about their fears and desires, their conflicts and their anguish about food, fat and femininity.

We haven't accumulated decisive evidence in favour of either side of the question. Some groups report that they work best on a closed basis. The feelings of acceptance, encouragement and attentive listening come from the stability of the group, from getting to know each person well and being able to rely on the security that comes from continuity. Others have written to say that bringing in new members from time to time energises the group; still others report that they have not been able to agree on this issue amongst themselves.

Each group will have to decide for itself. If there are disagreements among members, you may be able to resolve them through a third option – keeping the group closed for a certain period of time (say three months) and then opening it up to a new participant who is 'interviewed' and accepted by all group members.

You may want to bring in more members for a variety of reasons. The group may be too small, a friend of one of the existing members may have become interested, or perhaps people have left the group. When a new member joins, the group will inevitably go through a period of adjustment. The newcomer can feel awkward, and a group that has become set in its ways will feel jolted. On the other hand, the entry of new members often produces an upswing in the energy level of a group that is very positive. The old group members have a chance to share the process they have been through together and, in explaining how the group works to a newcomer, they put into their own words what they have learned about themselves and about doing self-help therapy.

Because the course of a group can last several years, it is inevitable that its composition will change in that time. You may find yourself going through several phases in relation to this issue. One pressure that can arise towards including new members when you aren't seeking more is when there is no other group in your vicinity. News of your group and its work may bring you telephone calls and letters asking for help. I think the best thing to do in those circumstances is to see if there are two people in your group who would be willing to help another group get off the ground. They could, with the potential new members, call a meeting for interested people, share what they have learned so far and then leave it in the hands of the new group.

As compulsive eaters we have a tendency to try to absorb or accommodate ourselves to everyone else, even at the expense of our own needs. It is important to keep your needs in the foreground in this instance and not sacrifice your group security for the sake of being responsive to another sufferer. It is essential to draw the lines between you and others, strange as that may seem. So, in considering these issues, make sure you as a group are expressing what you as individuals most want and need.

Making It Work

The group can only work for you if you put a lot into it. There is a tremendous temptation to hope that, once you are in a group, your problems will just disappear. I cannot stress strongly enough that this will not happen. Only by active observation and intervention will your eating and body concepts shift.

Give yourself the time to work on the problem. Make your group session a priority event in your week; allow yourself to bring up your fears, despairs, frustrations, worries and advances in the group. Learn from your own experience and from each other.

Self-help groups can teach us a great deal about our inner lives and the richness they contain, which is often concealed by preoccupations with fat and compulsive eating. The atmosphere generated in many groups is one of tenderness, concern and purpose. Be patient with yourself and strive to get what you need for yourself from the group. And very good luck.

Part II
PSYCHOLOGICAL EXERCISES

How to Use the Exercises

Throughout the book you will have noticed the symbol
★ referring you to this section of the book and to a particular exercise here. When you do these exercises, make sure
you have plenty of time. Don't rush them; they will be of
little benefit to you that way. When you plan to do an
exercise, set aside a good half hour. This applies to all
exercises except 'Breaking into a Binge', which you will
find useful as a quick intervention if you are bingeing.
Before you do any of the exercises, you might want to get
yourself a blank 120-minute tape. Slowly read into your
tape recorder the exercises, leaving good pauses where the
dots are. As a rough guide, each exercise takes about 7 to
10 minutes to tape. You may prefer to ask a friend to do
this for you or you may wish to send for a prerecorded
tape I have made of some of the exercises (available for $8
from Tapes, Suite 101, 80 East 11th Street, New York, NY
10003). Whatever method you choose, you will find it
extremely helpful to be able to close your eyes and listen
to a tape rather than having to interrupt your fantasies to
read the exercises.

Sit down in a comfortable chair with the tape recorder close at hand so that you can turn it on and off without moving from the chair.

Stay in your chair and sit quietly after you turn off the tape before you go on to the questions that follow several of the exercises.

The exercises are designed to help you consider aspects of your emotional life in a new way. I have attempted to help you create different scenes in your imagination by feeding in various ideas from which you can take off. Not everyone has an easy time fantasising at first (although many women love it straight off) and some women say they feel a bit silly initially; some balk at the idea of sitting quietly, eyes shut, doing a guided fantasy. Most often what prevents us from getting into fantasising in this way is a nervousness or embarrassment about letting ourselves go or a worry that we aren't doing it right. Sometimes you may notice that, instead of pursuing the fantasy I have tried to outline for you, your mind is wandering off in an altogether different direction and you can feel confused about what to do. You may not be able to fantasise at all and feel distracted by the unrelated thoughts that zoom through your mind. You may find yourself tuning into the fantasy halfway through or intermittently; the long pauses between the short phrases are there to help you relax and create whatever mental images you can. A woman who does the exercises in a group can feel a bit uncomfortable if she comes up with a less elaborate fantasy than the other members, but in all of these reactions the important thing to do is to *stay with your experience, try not to panic, and be as open as you can* to whatever – however off the topic it may seem – floats through your mind. Don't be discouraged if you don't have a rich fantasy the first time you attempt one.

322

The more you do the fantasies the more you will get out of them and the more attuned your mind becomes to doing them. Each time you do one you will notice that you can gather new information about yourself. Sometimes the differences will be almost imperceptible, at other times you will be astonished at how varied your responses can be.

The Ideal Kitchen

★

Sit down, get comfortable, and relax. I'd like you to close your eyes and imagine that you are contentedly on your own for a couple of days at a rather magical place that has everything you would possibly want . . . Take your pick of location – sun, sea, mountains, forest, city . . . whatever really pleases you . . . You are staying in a little apartment that is part of a beautifully designed holiday complex. Each apartment has its own kitchen, although you can order anything you like from a main kitchen to be brought to your room or you can eat in a public dining room . . . Soak in as many details as possible of this gorgeous holiday spot where you've chosen to be for a couple of days on your own . . . Now I'd like you to go into the kitchen in your apartment and just take a look at the supplies that have been laid out for you . . . Remember, this is a magical place, so you won't be at all surprised to find your most favourite foods are there . . . As you inspect the fridge, the fruit bowl, the cheese tray, the cookie tin, the bread board, and so on, you notice how very well the food has been chosen for you . . . How does seeing all this food in this setting make you feel? . . . Perhaps you sigh contentedly, perhaps you feel overwhelmed, perhaps you feel safe . . . While you are looking at the food and experiencing your feelings and enjoying being on your own, imagine that you leave the food temporarily to run yourself a bath . . . In the fantasy the bath is now full and I'd like you to get into it and relax . . . Feel the pleasure of being in this place with all your favourite foods put there especially for you . . . Focus on the positive aspects . . . Lie back in your bath and give yourself enough time to see what it is you feel like doing as soon as you are out of the bath . . . Are you hungry? . . . If so, what would you like to eat and how? . . . Do you wish to be on your own or with other people? See what feels absolutely right for you . . . Having thought through what would suit you best . . . Now imagine yourself eating if you *are* hungry . . . Perhaps you aren't inclined to eat right now but want to take a nap, sunbathe, chat with someone, swim, ski, read, walk, watch TV; see what it is you would really like to do, and in your mind's eye, pursue the activities that feel right to you . . . Nobody else's needs will intrude here; you can really choose what is exactly right for you . . . Reflect on how it feels to know that, when you are hungry, you will have a gorgeous treat awaiting you . . . Now I'd like you to stay in that frame of mind but bring yourself back to the here and now and consider the possibility of giving yourself the exact food you are longing for when you next get hunger signals . . . Can you do that? . . . If it seems difficult, is it because you feel money is standing in your way? . . . Think through your food budget and see whether you couldn't cut down on something else that you don't really enjoy in order to buy some of what you want . . . Do you feel you are not entitled to the foods you really want? . . . Try and feel any resistances you might have to looking after yourself well with food . . . Now imagine that you are free of any impediment to enjoying the food . . . How does that make you feel? . . . Now rouse yourself out of the fantasy and come back to the room you're sitting in. Open your eyes and do something you find relaxing – you can just stay in your chair if you wish, or you might want to take a bath for real . . . Choose an activity that will allow you to think for another few minutes uninterruptedly. If you're using a tape, turn off the cassette while you do this. When you are ready, return to this exercise. Sit down and close your eyes again and reflect back over the last 24 hours of your life. See if you can pinpoint those occasions when your eating satisfied and pleased you and those when it didn't . . . Try to figure out why your eating wasn't satisfying . . . Was it the food, was it the people, was it the way you ate? . . . As you are relaxing, be aware of as many details of each eating situation as you can . . . Now turn your attention to the foods you would like to have in your kitchen now, and what you would most like to eat . . . Try and stay with this feeling, picking out the exact food or beverage you would really like . . . When you are ready, open your eyes, and refer to the questions that follow this exercise.

★

1. **How do you feel about the food in your own kitchen at present?**

2. **Does it include foods that you especially like?**

3. **What are your favourite foods? Are they new discoveries? Are they foods from your childhood?**

Make a list. Do you have particular moods that go with particular foods?

4. How did you feel with all your favourite foods in the holiday apartment?

5. Do you like anticipating what you will eat the next time you are hungry, or do you gain more satisfaction by spontaneously responding to that hunger? Remember your favourite foods for those occasions when you are hungry but don't know what to eat.

6. Does having nice food worry or upset you? If so, what do you fear it will do to you?

Breaking into a Binge

★

Sit down, close your eyes, and take a few deep breaths . . .
The fact that you have been able to pry yourself away from
the food to listen to the tape is a big step in the direction
of breaking away from your binge. Try and feel the relief
of having interrupted the binge . . . Now I'd like you to
think back to when you were first aware that you were
going to be eating this way on this occasion . . . Did it
start before you even began to eat, or did it flow out of a
satisfactory, or perhaps unsatisfactory meal? . . . Bring to
mind all the details . . . where you were, who you were
with, the general atmosphere . . . Try and pinpoint the
sensation you experienced in the binge . . . What foods
did you go for? . . . Were you concentrating on taste or
texture or was the food eaten in such a way that you
couldn't discriminate? . . . Were you looking for something?
. . . Were you depriving yourself of a particular food that
you finally succumbed to or does it feel more as though you
were trying to avoid some feelings? . . . What is it that
you are searching for in the food? . . . Try and feel what

it is that you really want . . . Try to put that wanting into words or into an image . . . Feel again the relief of having torn yourself away from the binge . . . What can you do now to give yourself something more truly nourishing? . . . Do you want to have a cry, a bath, a nap? . . . Do you want to reach out to someone . . . write to them or ring them? . . . Do you want a hug from someone special? . . . Try and find an appropriate response to your longing . . . Don't deny the longing, even if you can't find the right response . . . Try and accept it. It won't eat you up, above all don't expect the food to satisfy it . . . Be aware of your emotional hunger and take a few moments to let yourself experience it directly . . . Decide in a relaxed way what you'd like to do after finishing this exercise and, when you are ready, open your eyes.

★

Increasing Your Food Awareness

★

Close your eyes and get comfortable . . . In this fantasy
you will have the chance to go through a few minutes of
your past again, and increase your awareness of your food
habits . . . Remember back to the most recent time this
week that you either ate more than you were wanting or
that you were drawn to eating and started to eat but knew
you weren't hungry . . . It will help you to recreate the
feelings if you remember the details and particulars of the
situation . . . Were you on your own or with others, in
your kitchen or in a public place? . . . Draw the scene as
vividly in your mind's eye as you can, so that it's as though
you were observing a film of yourself in the situation . . .
And now I'd like you to replay the incident slowly, frame
by frame . . . Start by focusing on what was happening just
before you ate when you weren't really hungry . . . Does
the scene feel familiar? . . . Is this the time you usually
overeat? . . . Is this one of those persistently difficult times
you have around food? . . . Had you prepared to eat or
did you just sort of stumble into the refrigerator or candy

store or whatever? . . . Were you at a friend's house and didn't know how to, or feel able to refuse her offer of food? . . . Now that you've set the scene, focus in on the emotional state just before you ate . . . How were you feeling? . . . Can you give your feelings a name? . . . Let whatever feelings you were having then come to the surface now . . . Carefully consider those feelings before moving on in this exercise . . . Now, I'd like you to imagine you are eating the food. What are you eating? As methodically as you can, see how much of the food you actually tasted, at what point you felt physically full, and how long you continued to eat after that point . . . Were you grabbing desperately for the food or were you eating calmly? . . . See if you can come up with words that precisely describe the way you were eating . . . See if you can distinguish exactly what kind of satisfaction you were getting from the food . . . Now I'd like you to return to the point *before* you started to eat or found yourself eating more than you were needing . . . Focus in on your emotional state . . . If you can't quite get it into focus, think back over the various incidents of the day up until that point and see if you can recapture how you felt . . . Was it a day when your emotions were seesawing? . . . Did you receive some disappointing news? . . . It's even possible, of course, that everything was going well before you ate . . . There are no formulas here; just take your time to see what you were actually feeling . . . Now I'd like you to imagine that, instead of eating or overeating, you stay in this emotional state . . . See if you can replay the scene from this point on, except this time allow yourself to not eat . . . Give yourself time to live through any immediate anxiety that not eating might produce, and see what then comes up for you . . . Are you being overwhelmed by uncomfortable feelings, or is not

eating much less difficult than you had anticipated? . . .
Allow yourself plenty of time to see what the desire for
food may have been covering up in terms of other wishes
. . . Allow yourself to be filled up with your emotions . . .
Now gently rouse yourself from this exercise, open your
eyes, and go back to the book.

★

Expressing Your Feelings

★

This exercise is designed to help you express your uncomfortable feelings in a way that feels right and satisfying to you. Close your eyes now and relax, and remember back to the last time you felt either angry, envious, competitive, jealous, sad, or depressed, and couldn't seem to get rid of the feeling. Choose any one of these feelings. When you do the exercise another time, you can choose another feeling. Having settled on which feeling you would like to explore, think over how often during the last few weeks you have felt this particular feeling and under what circumstances . . . Choose one of those times, preferably the one that is the most emotionally charged, and try to recapture in detail the surrounding circumstances that sparked off this feeling in you . . . Who else was involved? . . . As you are recreating the scene, are you aware of wanting to dilute the feeling? . . . of judging yourself? . . . Are you blaming someone else? . . . Give yourself a chance to explore the reality of the situation and just notice the internal voices that interfere with your experiencing the feeling directly

. . . Do you often hold back from expressing to people what you are feeling? . . . Are you all choked up with feeling? . . . Imagine for a moment that you are able to say or express whatever you feel . . . Imagine yourself telling whoever else is involved what impact they had on you . . . If that feels impossible, try telling a friend about how this person made you feel . . . Now try and tell the person directly . . . Don't be apologetic, just tell them in a straightforward way about the impact the interaction had on you . . . Don't allow yourself to get sidetracked into being oversensitive to what they might be feeling right now . . . Focus instead on what *you* need to say to them . . . See yourself doing it; it doesn't matter how many false starts you have . . . Try again to express yourself as accurately and fully as you can . . . How does it feel to be communicating your feelings? . . . How does it affect the picture you have of yourself? . . . Now think about whether you would actually like to tell this person in reality what you expressed during this fantasy . . . Perhaps you'd like to write them a letter full of feelings, which you can choose to either send or not send . . . Perhaps you'd like to tell them directly how they made you feel . . . Sort out what feels right for you to do in order to feel satisfied and complete . . . We are coming to the end of this exercise now, so see what you are able to take from it that you can use the next time these feelings well up in you . . . Try to focus on one specific intervention that you feel you could use to express yourself, and when you are ready, open your eyes.

★

Exploring Your Feelings

*

Think about an emotion that is particularly troubling to
you. What would you call this feeling? Is it anger, frustration, resentment, despair, guilt, competition, envy, jealousy,
hatred, depression? . . . Now experience this feeling, and
think back to what triggered it off . . . Were you disappointed? Was it something someone said? Did the feeling
come up because of something you felt unable to do? . . .
Be aware of the circumstances that caused this feeling to
erupt in you . . . Do you have this feeling often? . . . What
other kinds of situations can set off this feeling in you?
. . . Allow yourself to experience the feeling as fully as you
can . . . What would you like to do right now? . . . See if
you have any spontaneous urges to express this feeling —
through crying, shouting, shaking or whatever . . . Notice
any thoughts going through your mind that interrupt your
experiencing the feelings fully . . . Let the thoughts pass
quickly through your mind as you allow yourself to be
aware of the intensity of your feelings . . . As you are reliving
the circumstances that brought this feeling up in you, see

if you can catch a whiff of any other feelings . . . perhaps feelings that are unfamiliar to you . . . Focus in on these feelings . . . Let them fill you up . . . Let go of all your thoughts and judgments, and let yourself experience your feelings fully . . . It's okay to be frightened of them – just try letting them come to the surface for a minute or two . . . You'll find that once you've actually experienced them, the feelings won't seem so scary . . . Remember that these are feelings you walk around with all the time. They are *already* a part of you. They have the power to confuse and frighten you only because they are usually hidden away . . . Allowing yourself the space to let them come up in this way shows you that you *can* handle them . . . Try and relax for a minute now . . . Think back over the feelings you have experienced during the course of this exercise . . . and concentrate on following your breathing, in and out, in and out.

★

Fat/Thin Fantasy

★

This exercise is designed to help you understand how you express yourself through your body and help you come to grips with the emotional issues you have attached to different body states. If you can do this exercise frequently it will provide you with a rich picture of the conscious and unconscious meanings of fat and thin for you. Since these meanings vary, and different moods can illuminate different meanings, the more often you do the exercise, the more you will get out of it. Now I'd like you to close your eyes, get as comfortable as you can, follow your breathing, in and out, in and out, and relax. I'd like you to imagine that you are at a party . . . This can be either a real party or an imaginary one . . . It might be a dancing party, a talking party, a small intimate party . . . Set the scene and notice how you are feeling . . . What are you wearing? . . . How do you feel in these clothes? . . . Try and feel yourself in your body . . . Now notice your behaviour at this party. Are you an observer? . . . Are you actively mixing with other people; do you feel withdrawn? . . . As you observe yourself at this party, I'd like you to imagine that you are getting fatter . . . You are now quite large . . . How do you feel at this size? . . . Try and be aware of the nuances of feelings about being this size . . . You may have both negative and positive feelings about being this size . . . What are you wearing and how do you feel about your clothes? . . . What is going on at the party and how are you interacting with the other people there? . . . Are you on your own or are you talking, dancing, eating with others? . . . Do you feel comfortable or would you like to leave? . . . Can you initiate contact or do you feel you must wait until you are sought out? . . . Now I'd like you to imagine your fat is communicating with the people at the party . . . It is saying something that I'd like you to put into words . . . What is your fat saying to others? . . . Is there any way in which you feel it helps you to be *this* size in *this* situation? . . . Does being fat allow you to do or say certain things or act in particular ways? . . . Now imagine that your fat is peeling or melting away and, in this fantasy, still at the same party, you are now your ideal size . . . Can you see yourself? . . . Can you feel yourself at your ideal size? . . . Notice what you are wearing . . . What do these clothes say about you? . . . What do you see from the perspective of being your ideal size? . . . Do you view the party with different eyes? . . . What or who do the people at the party see when they look at you? . . . How do you feel? . . . Are you sure of yourself or do you feel vulnerable? . . . How are you getting on with the others at the party? . . . Are there differences between how you interacted with people when you were fat and how you are getting on now? . . . What is the quality of your contact with others? . . . Focus on the positive feelings coming up in you about your being your ideal size . . . Are you being seen as you? . . . Are you being admired for your body? . . . Now see if you notice any disconcerting feelings about being your ideal size at this party? . . . Is there anything scary or unpleasant about being this size? . . . Now I'd like you to imagine that you are fat once again, still at this same party . . . Does the atmosphere change? . . . How? . . . How do you feel within yourself? . . . Can you contact any feelings of relief about being larger again? . . . Allow yourself time to experience whatever feelings are coming up. Notice your responses to other people and how you feel about yourself . . . See what messages this fat you is sending out . . . Is there any way in which it helps you to be fat at the party? . . . Are there any conflicts you seem able to avoid? . . . Are there some very private feelings concealed in the fat? . . . When you are ready, I'd like you to imagine that once again, at this party, you are your ideal size . . . How do you feel? . . . Allow yourself to experience the many complicated feelings you may have . . . Notice how you are in your 'slim' clothes and how you feel in your body . . . Do you feel *you?* . . . Particularly note any difficult feelings that come up for you in being your ideal size . . . See if you can pinpoint any feelings that might have made it hard for you to stay at this size in the past . . . Now I'd like you to look back over this entire fantasy exercise and see what new information came up for you about yourself . . . When you are ready, turn to the questions below.

★

1. **What positive aspects of fatness emerged that you hadn't realised you felt?**

2. **What emerged about aspects of your personality that you express through your fat?**

3. How might you express that part of you if you were your ideal size?

4. What emerged about you at your imagined 'ideal' size?

5. What fears came up for you about being slim?

6. What aspects of your personality are you currently suppressing that you imagine go with slimness?

7. How might you express those aspects now?

Mirror Work

★

Sit down in the chair and close your eyes, follow your
breathing for a moment and try to get a feel of your
body from inside, and a mental picture of how you look
sitting in the chair . . . Imagine yourself as you are now
and sit in a position that expresses how you feel about
your body . . . Now strike a confident pose . . . now an
eager one . . . now an open attitude to the world . . . now
a withdrawn stance . . . Do all this with your eyes closed
. . . Just feel the internal changes and the shifts you are
required to make . . . Now I'd like you to imagine that
you are your ideal size . . . What are you spontaneously
expressing in this pose? . . . Now try a series of poses just
as you did before, only at your ideal size . . . open, withdrawn, eager, confident, reticent, and so on . . . Notice
how rich a repertoire of physical expression you have . . .
When you have familiarised yourself with the various
feelings, review what was different about them at different
imagined body sizes . . . What aspects of the ideal size
would you like to express right now? . . . What are you

afraid of, or what do you not want to express right now?
. . . Did you discover anything at all difficult or surprising
about feeling yourself into your ideal size? . . . Now open
your eyes, stand up and take a good look at your whole
body in the mirror . . . Follow the outlines of your body
and get a picture of the whole of you rather than focusing
in on details . . . Try not to judge, just look. Stand comfortably and try to project a feeling of accepting and liking
yourself . . . Keep your back straight and turn sideways
so that you get another picture of yourself . . . Just look,
try not to judge . . . Now turn forwards and then to the
other side . . . Just look, try not to judge . . . Turn forwards
again and, starting with your toes, look all the way up
your body and, when you reach your head, look from
your head all the way down . . . As you look at yourself
in the mirror, try to see yourself with accepting eyes . . .
Turn to your right, stand as though you are now your
ideal size and look into the mirror . . . Now turn to the
other side . . . What do you see? . . . Now turn front-
wards and resume your usual stance . . . What are the
differences? . . . Now sit down on the chair as if you were
your ideal size . . . What do you see? . . . How would it
be for you to hold this position regularly? . . . Would it
express more clearly how you feel about the inner you?
. . . Would you appear to be too confident? . . . Hold this
position for a minute and, when you are ready, go on to
the questions below.

★

**Give yourself time to respond to these questions,
as they can help you deepen your understanding of
how you relate to your body.**

1. Were you able to feel comfortable looking at yourself? Describe what you felt. As you do the exercise regularly, notice the small changes in self-acceptance.

2. What did you notice about the differences between the way you held your body to express the various emotional states? What did you notice when you tried to project yourself at your ideal size? What aspects of you came forwards?

3. Try incorporating the positive aspects of how you hold your body at your ideal size into how you are in your body now. Start off by doing it for a few minutes each hour.

Part of the Body

*

I'd like you to lie down, get as comfortable as you can. Close your eyes and observe your breathing . . . Try to feel your body physically . . . Feel your breath as it travels through your body into your arms and legs, chest and diaphragm . . . Now I'd like you to focus on the part of your body that you currently feel most unhappy about – it could be your legs, your stomach, your thighs, your breasts . . . Review your feelings about this part of your body and see if you can get back to when you first became aware of it as a part of you that you weren't comfortable with . . . Let whatever memories that come to mind emerge . . . Now I'd like you to pinpoint what exactly it is about this part of you that you feel so rejecting of . . . How would you describe that part of you? . . . What does that say about you? . . . What emotions is this part of your body expressing? . . . Now I'd like you to imagine that you are your ideal size . . . What happens to this part of you? . . . Can you actually visualise how you would be or are you superimposing part of someone else's body onto your own? . . .

344

Are you seeing yourself as you once were? . . . Try and feel your body changing . . . If you really feel that this part of you would be more acceptable smaller, try to imagine yourself smaller and see how that feels . . . What does this part now express about you? . . . How do you feel in your body? . . . What does it mean to you not to have something you dislike about yourself to focus on? . . . Do you feel more comfortable or is there something strangely missing? . . . Let yourself experience whatever feelings come up in you whether they are positive, negative or confusing . . . Now I'd like you to go back to your body as it is in reality, including the part that gives you so much distress, and just feel it again . . . Do you get any further associations to this part and what you so dislike about it? . . . What does this expose about you? . . . Really let yourself explore this part of your body rather than judge it . . . Try and experience it as a part of you . . . Integrate it into the rest of your body . . . Now imagine again that you are your ideal size . . . What happens to this part of your body? . . . What does being your ideal size allow you to do in your imagination? . . . Do you approach the world differently? . . . Now think of a difficult situation you experienced this past week. Let the details of the situation come to life, and put yourself back into that situation but at your ideal size . . . Would it be different? . . . Really see how it would be and think it through . . . Now I'd like you to open your eyes and use the questions below to help you reflect on your experience in this exercise.

★

1. What kind of associations did you come up with to this part of your body?

2. Do any other members of your family share the same concern about this part of their body?

3. If so, how do you feel about that part of their body?

4. Now spend some time exploring the themes that came up for you when you were doing the fantasy. Think through in detail your first awareness of your discomfort with this part of your body. What kind of role does this discomfort play currently, and what are the emotional issues this discomfort is masking? Are you perhaps assigning it more power than it has? Does being preoccupied with this part *help* you in any way?

5. Why do you so dislike this part? Is it because it doesn't conform to a stereotype? If in the fantasy you superimposed someone else's body part on to yours, whose was it – and what does that mean for you? If you saw yourself younger, what was so special about that particular time?

6. What is the actual bodily function of this part of your body? How well does it perform its physical function? How do you feel about its function?

The Family Meal

★

This exercise is designed to help you contact the emotional resonances of your childhood eating and to help you see how they affect your current eating patterns. Sit back, relax, close your eyes . . . Imagine that you are at a family dinner at your parents' home. It could be a special occasion, such as Christmas or a birthday. Choose a time when as many family members are there as possible . . . It could be a real situation or a fantasised one . . . If it helps you, remember back to a specific family occasion around the dinner table . . . Who is there? . . . How do people get on with each other? . . . Are there many sources of friction between the people? Are there unmentionable subjects and tense areas that everyone avoids, or do the tensions come to the surface? . . . Or is there perhaps a good feeling about all of you being together? . . . Notice the details of the situation and try to really feel yourself in the situation . . . Who do you feel closest to? . . . How does whatever is going on between people at the table get expressed through the food? . . . Notice how other people are eating . . . Now notice what is going on for you with food . . . How comfortable are you with your eating? . . . Really see yourself sitting there and describe your eating to yourself quickly and simply . . . Now it's time for the dishes to be cleared away . . . Who participates? . . . Who doesn't? . . . Is anyone eating what's been left over? . . . Observe yourself and your impulses . . . Now I'd like you to remember back to when you were much younger, and conjure up a picture of your family's eating habits. What do you remember of them? . . . Paint the picture as vividly as you can . . . Did you all eat together, or in separate shifts? . . . Did your mother do all the cooking? . . . Did you wish that she would behave differently in some way? . . . Did you wish that she would sit down more often? . . . Did she eat robustly, with pleasure, or pick at her food? . . . Were you encouraged to eat everything on your plate? . . . If you were, what would happen if you didn't? . . . Who served the food? Did each individual take their own, or did one of your parents serve you? Who decided what was the right size portion for you? . . . What was the atmosphere like at the table? . . . Did you look forward to mealtimes or not? . . . What happened there besides eating – was it a place for talking, shouting or disciplining? . . . Remember as many details as you can, both about the atmosphere and about how you and the other family members were eating . . . Now I'd like you to think about your current eating situation in your present living arrangement . . . What are meals like for you now? . . . What is the atmosphere like at the table? . . . Who does the cooking? . . . How do you feel about that? . . . If you live alone, how do you feel about eating alone? . . . What do mealtimes mean to you? . . . Are they social occasions, a time of getting together, or are they fraught, or unpredictable, lonely or upsetting? . . . Be aware of the aspects of your mealtimes that give you pleasure . . . Now notice those aspects that cause you discomfort . . . Are there emotional continuities between your present eating situation and the way you felt as a child and as an adult about eating with your family? . . . Reflect now on whether you may be trying to make up for or trying to recreate the meals of your childhood . . . What are you looking for in a meal with others? . . . Now think back to the tables you've been fantasising sitting at in the last few minutes and scan them for anything else you may not have noticed the first time . . . How might you relate what you've noticed about how you eat now and how you might want to eat? When you are ready, open your eyes, and return to the book.

★

The Chinese Meal

*

Sit down, get comfortable and relax. Now I'd like you to imagine you are with a group of friends at a Chinese restaurant that you like . . . How many people are at the table? . . . Do any of them have problems around food or are you the only one with a compulsive-over-eating problem? . . . Do you anticipate this communal meal with pleasure or nervousness or a mixture of both? . . . Use this opportunity to observe how you conduct yourself at such a meal, how you feel about the food on the table and how the other people handle this way of eating together . . . How is the ordering done? . . . Does each person choose a dish for themselves, or to share, or is the whole menu decided by everyone together? . . . Do you feel comfortable or uncomfortable with the arrangement? . . . Are you participating actively in choosing the food? . . . Are you engaged in conversation? . . . Once the ordering is done, notice how you are feeling as you await the arrival of the food . . . Are the ordered dishes mostly food that you like? . . . Are you worried about appearing greedy?

... Are you worried about overeating? ... Are you worried about not getting enough food? ... The food has now arrived ... Does it all come at once or one dish or two at a time? ... Are the first dishes to appear your favourites? ... How are you feeling about the food at this point? ... Slow down ... Take a few deep breaths and think about the meal, alerting yourself to the areas that can cause you difficulty ... Plan how you could intervene at such times so that you won't be eating in an unaware fashion; for example, if you are inclined to put more food on your plate than you really want to insure you get enough, and then you habitually overeat rather than stop when you feel satisfied, try a different response – either plan to observe your eating closely enough so that you are not eating 'unthinkingly', or take less food on your plate initially and see how that feels ... Do you feel deprived or restricted? ... As this is a fantasy, you can be absolutely sure that there will be plenty of food for you. It will not run out. Bearing that in mind, how do you feel putting smaller amounts on your plate, knowing you can always take more? ... Perhaps you'd prefer to eat one dish at a time ... In this fantasy you can tell your friends that that is what you are doing and they will make sure to leave you as much as you might want of everything ... What kind of feelings are you experiencing now? ... Are you able to relax and enjoy the food and taste each mouthful? ... Can you distinguish between the tastes you like and those you don't? ... Try and stay in touch with your eating as you socialise with the people at the table ... Now relax and continue with the meal, only this time I'd like you to act as you usually would on such an occasion ... Now I'd like you to reflect back on these last few moments: What was going on for you? ... How were you relating to the other people and how did you feel about the way you were eating? . . . See if you can spot moments of tension or compulsive eating . . . Focus now on any difficulties you're having . . . Try to replay that difficult part of the meal, but with your concentration turned to your eating . . . How might you be able to intervene differently? . . . You are now full . . . Has it been a satisfying or disappointing meal? . . . Notice the feelings in your body that let you know you've had enough food . . . Do you feel inclined to continue eating the food that is still on the table and perhaps in your dish, or are you quite content to stop? . . . If you are having difficulty stopping, try and put into a few words what you are still wanting . . . See if you can discover exactly what you want to best satisfy that hunger . . . What will you have to face if you stop eating when you are no longer hungry? . . . Now bring back the meanings and feelings of a communal meal like this for you. Do you feel mostly pleased, or mostly uncomfortable? . . . What would need to be happening around the table and in relation to the food to make it absolutely right for you? . . . Pinpoint whatever would make this a pleasant experience for you and consider what you could do the next time you have a meal like this . . . Remember what you did to intervene successfully when you felt like eating but were not hungry . . . When you are ready, open your eyes and reflect on the exercise.

★

The Supermarket Fantasy

★

Close your eyes . . . Now I would like you to imagine
you are in your kitchen . . . Look around the room and
make a note of all the food there . . . in the refrigerator
. . . closets . . . cookie tin . . . freezer . . . It probably is
not too hard for you to form a complete picture because
undoubtedly you know where everything is or is not,
including any goodies or dietetic foods . . . Look around
the room and see how it is affecting you . . . Is it painful
to see how pathetic the foods are that you generally
keep there or allow yourself to eat? . . . See what your
kitchen says about you . . . Now go to your favourite
supermarket or shopping mall or a place where there is
a wide variety of stores under one roof – vegetable
market, butcher, delicatessen, dairy, bakery, take-out food
store – and I would like you to imagine that you have
an unlimited amount of money to spend . . . Take a
couple of supermarket carts and fill them up with all
your favourite foods . . . Go up and down the aisles or
from counter to counter and carefully select the most

appetising foods . . . Be sure not to skimp . . . If you like cheesecake, take several, take enough so you feel that there is no way you could possibly eat it all in one sitting . . . Be sure to get the specific ones you really like . . . There is no hurry, you have plenty of time to get whatever you want . . . Cast your eyes over the wonderful array of foods and fill up your cart . . . Make sure you have everything you need and then get into your car or a cab with your boxes of food and go to your home . . . There is nobody in the house and nobody will be around for the rest of the day; the house – especially the kitchen – is all yours for you to enjoy . . . Bring the food into the kitchen and fill up the room with it . . . How do you feel surrounded by all of this food just for you? . . . Does it feel sinful or is it a very joyful feeling? . . . Do you feel reassured or scared by the abundance of food just for you? . . . Just stay with the food and go through the various moods that come up . . . Remember nobody will disturb you, the food is there just for you, enjoy it in whatever way you want to . . . See if you can relax in the knowledge that you will never again be deprived . . . And now I would like you to go down the road to mail a letter . . . How do you feel about leaving the house and all the food? . . . Does it give you a warm feeling to know that when you go back it will all still be there for you undisturbed? Or is it a relief to get away from it? . . . You have now mailed the letter and are on your way back to the house . . . Remember as you open the door that the food is all there just for you and no one will interrupt you . . . How does it feel to be back with the food? . . . If you found it reassuring before, does it continue to be so? If you found it scary, can you find anything comforting about being back in the kitchen with all this food? . . .

Slowly come back to the room you are actually in now with the knowledge that your kitchen is full of beautiful foods to eat that nobody is going to take away from you . . . and, when you are ready, open your eyes.

★

Food Chart

TIME OF DAY	CIRCUMSTANCES UNDER WHICH I APPROACHED FOOD: WAS I PHYSICALLY HUNGRY? IF SO, DID I ALLOW MYSELF A FREE CHOICE OF FOODS?	WHAT WAS I FEELING BEFORE EATING? WAS I EMOTIONALLY HUNGRY? IF SO, FOR WHAT?

WHAT AND HOW I ATE	DID THE FOOD SATISFY ME, OR NOT?	FEELINGS AFTER EATING

Acknowledgements

FAT IS A FEMINIST ISSUE: Thanks are due to many, many people. First to Carol Munter, the original compulsive eating and self-image group, and all the women with whom I have worked and who have shared their feelings about their bodies with me. Without these people there would be no book and nothing to say. Thanks too to all those people who have generously encouraged, helped and supported me in this work in one way or another over the past six years. They include Dale Bernstein, Patrick Byrne, Warren Cohen, Anne Cooke, Clare Dennis, Luise Eichenbaum, Peggy Eliot, Ian Franklin, Barbara Goldberg, Clara Caleo Green, Rose Heatley, Altheia Jones Lecointe, Eddie Lebar, Bob Lefferts, David McLanahan, Laurence Orbach, Ruth Orbach, Rosie Parker, Jeremy Pikser, Cathy Porter, Ron Radosh, Olly Rosengart, Julie Saj, Steve Sandler, David Skinner, DeeDee Skinner, Laura Schwartz, Michael Schwartz, Ann Snitow, Jimmy Traub, Redesign, Spare Rib and the Women's Therapy Centre.

Finally, four people have come through with support in immeasurable ways. Sara Baerwald has provided consistent no-nonsense support from afar. Malinda Coleman miraculously dropped everything to provide crucial help at a critical time. Gillian Slovo cared for me very well in the final stages. Joseph Schwartz came through in unimaginable ways providing love, support, patience, criticism, handholding and chicken soup throughout – my love and deep appreciation cannot express how important this has been to me.

All the case histories in this book are true. The names and places have been changed to protect the privacy of individuals and their families.

FAT IS A FEMINIST ISSUE II: Thanks to Nina Shandloff and Linda Healey for thoughtful editing, to Sara and Ed Lebar for housing me, to Judy Lever for discussion on compulsive eating and pregnancy, to all the women who replied to the questionnaire, to Mira Dana and The Women's Therapy Centre and to Sara Baerwald, Sally Berry, Carol Bloom, Luise Eichenbaum, Joseph Schwartz and Gillian Slovo for being who they are.

Useful Websites

www.any-body.org
Any-body.org: the group started by Susie Orbach, Althea Greenan, Joanna Orpin, Jess Miller and others arguing for body diversity.

www.showmethedata.info [Link correct at time of publication – link since been removed]
Show Me The Data: takes a critical look at statistics on weight-loss and diet claims made in the press and elsewhere.

www.about-face.org
About Face: a San Francisco-based non-profit group, combatting negative and distorted images of women in the media.

www.cswd.org
The Council on Size & Weight Discrimination: a not-for-profit advocacy organisation working to end discrimination against people who are heavier than average. This is packed with information with special attention to children.

www.fightmannequinism.org/forthepress/index.asp
US-based site that equates the lack of citizenship and political awareness amongst youth to becoming a mannequin.

www.bodybodyproject.com
bodyBODY: You Can't Tell By Looking: uses different art forms to show audience members that they are not alone in their experiences navigating cultural, media and familial messages about their bodies.

www.size-acceptance.org
International Size Acceptance Association (ISAA): Their mission is to promote size acceptance and fight size discrimination throughout the world by means of advocacy and visible, lawful actions.

www.ywcascotland.org/campaigns/bodyimage.html [Link correct at time of publication – link since been removed]
The YWCA Body Image Survey, 2003

Useful Reading

Effective self-help for eating and body image problems:

Berg, Frances, *Children & Teens Afraid to Eat* (Hettinger, North Dakota: Healthy Weight Network, 1997)

Cooke, Kaz, *Real Gorgeous* (London: Bloomsbury, 1995)

Hirschmann, J.R. and Munter, C.H., *Overcoming Overeating* (Massachusetts: Addison Wesley, 1988)

Hirschmann, J.R. and Zaphiropoulos, L., *Are you Hungry?* (New York: Random House, 1985)

Orbach, Susie, *On Eating* (London: Penguin, 2002)

Orbach, Susie, *Hunger Strike* (London: 1986, Penguin, 1993)

Roth, Geneen, *Why Weight? A guide to overcoming compulsive eating* (New York: Penguin, 1993)

Understanding the background to body worries:

Chernin, Kim, *The Hungry Self*, (New York: Times Books, 1985)

Orbach, Susie, *Hunger Strike* (London: 1986, Penguin, 1993)

Wolf, Naomi, *The Beauty Myth* (London: Chatto & Windus, 1990)

Critiques of food and diet industry:

Bennet, William and Gurin, Joel, *The Dieter's Dilemma* (New York: Basic Books, 1982)

Campos, Paul, *The Obesity Myth* (New York: Gotham Books, 2004)

Critser, Greg, *Fat Land* (London: Allen Lane, 2003)

Ruppel Shell, Ellen, *The Hungry Gene* (Oak Lawn, Illinois: Atlantic Press, 2002)

Schlosser, Eric, *Fast Food Nation* (London: Penguin, 2002)

For professionals:

Aron, Lewis and Sommer-Anderson, Frances, (eds.), *Relational Perspectives on the Body* (Hillsdale, New Jersey: The Analytic Press, 1998)

Bloom, Carol, et al., *Eating Problems: A Feminist Psychoanalytic Treatment Model* (New York: Basic Books, 1994)

McDougall, Joyce, *Theatres of the Body* (London: Free Association Books, 1989)

Petrucelli, Jean and Stuart, Catherine, (eds.), *Hungers and Compulsions: The Psychodynamic Treatment of Eating Disorders and Addictions* (Lanham, Maryland: Jason Aronson, 2002)

Further reading:

Allon, Natalie, 'Group Dieting Interaction', (unpublished doctoral dissertation, Brandeis University, Waltham, Massachusetts, 1972)

Becker, Anne E., *Body Self & Society: The View from Fiji*, (Philadelphia: University of Pennsylvania Press, 1996)

Belotti, Elena Gianini, *Little Girls* (London: Pluto Press, 1975)

Bernard, Jessie, *The Future of Motherhood* (New York: Viking Press, 1975)

Bloom, Carol, 'Training Manual for the Treatment of Compulsive Eating and Fat', (Master's thesis, State University of New York at Stony Brook, 1976)

Bordo, S., *Unbearable Weight: Feminism, Western Culture & the Body* (Berkley, California: University of California Press, 1993)

Boston Women's Health Book Collective, *Our Bodies, Ourselves* (New York: Simon & Schuster, 1971)

Bruch, Hilde, *Eating Disorders* (New York: Basic Books, 1973)

Chernin, Kim, *The Obsession* (New York: Harper and Row, 1981)

Chesler, Phyllis, *Women and Madness* (New York: Doubleday, 1972)

Dana, M. and Lawrence, M., *Women's Secret Disorder: A New Understanding of Bulimia* (London: Grafton, 1988)

de Beauvoir, Simone, *The Second Sex* (London: Jonathan Cape, 1968)

Deutch, Helene, *The Psychology of Women*, vols. I & II (New York, 1973)

Donovan, Lynn, *The Anti Diet* (New York: Nash Publishers, 1971)

Ehrenreich, Barbara and English, Deirdre, *Witches, Midwives and Nurses* (New York: Compendium Books, 1974)

Eichenbaum, Luise and Orbach, Susie, *Understanding Women* (London: Penguin, 1983)

Eichenbaum, Luise and Orbach, Susie, *What Do Women Want?* (London: Michael Joseph, 1983)

Ernst, Sheila and Goodison, Lucy, *In Our Own Words* (Boston: Houghton Mifflin, 1981)

Figes, Eva, *Patriarchal Attitudes* (Greenwich, Connecticut: Stein and Day, 1970)

Friday, Nancy, *My Mother, My Self: The Daughter's Search for Identity* (New York: Delacorte Press, 1977)

Gerrard, Don, *One Bowl* (New York: Random House, 1974)

Grosz, Elizabeth, *Volatile Bodies: Towards a Corporeal Feminism* (Bloomington, Indiana: Indiana University Press, 1994)

Kiell, N., (ed.), *The Psychology of Obesity* (Springfield, Illinois: Charles C Thomas, 1973)

Lawrence, M., *Fed Up and Hungry* (London: The Women's Press, 1987)

Maccoby, Eleanor Emmons and Jacklin, Carol Nagy, *The Psychology of Sex Differences* (Stanford, California: Stanford University Press, 1974)

MacLeod, Sheila, *The Art of Starvation: Anorexia Observed* (London: Virago, 1981)

Mahler, Margaret, et al., *The Psychological Birth of the Human Infant* (New York: Basic Books, 1976)

McBride, Angela Barron, *The Growth and Development of Mothers* (New York: Harper & Row, 1973)

McBride, Angela Barron, *Living with Contradictions: A Married Feminist* (New York: HarperCollins, 1977)

Mitchell, Juliet, *Psychoanalysis and Feminism* (New York: Random House, 1974)

Orbach, Susie, *What's Really Going on Here?* (London: Virago, 1994)

Orbach, Susie and Eichenbaum, Luise, *Bittersweet: Love, Competition & Envy in Women's Relationships* (London: Arrow, 1988)

Pearson, Leonard and Lillian, *The Psychologist's Eat Anything Diet* (New York: Wyden Books, 1973)

Rainer, Tristine, *The New Diary* (London: Angus and Robertson, 1980)

Reich, Wilhelm, *The Sexual Revolution* (New York: Farrar Straus Giroux, 1971)

Rich, Adrienne, *Of Woman Born: Motherhood as Experience and Institution* (New York: Norton, 1976)

Rosaldo, Michele Zimbalist and Lamphere, Louise, eds. *Woman, Culture and Society* (Stanford, California: Stanford University Press, 1974)

Rubin, Theodore Issac, *Forever Thin* (New York: B. Geis Associates, 1970)

Sager, Clifford J. and Kaplan, Helen Singer, (eds), *Progress in Group and Family Therapy* (New York: Brunner/Mazel, 1972)

Schiffman, Muriel, *Gestalt Self Therapy* (Berkeley, California: Self Therapy Press, 1980)

Southgate, John, et al., *The Barefoot Psychoanalyst* (London: The Association of Karen Horney Psychoanalytic Counsellors, 1978)

Strouse, Jean, (ed.), *Women and Analysis* (New York: Grossman Publishers, 1974)

Thompson, Clara, 'Penis Envy in Women', *Psychiatry* 6 (1943)

Williams, Elizabeth Friar, *Notes of a Feminist Therapist* (New York: Dell, 1977)

Winnicott, D. W., *Mother and Child: A Primer of First Relationships* (New York: Basic Books, 1957)

Zaretsky, Eli, *Capitalism, the Family and Personal Life* (London: Pluto Press, 1976)